All Generations Shall Call Me Blessed

All
Generations
Shall
Call
Me
Blessed

Francis A. Eigo, O.S.A.
Editor

The Villanova University Press

Copyright © 1994 by Francis A. Eigo, O.S.A.
The Villanova University Press
Villanova, Pennsylvania 19085
All rights reserved
Library of Congress Cataloging-in-Publication Data
All generations shall call me blessed / Francis A. Eigo, editor.

    p.   cm.
  Includes index.
  ISBN 0-87723-061-7 : $8.95
  1. Mary, Blessed Virgin, Saint. I. Eigo, Francis A.
BT602.A436 1994
232.91 — dc20
                                        94-4971
                                          CIP

To
the memory
of
Joseph Papin:
Founder
of the
Villanova University
Theology Institute

Contents

Contributors

DORIS K. DONNELLY, a professor of Religious Studies at John Carroll University where her specializations are spirituality and sacramental theology, has authored several dozen articles for scholarly publications and published several books, including *Spiritual Fitness, Mary: Woman of Nazareth* (editor), and the forthcoming *Spiritual Principles at Work*.

CAROL FRANCES JEGEN, B.V.M., professor of Religious Studies at Loyola University Mundelein and nationally known lecturer and retreat director, lists among her publications articles for various journals as well as such books as *Mary According to Women* (editor and contributor), *Jesus the Peacemaker, Restoring Our Friendship with God*, and *Thank God, Prayers of Jews and Christians Together* (coauthored with Rabbi Byron Sherwin).

ELIZABETH A. JOHNSON, C.S.J., a member of the Department of Theology of Fordham University and nationally known consultant, advisor, and lecturer, has published articles on the mystery of God, Jesus Christ, Mary, feminist theology in scholarly journals and numbers among her books *Consider Jesus: Waves of Renewal in Christology* and the prize winning *SHE WHO IS: The Mystery of God in a Feminist Theological Perspective*.

ALICE L. LAFFEY, currently Associate Professor of Old Testament on the faculty of the College of the Holy Cross, is an internationally known lecturer and has authored a number of Old Testament Monographs, articles for books and journals, book reviews, and books, including *The Pentateuch: A Cosmic-Liberation Perspective*.

MARY T. MALONE, Chairperson of the Department of Religious Studies of the University of St. Jerome's College, Waterloo, Ontario, has lectured widely, has written articles for various journals, and includes among the books she has authored *Who Is My Mother? Rediscovering the Mother of Jesus*.

SANDRA L. ZIMDARS-SWARTZ, a member of the Department of Religious Studies of the University of Kansas, is a lecturer, a writer of articles for books and journals, and the author of books, including the highly successful *Encountering Mary: From La Salette to Medjugorje*.

Introduction

This twenty-sixth volume of the *Proceedings of the Theology Institute of Villanova University* attempts a study of Mary of Nazareth from a variety of viewpoints. After Elizabeth A. Johnson's introductory essay, Alice L. Laffey examines images of Mary in the Christian Scriptures. Following Mary T. Malone's consideration of Mary as an advocate of justice is Doris K. Donnelly's answer to the question of Mary as a possible sign of contradiction to women. Then, Sandra L. Zimdars-Swartz treats images of Mary in popular devotion, and Carol Frances Jegen brings the study to a close with her essay on Mary and the Church of the Future.

Very special thanks are due to a number of people who have figured in the planning and execution of the Theology Institute: the members of the Theology Institute Committee (Walter Conn, Edward L. Hamel, O.S.A., Bernard A. Lazor, O.S.A., Thomas Ommen, Gaile Pohlhaus, Suzanne Toton); the presiders (Bernard Lazor, Edward Hamel, Joseph Loya, O.S.A.); my assistant, Patricia Fry; the essayists, and, above all, the administrators of Villanova University.

Francis A. Eigo, O.S.A.
Editor

Toward a Theology of Mary: Past, Present, Future

Elizabeth A. Johnson, C.S.J.

INTRODUCTION

Standing, as we are, at the cusp of the third millennium, this volume affords us the opportunity to cast our thoughts in two directions: back over two thousand years of Marian theology and piety and ahead to the way the relationship between the Christian people and Miriam of Nazareth may be shaped in the future. We do so with the intention of moving *toward* a theology of Mary that will serve the Church in that future. Theology, in Anselm's well known dictum, is the effort of faith seeking understanding of what it believes. A theology of Mary is a search for understanding of this woman in the light of God's gracious kindness that appeared on our earth in Jesus Christ. Who is she; what is her importance in the Christian story; and what is her meaning in the life of faith?

Our search for understanding is a monumental task. One could drown in the profusion of images, titles, theological tracts, doctrines, devotions, dogmas, and just plain pious fantasies that have emerged around this woman in the course of history. In addition to this plurality of Marian expressions, our task is further complicated by the ambiguity of their meaning. Certain aspects of Marian doctrine and devotion are clearly coherent with the central confession of Christian faith and help to express it. Just as clearly, other facets are aberrations, exaggerations, errors. But, even here a sympathetic, critical probing reveals that what is often going on is an attempt to compensate for deficiencies in the way the faith is being officially proclaimed

1

and personally experienced. As with contemporary theology in general, plurality and ambiguity mark the Marian tradition, presenting a challenge to thought as we seek "toward" a theology of Mary.[1]

In this essay, I propose to chart a reflective path through this material in five steps. First, we will reconnoiter the past with brief soundings of key developments in the first and second millennia. Second, we will seek to understand the Marian heritage we have received by discussing contemporary interpretations of this history. Third, with the past somewhat in hand, although not definitively judged, we will move to the present, highlighting the Second Vatican Council and the checkered situation of Marian thought and practice in the postconciliar world Church. Fourth, we will examine a number of dynamic factors that are now shaping future forms of Marian theology. Finally, with these factors in view, I will propose a series of theses for a future theology of Mary, a theology that will name her as our companion, friend, and faithful sister within the community of disciples.

I. TWO MILLENNIA, TWO DIRECTIONS

The danger of painting history in large brush strokes is that one omits particular distinctions and nuances, thereby ignoring the plurality and ambiguity inherent in any tradition and risking distortion. However, in the interest of gaining a modicum of clarity about the two thousand years of Marian tradition, such large brush strokes may be helpful. Particularly for a theology of Mary, which seeks specifically to understand the meaning of this woman within the context of Christian faith in God, broad lines are necessary in view of the immense sprawl of the historical phenomenon.[2]

Painting a big picture, I propose that the two millennia of Catholic Christianity have been marked by two roughly different directions. During the first thousand years, theology understood Mary within the economy of salvation centered in Jesus Christ. Her meaning was found within the larger meaning of that reconciliation brought about by God in Christ, the focus being kept on the Incarnation. By contrast, the second thousand years saw an increasing tendency to isolate Mary from this context, resulting in ever more rarified reflections on her privileges, powers, and glories. While examples of the second millennium's isolating tendency can be found in the first, and while at its best the second millennium preserved a gospel-oriented view of Mary, these two tendencies do describe the major currents of Marian theology in each era. As the Second Vatican Council checked the isolating trajectory of the second millennium in no uncertain terms, we may consider that we are now living at the beginning of a third major configuration.

The First Millennium

In light of what was to develop later, it is remarkable that the first three Christian centuries saw no discernible official veneration or theology of Mary. The new Church, which was actually a communion of local churches, was under persecution for its perceived disloyalties to state authority, and a number of its members were put to death. Veneration of these martyrs, graphic icons of Christ who witnessed, as had he, even to the shedding of blood, flourished in the early Church. By holding their memory and their bones dear, living Christians hoped for courage and inspiration when their own moment of testing arrived. Since Mary was not a martyr, she did not receive the community's regard in this formal way.

The main vehicle for driving theological attention to Mary was the growing inquiry into the function and identity of Jesus Christ. The earliest Christological heresy, Docetism, held that the body of Jesus was not truly human flesh. Seeking to honor the transcendent dignity of God by protecting divinity from contact with the material world, this view argued that Jesus' body was a kind of camouflage that allowed God to appear, to be seen and heard, but it was not the same stuff of which Adam and Eve and their descendants were made. To counteract this idea, which strikes at the reality of the Incarnation and therefore nullifies salvation, theology turned to Mary. Her historic pregnancy was evoked to insure the human authenticity of Jesus' flesh, taken from her. One Docetic group, the Valentinians, had advanced the notion that Jesus passed through Mary the way water passes through a tube: two different substances, one not affecting the other.[3] In contrast to this, the Apostles' Creed incorporated the phrase that Jesus was born *of* the Virgin Mary, that is, out of her flesh. The first post-biblical creedal affirmation of Mary was in defense of the humanity of Jesus.

Once the divinity of Christ had been formally confessed at Nicea (325), conflict flared over the way to understand the unity of human and divine natures in the one and the same Jesus Christ. On the one hand, the school of Antioch endorsed a moral view of the unity of natures, seeing Jesus Christ as the human being in whom the divine Word dwells, similar to the way God dwells in the Temple. While presenting a rather weak view of unity in Christ, so that he could be said to act at times through one nature (hungry in his humanity) and at times through his other nature (working miracles through his divinity), this Christology had the advantage of preserving the distinction of natures and thereby Jesus' genuine humanity. In this school, the preferred title for Mary was *Christotokos,* Christbearer, meaning mother of this human being who is indwelt by the Logos and who is thereby the Christ. On the other hand, the school of Alexandria argued for a stronger, ontological form of union in which the divine Son of God personally appeared in human form. While safeguarding the unity of the person of Christ, this notion tended to dilute his humanity, seeing it as somehow mixed with, or swallowed up by, transcendent divinity. In this view, Mary may truly be called *Theotokos,* the Godbearer or Mother of God, because she is the mother of the one who is personally the Word of God. The Marian title itself bore the brunt of this dispute, but the essence of the controversy was Christological. When the Council of Ephesus (431) opted for the *Theotokos* title, this theological affirmation of Mary became the safeguard for the personal unity of Jesus Christ.

Other developments in the first millennium follow this same pattern. If Jesus Christ is the Second Adam whose fidelity heals what the sin of the first Adam has wounded, then by extension Mary is the new Eve whose willing cooperation with God reverses the disobedience of the first. If Jesus Christ is conceived by the Holy Spirit, then Mary's virginity is a sign of the creative new beginning God makes with the human race in the birth of this child. If Christ is Head of the Church, then Mary is a type of the Church, modelling the faith, charity, and spirit of service that are the true marks of discipleship. In every instance, theology of Mary is shaped by the story of salvation coming from God in Jesus.[4]

By keeping our gaze fixed steadfastly on theology, I have, of course, neglected some other dynamic factors that also shaped the first millennium's Marian tradition. There was, above all, popular piety, not confined to simple people, the *rudes,* but shared by priests and bishops as well. This devotion was expressed in such devotional prayers as the *"Sub tuum praesidium"* that invokes Mary's protection against danger; in such apocryphal writings as the *Protoevangelium of James,* that gives imaginative details of Mary's childhood, marriage, and birth-giving, and the *Transitus Mariae,* that recounts her journey to heaven at the end of her life[5]; in mass demonstrations in favor of the *Theotokos* title in Ephesus, reminiscent of earlier rallies in favor of the great goddess Diana of the Ephesians recounted in Acts

(19:23-41); and in the shrines and churches dedicated or rededicated to Mary. Even when led or moved by popular piety, however, theology of Mary kept its connection with the Incarnation, understanding Mary as a participant within the larger, public story of salvation in Christ.

Second Millennium

Factors already at work, such as the growing juridical character of Church office and the Church's penitential system, effected a shift in the Marian theology of the second millennium. Now, interest focused more intensely on each person's subjective need for salvation, a desired outcome of life that was difficult to achieve. In this situation, the mother of the Redeemer came to be seen as a particular help to sinners, a heavenly power who would take the sinner's side. Consequently, reflection about her meaning became detached from the more objective story of salvation history, proceeding in an isolation that grew more intense as the millennium progressed.

The mediatory role of Mary is a case in point.[6] In earlier theology, while the term was little used, the idea of Mary as a "mediator" had been rooted in her unique role in the Incarnation, whereby the Son of God became a human being in order to save the sinful human race. Having given her free consent in faith, she conceived him in her body and, through her physical pregnancy and childbirth, delivered to the world its Savior. Thus, she was understood to be the means by which God came to earth, the female mediator of Christ's saving presence in history. As a corollary, it was envisioned that, in a special way among the apostles, martyrs and other saints, Mary in heaven joined in the prayer of Christ for those still struggling on earth, praying for them with a maternal love.

In the medieval West, Mary's mediation became connected not only with Christ's coming to earth, but also with sinful humanity's coming back to God: "Just as the Son of God has deigned to descend to us through you, so we also must come to him through you. . . ."[7] This insight found expression in the popular images of Mary as the neck connecting Christ and his body the Church and as the aqueduct through which the graces of Christ flow. With eloquent rhetoric, Bernard of Clairvaux preached that it is God's wish that we venerate Mary with great tenderness, for God "wills us to have everything through Mary."[8] True, he goes on, the Father has given us Jesus as our efficacious Mediator; he is our merciful brother, made of our flesh. But we might tremble to approach him, for he is also God of

awesome divine majesty. If we wish to have an advocate with
him, let us have recourse to Mary, for she is wholly sweet and
gentle, full of mildness and mercy. The Son will hear his
mother, the Father will hear his Son, and so we will receive divine favor.

A fearsome edge was given to this mediating role of Mary by
the emphasis placed by medieval theology on Christ as the Just
Judge and on each person's subjective need for salvation, a desired outcome of life that was difficult to achieve. In this situation, the mother of the Redeemer came to be seen as a
particular help to sinners, a heavenly power who would take
their side. Being the mother of the Judge as well as of the ones
on trial, Mary could soften the heart of her Son and obtain
mercy for sinners, undeserving though they be. The resulting
contrast between Christ and Mary was expressed by many medieval writers and preachers: "The Blessed Virgin chose the
best part because she was made Queen of Mercy, while her Son
remained King of Justice; and mercy is better than justice."[9]
Mary, then, was a potent protector of her clients, warding off
the just anger of Christ. Given her power to influence even
Christ the Lord, she was also credited with being able to protect
people from the attacks of the devil and the earthly misfortunes
of famine, plague, and war. As a consequence, reflection about
her meaning became detached from the more objective story of
salvation history, proceeding in an isolation that grew more intense as the millennium progressed.

Toward the end of this period, Bernardine of Siena (d.1444)
trenchantly summed up the general perception when he
preached:

> Every grace which is communicated to this world has a threefold
> procession. For from God to Christ, from Christ to the Virgin,
> from the Virgin to us, it is dispensed in a most orderly fashion
> . . . I do not hesitate to say that she has received a certain juris-
> diction over all graces . . . They are administered through her
> hands to whom she pleases, when she pleases, as she pleases, and
> as much as she pleases.[10]

It is little wonder that devotion to Mary blossomed in a profusion of prayers, hymns, cathedrals, pilgrimages, poems, miracle stories, dramas, songs, images, and practices, an
outpouring that is impossible to codify.

Some of this material is beautiful and doctrinally sound.
From a theological point of view, some of it is superstitious and
fanciful. As the second millennium reached its midpoint, the
situation had deteriorated to the point where, in the words of
René Laurentin:

Repelled by a desiccated intellectualism, people sought life on the imaginative and sentimental plane. Throughout this period of decadence, popular enthusiasm for the Blessed Virgin never faltered, but the adulterated fodder it was nourished on consisted of trumpery miracles, ambiguous slogans, and inconsistent maunderings."[11]

The Reformation critique brought an end to some of the more blatant expressions of the mediating role of Mary, and the reforming Council of Trent called for correction of abuse. However, due to the polarizing of the divided churches, a new way forward was not forged. Instead, devotion to Mary became a badge of Catholic identity over against Protestant identity which sought salvation in Christ alone. Themes of Mary's universal mediation of God's grace and her protection of the sinner continued to resound in the writings of Popes, theologians, spiritual guides, and preachers, and her glories were acclaimed accordingly. This post-Reformation period saw the proliferation of new expressions of honor, such as papal proclamation of two Marian dogmas, the Immaculate Conception (1854) and the Assumption (1950); innumerable religious orders founded in Mary's name; new customs, such as the wearing of the Miraculous Medal; and pilgrimages to new sites of Marian apparitions, such as Lourdes and Fatima. In a very precise expression of this mindset, the term "mariology" was coined in the seventeenth century to describe the distinct body of theological thought that concentrated on Mary, her privileges, and her universal role in salvation. Toward the end of the second millennium, as this pattern of thought flourished with its own treatises and societies, Mariology had indeed gone off on its own track.[12]

Before considering Vatican II, which preserved the best of this Marian tradition while correcting its isolating tendencies, let us try to understand developments to this point.

II. INTERPRETATIONS:
MARY IS A COLLECTIVE NOUN

Granted its complexity, no one interpretation is adequate for the entire phenomenon. Scholars of different disciplines have ventured a number of explanations, each of which sheds its own light. Such exegesis of the Marian tradition also suggests ways in which it might be critically reappropriated for a theology of the future.

— The burgeoning study of the history of religions sees the Marian phenomenon as an example of mother worship. Given the presence of female deities in the religions of the ancient

Near East and pre-Christian Europe, the Marian cultus is actually an expression of faith in the divine under the guise of female symbolism: Mary is the female face of God.[13]

In truth, morphological similarities between the post-Constantinian ecclesial cult of Mary and the pervasive cults of the Great Mother in the Mediterranean world are simply a matter of historical fact. For example, natural sites where female deities had been honored with pilgrimage and prayer became associated with Mary: Grottoes, Springs, promontories, mountains, lakes, woods. Shrines and temples to the goddess were rededicated to Mary the Mother of God, outstanding examples being found in Rome, Athens, Chartres, and Ephesus. Artistic symbols of the goddess accrued to Mary: the dark blue cloak, turreted crown, link with the moon and the stars, the fertile dark of the black madonna. The iconography of Mary seated with her child facing outward on her lap was patterned on the pose of Isis with Horus, the mother herself an upright royal throne on which the god-king is presented to the world. Hymns, prayers, and such titles as Queen of Heaven resonate with praise and petition formerly directed to the Great Mother.

While the pattern of Christian Trinitarian faith officially held firm in the midst of this early process of inculturation, there is question about how deeply this pattern reached in the minds and hearts of believers so recently accustomed to the beneficence and maternal power of female deities.[14] Indeed, as our soundings in the Marian tradition have indicated, in piety and theological reflection Mary has at times replaced each of the persons of the triune God and their functions. From the perspective of the history of religions, this is to be expected as the human heart seeks the female principle.

— In the different view of historians concerned with social, political, and economic factors, the growth of the Marian tradition signals shifts in the distribution of civil and ecclesial power. Peter Brown's illuminating study of the cult of the saints, for example, links this cult with the patronage of the educated upper classes and the strengthening of ecclesiastical office as bishops gained control of relics and shrines.[15] This has obvious implications for the cult of Mary. The financial well-being of the clergy also enters the picture. Benedicta Ward, for example, shows the way, in order to gain funds to rebuild the cathedral destroyed by fire in 1112, some canons of Laon went on tour with a relic of the Virgin's hairs. Healings, as well as a desire to honor Mary, brought donations into their purse:

> The party returned to Laon with considerable funds, enough to
> continue the rebuilding through the winter. During Lent, how-
> ever, money ran out and a further, more ambitious tour was
> planned. This time the canons were to take the relics to En-
> gland. . . .[16]

The ascendancy of juridical papal power and its exercise in the
proclamation of the two modern Marian dogmas is yet another
instance of the way this cultus is connected with the body politic
of the Church, when viewed through the lens of social analysis.[17]

— Psychology, too, has taken its turn at interpretation. Ana-
lyzing the cult of Mary from an exclusively Freudian point of
view, Michael Carroll argues that male devotion to Mary per-
mits men to dissipate their repressed, incestuous desires for
their mothers in a socially acceptable manner, while female devotion to Mary enables women to release their own incestuous
desires by identifying with a woman who became pregnant by
her Father and bore his baby.[18]

By contrast, the Jungian school of interpretation sees devotion to Mary restoring wholeness by giving play to the under-
valued feminine archetype. Jung himself saw in Pius XII's
proclamation of the dogma of the Assumption an unintended
affirmation of the divinity of Mary. He considered the 1950 definition the religious event of the century, for it balances the
dominant masculine archetype of the Trinity that expresses itself in rationality, assertiveness, and independence with the
feminine archetype of Mary, symbol of bodiliness, sensitivity,
relationality, and the desire to nurture.[19] In this tradition, others, such as Joan Chamberlain Engelsman, argue that the feminine archetype, suppressed in the Christian view of God and
Christ, reappears in Mariology, although in a partial and distorted way (lacking female rage, for example). Although osten-
sibly meant to glorify her son, Jesus Christ, popular piety and
theological speculation about Mary have both produced an unexpected result:

> Mary emerged as a powerful figure in her own right, with many
> attributes formerly attributed to the Hellenistic goddesses.
> Clearly this is an example of the return of the repressed feminine
> which found a weak spot and, by opening another path for itself,
> came to light without the acquiescence of the ego and without its
> understanding.[20]

— In addition to the history of religions, social history, and
psychology, the field of theology itself has produced varying
readings of the Marian tradition. What may be called mainline
Catholic theology interprets the best of postbiblical tradition as
a legitimate development of doctrine and piety. The title

Mother of God, for example, rooted so deeply in Christological awareness, or the Hail Mary prayer that weaves together several biblical salutations together with the petition to "pray for us": each rightly carries the intuition of faith in cultural categories of a particular age. In this sense, the Marian tradition may be seen as an intrinsic part of that wider, living tradition that marks the history of the whole Church.

— From this same theological perspective, the excesses that characterized certain Marian developments in the second millennium can be attributed to deficiencies in official theology. Yves Congar, for example, argues that, under the pressure of a monophysite tendency, the divinity of Jesus Christ was stressed to the point where his real humanity slipped from view. In this situation, the totally and simply human Mary seemed more approachable. In addition, the gracious mercy of God in Christ was partially eclipsed by a preached emphasis on God's just judgment and by the detailed penitential system of the Church. Because of her image as a mother, who does not want even one of her children to be lost, Mary assumed the role of mercifully interceding for sinners and even of turning away Christ's wrath. Thus, a deficient Christology lies behind the over-enthusiasm for Mary's powers.[21]

— In a parallel way, other thinkers, such as Heribert Mühlen, note that, in the absence of a vital theology of the Holy Spirit, Mary, in fact, took over the place and function of the Holy Spirit in the conferring of grace. For example, Catholics have said of Mary that she forms Christ in them; that she is spiritually present to guide and inspire; that she is the link between themselves and Christ, and that one goes to Jesus through Mary. But, are these not precisely the roles of the Spirit of Christ? Biblically, it is the Spirit who makes Christ present, forms Christ in believers, guides and inspires. Attributing such roles to Mary is an indication of an underdeveloped understanding of the third person of the Trinity.[22]

— In addition to Christology or Pneumatology, some Catholic theologians also appeal to linguistic theory to interpret what may at first appear to be Marian overstatements. Rather than language about Mary being taken literally in a spatial, temporal, material way, it should be seen as metaphorical. Michael Schmaus, for example, judges that, even when official prayers apply to Mary titles which were originally predicated of Christ, as the *Salve Regina* prayer does by calling Mary "our life" and "our hope," such enthusiastic expressions are not intended to be theological assertions. They are pieces of poetry and should be interpreted by a hermeneutic suitable to the literary genre of

poetry, which is different from a hermeneutic of dogmatic statements.[23] Karl Rahner has thought in a similar vein, writing:

> Vatican II by no means ascribes to Mary the title and function of
> a Mediatrix in the strict theological sense, but rather takes the
> freer language of pious affection under its protection when the
> latter has recourse to the title 'Mediatrix'.[24]

— Protestant theologians offer a much more stringent interpretation of these Mariological developments. While affirming
the biblical view of Mary as the mother of Jesus and a woman of
faith and while accepting the conciliar title of *Theotokos* in the
light of its significance for Christ, they view much of the second
millennium critically, seeing what happened as nothing less
than a distortion of the Gospel. Promoting Mary to such prominence sells out the blessed word of promise that God's saving
mercy is freely and graciously offered through Christ alone.
Seeking Christ's favor through her intercession or other practices of piety subverts the Gospel truth that we are saved by faith
in Christ, not by our own personal efforts or merits. Thus, one
is not dealing with deficiencies in Christology or Pneumatology
or with linguistic, poetic license, but with plain error. In the
inimitable language of Karl Barth:

> We reject Mariology, (1) because it is an arbitrary invention in
> the face of Scripture and the early Church, and (2) because this
> innovation consists essentially in a falsification of Christian
> truth. . . . In the doctrine and worship of Mary there is dis-
> closed the one heresy of the Roman Catholic Church which ex-
> plains all the rest.[25]

Comparing the whole development to cancer, he argues that
"Mariology is an excrescence, i.e., a diseased construct of theological thought. Excrescences must be excised."[26] While not so
sharp in rhetoric, those who embody the spirit of the Reformation in ecumenical dialogue today are just as strong in judgment.[27]

— Arguing in a manner that makes ecumenical hair stand on
end, some Latin American theologians endorse what Reformation sensibility sees as distortion. Honoring the people as a locus of theology, they explain that Marian maximalism, so
characteristic of piety and thought of millions in Latin and Hispanic cultures, expresses an experience of the divine in female
form. For Leonardo Boff, Mary functions as the maternal face
of God, the woman who is ontologically divinized to become the
human embodiment of the Holy Spirit.[28] In Virgilio Elizondo's
evocative phrase, "The Marian devotion of the poor leads the
universal Church to a new appreciation of the very selfhood of

God,"[29] namely, to the female character of the divine, that needs
to take its place in human consciousness in connection with the
male. Revelatory of divine characteristics, Mary radiates all-
encompassing warmth and love, immediate presence, inspiring
energy, intimacy, and care for the little people, in the manner of
the Divine mother everywhere.

— While somewhat sympathetic to this view, North American
and European feminist theology mounts a far-ranging critical
interpretation of the whole Marian tradition. Guided by the
critical principle of the full humanity of women and having as
its goal the mutual participation of women and men in a community of the discipleship of equals, feminist theology sees both
Marian maximalism and minimalism as a creation of the patriarchal imagination. This creation, whether consciously intended to or not, functions to maintain male dominance by
giving women a Marian ideal that keeps them in their pre-
assigned, private, politically powerless place.

Official theology presents Mary, not as a real, historical
woman, but as the theological personification of the patriarchal
ideal of the feminine: beautiful, but not threatening; nurturing,
but not challenging; open to receive, but not taking initiative
from her own personal center. As female, her main virtue is
humble receptivity to the will of God, the sovereign God always
being imaged as male. She does not conceive and give birth and
remain sexually active like other women, for her virginity is
perpetual. Bleached of sexuality, totally devoted, lacking critical
intelligence and leadership potential, willingly obedient, all
heart, the official Mary directs the energies of the male celibate
culture that created her to the higher, spiritual feminine that
elevates the soul.

At the same time that this Marian symbol of the spiritual
feminine is exalted, a strong misogynism toward the sexually
active, maternal, and public roles of real historical women
grows apace. Throughout the tradition, female sexuality and
initiative are consistently blamed for the entrance of sin into the
world, in the beginning and forever after. Women's humanity is
denigrated in theory, and their gifts are excluded from public
service. Used as a tool of this subordination, the idealized Mary
stands out "alone of all her sex," an unreachable norm by which
all other women are judged to be deficient.[30] As one woman in
South Africa expressed it to me, explaining the reason her
prayer group had dropped certain invocations from the Litany
of Loreto, to call Mary "Mother inviolate, Mother undefiled"
casts all other mothers into impurity and defilement.

Since the dualistic mentality undergirding patriarchy divides the world into clear polarities, the Marian symbol is frequently not allowed to function as a model for men despite the biblical, conciliar, and theological notion that Mary is a type of the Church. Rather, Mary becomes a model for women only. This identification is promoted within a system where Christ's pre-eminence over Mary is the pattern for men's rule over women. Not only can women never be fully like Mary, but, even if they were, the result would be to sediment them in a subordinate position.

A case in point is John Paul II's encyclical on Mary that, despite some excellent passages, is pervaded with this sensibility. Noting that, even though she was present in the Upper Room when the Holy Spirit descended, "Mary did not directly receive this apostolic mission. She was not among those whom Jesus sent 'to the whole world to teach all nations',"[31] the letter goes on to say that the Marian dimension of Christian life takes on a special importance with regard to women and their status:

> Here I simply wish to note that the figure of Mary of Nazareth sheds light on womanhood as much by the very fact that God, in the sublime event of the incarnation of his Son, entrusted himself to the ministry, the free and active ministry of a woman. It can thus be said that women, by looking to Mary, find in her the secret of living their femininity with dignity and of achieving their own true advancement. In the light of Mary, the church sees in the face of women the reflection of a beauty which mirrors the loftiest sentiments of which the human heart is capable: the self-offering totality of love; the strength that is capable of bearing the greatest sorrows; limitless fidelity and tireless devotion to work; the ability to combine penetrating intuition with words of support and encouragement.[32]

What feminist analysis reveals in this passage is an ideological use of Mary to stereotype and domesticate women. However praiseworthy the virtues enumerated may be, their one-sided listing as "feminine" virtues pours women's potential into the mold of the patriarchal feminine and consigns them to the private sphere. In the end, women are encouraged to give willing service to men as the totality of their Christian vocation — since for whom else are the work to be done, the tears to be shed, the words of encouragement and support to be spoken?

It is true that, while official Mariology reflects a sexist ideology, one can also sense the hidden, repressed power of femaleness breaking through in the tradition:

> There is the Mary of the people who is still the earth mother and who is venerated for her power over the secret of natural fecun-

dity. It is she who helps the woman through her birth-pangs, who assures the farmer of her new crops, new rains, new lambs. She is the maternal image of the divine who understands ordinary people in their wretchedness.[33]

Even the official Mary breaks her bonds and appears as a woman, immaculate and powerful. There are subintended meanings in the modern Marian dogmas that endorse women's goodness, women's strength, women rising.[34] These breakthroughs, however, do not remedy the fatal flaws in the Marian tradition of the Church. It has divided the one woman Mary from all other women, used Mary's relation to Christ to subordinate women to men, and designed a set of virtues calculated to suppress women's desire for equality and self actualization.

To sum up: interpretations of the Marian heritage range from the history of religions to social history, from Freudian to Jungian psychology, from the development of doctrine to deficiencies in the doctrine of Christ or the Spirit, from poetic license to the Reformation critique, from Latin American maximalism to feminist theology's critique of patriarchy. The ambiguity and pluralism of the Marian tradition itself are matched by the varied and conflicting nature of these interpretations. Indeed, "Mary" is a collective noun.

III. CHECKERED PROFILE

Marian theology and devotion were pointed in a new, yet ancient, direction by the Second Vatican Council (1962-65). In most basic terms, what the Council did was to reconnect reflection on Mary with the great themes that are at the heart of the Christian faith. To do so, it had to reconcile opposing forces: the promoters of the Marian Movement on the one hand, who had come into the Council seeking a new dogmatic definition of Mary as Mediatrix of Grace, and proponents of the biblical, liturgical, and ecumenical movements on the other hand, who sought a change in direction away from Marian maximalism. After spirited, emotional debate, and by the narrowest vote of the Council (1114-1074), the Council opted to include its teaching on Mary within the developing "Constitution on the Church," thus connecting her once again to the whole communion of saints, living and dead, united in the grace of Christ. The final text of this Constitution returns to biblical and early Christian sources to interpret Mary within two relationships: to Christ, through her historic maternity and her life's journey of faith, and to the Church of which she is a preeminent member and type. It also calls for the avoidance of exaggeration, fruitless and passing emotion, and vain credulity when Mary is honored. On balance, it affirms Mary's special participation in the saving mystery accomplished by the one mediator Jesus Christ, while braking the particular preconciliar way of developing this theme.[35]

While the Council was successful in ensuring what would *not* be the Marian wave of the future, it was not so fruitful in setting a positive direction. In the postconciliar period, traditional Mariology experienced a crisis, both its methodology and content having been passed by.[36] Intensely occupied with questions of Church, Christ, and moral issues set loose by the Council's deliberations, theology in general ignored the question of Mary.

One contribution stands out in these years for the clarity of its vision that does delineate a new direction: Paul VI's apostolic letter on Marian devotion, entitled *Marialis Cultus*.[37] Building on the Council, the Pope notes that some ways of honoring Mary, developed in previous eras, show the ravages of age and are not suitable to contemporary men and women. Thus, he calls for great creativity on the part of the Christian people and their pastors to do for our era what our forebears did for theirs, namely, develop ways to honor Mary according to our own cultural spirit. To facilitate this, he proposes four theological principles and four practical guidelines that should serve as criteria for the proper honoring of Mary.

Theologically, Christian belief is centered in basic understandings of the triune God, Jesus Christ, the Holy Spirit, and the Church. Any idea about Mary, therefore, that would theologically overshadow the one triune God, or impugn the mercy of Jesus Christ, neglect the sanctifying power of the Holy Spirit, or isolate this particular Church member from the whole body, is to be judged "out of order." On a more practical level, devotional practices should be imbued with biblical, liturgical, ecumenical and cultural sensitivity. In the latter regard, Paul VI gives the example of the emergence of women into all fields of public life. In this context, to present Mary as if she were timidly submissive or mindlessly pious repels contemporary people. Rather, she should be understood as one who fully and responsibly hears the word of God and acts upon it. Any practice, therefore, that ignores the great biblical themes of salvation history, does not accord with the dynamism of the Church's prayer throughout the year, gives ecumenical offense, especially with regard to the mercy of Christ, or is out of step with cultural advances is to be judged "out of order."

In my estimation, these precepts, wisely proposed as criteria for devotion, also serve well as criteria for renewed thought about Mary, into the third millennium. To what degree has such renewal occurred?

Where once uniformity prevailed, three decades of postconciliar development have resulted in a globally multifaceted situation regarding the Marian profile in the Church. The experience of Christians in different cultures reflects basic mentalities of their time and place, and this in turn affects their approach to Mary.

In Latin America, the veneration of Mary flourishes both in traditional ways as the great Mother of God, *Mater Dolorosa,* and Protector of struggling people, and in newer ways arising from base Christian communities as a woman of the people, herself poor, who announces and embodies God's gracious liberation. In eastern Europe and the Mediterranean countries, a thriving Marian cult is also visible, occasionally related to national aspirations, but more often the expression of a national character that is warm-hearted and affectionate. In Africa, the unseen presence of ancestors is foundational for the whole social fabric, including ethical values. Drawing on the genius of African peoples with their sense of the vital relationship between the living and the "living dead," the Church here experiences the living presence of Mary.[38] The ancient cult of ancestors is being adapted to veneration of the saints and Mary, with several Christian corrections: only God is powerful, so ancestors can do no harm; and Christ, rather than family blood ties, is the foundation for relation with the living dead. With these provisos, new forms of honoring Mary are developing. Catholic Christians in Asia, a minority within a minority in India, Indonesia, and elsewhere, find it necessary to keep their main focus fixed more centrally on Jesus Christ, while still reverencing Mary and the saints in creative, indigenous ways.

Perhaps most striking in this global panorama is the noticeable diminishment of private devotion and public theologizing about Mary in the democratic European and American countries on both sides of the North Atlantic. Theologically, this is being interpreted as a direct result of the new spiritual focus on Jesus Christ to which the Council gave impetus, along with new emphasis on Scripture and on the nourishment of the Eucharist. With access to God's mercy in Christ through Word and Sacrament assured, there is no longer a great, felt need for an approachable mother to mediate with distant divine powers.

Since this result has not occurred around the world, however, there are obviously cultural forces at play as well. The phenomenon, in all likelihood, is also due to the climate of secular culture, a powerful mood wherein the close connection between heaven and earth has broken down. Unlike their early Christian or medieval counterparts, post-Enlightenment, post-industrial Christians live in an environment marked by an historical and scientific mind-set that leaves very few gaps for God to fill. A practical atheism pervades the public life of these countries, finding its intellectual counterpart in the momentous question of whether there is a God at all.

The spiritual experience that results has attracted a host of commentators. For Karl Rahner, it involves entry into the spirituality of a bleak season where God is experienced as utterly incomprehensible and remote, even if known as the holy mystery who is ineffably near. For Constance Fitzgerald, this signals the classic mystical experience of impasse and dark night. For Sandra Schneiders, this dark night is not only individual, but a corporate purification. For Martin Marty, winter serves as metaphor for this season of the heart. For Martin Buber, the loss signals the eclipse of God. For Michael Buckley, our culture draws even believers into emptiness, silence, the cross, in accord with the dynamic of apophatic mysticism.[39]

For me, this shift in the experience of God is poignantly summed up in the contrast between the titles of the first and last books of my friend and colleague, William Hill, O.P., now seriously ill. He broke into print with *Knowing the Unknown God,* an exploration of the way the Thomistic category of analogy could lead the mind to God even in the contemporary world. God might be unknown, but we were possessed of a certain knowledge through the judgments we make. Now, his essays have been collected under the title, *In Search of the Absent God.* We are not in possession at all. Enmeshed in history and its suffering, we can but seek the hidden face of the living God.[40]

In this spiritual climate, sometimes characterized as postmodern,[41] people, as a rule, experience that those who have died have truly disappeared from this world. They are no longer accessible to the living in any direct fashion, as was possible to imagine in a previous age. Instead, as Karl Rahner describes it, they disappear into the dark mystery of God.[42]

If the main religious issue in Western intellectual culture is God and if the experience of even known loved ones who have died is that they are no longer accessible, then it is not surprising that interest in holy people of the past, including in a significant way Mary, has diminished. Existentially, Christians in a secular culture cannot seem to connect with Mary; intellectually, such a connection seems irrelevant to the burning religious questions of the day. As a result, theology of Mary, at least as traditionally carried out, is relegated to a marginal position.

In my judgment, the experience of the Church in so-called Third World countries has a great deal to teach those of us in a Western, secular culture that promotes unrestrained individualism rather than, in Robert Bellah's memorable phrase, habits of the heart that cultivate community.[43] Remembrance of ancestors in the faith, including Mary, within the communion of saints has potential to activate a consciousness sensitive to solidarity with others. However, such is not the present mentality of the majority of First World believers. Thus, the theses that I will propose in the last section of this essay are shaped by my own social location within a white, Western, middle-class culture wherein theology of Mary is of marginal interest.

IV. CURRENT CATALYSTS

Within Catholic Christianity in this culture, certain intellectual developments are contributing to a modest, renewed theology of Mary. These catalysts include biblical studies, justice and peace movements that attend to liberation theology, feminist theology, analysis of popular religion, and ecumenism. Since subsequent essays in this volume will deal with the first four of these, I will bring them into the picture only briefly to highlight their importance, while leaving their fuller exploration to my colleagues.

Biblical Studies

The growth of biblical studies has refocused theology's attention on the gracious abundance of God's mercy poured out in Jesus Christ and on the genuine humanity of the Word made flesh. Thus are removed two motives for the growth of Mariology in a compensatory way. Situating Mary within biblical truth returns theology to the contours it had in the first millennium. However, exact repetition is not possible due to the critical nature of today's biblical approaches.

Contemporary methods of reading the Gospels allow the voice of each author to be heard distinctly, rather than be submerged in a wider harmonization. The result, not surprisingly, is that the plurality and ambiguity of the biblical portraits of Mary become evident. Mark has a negative view of Mary and the brothers, depicting them as being "outside" the circle of Jesus' true family. Luke's picture, by contrast, is highly positive: she is the faith-filled believer, first to hear the word of God and act upon it. Less clearly categorized are the depictions of Matthew and John, both of whom position Mary as something of an outsider, yet one who plays a significant role in God's plan (see Matthew's genealogy and John's Cana story).[44]

In addition to distinguishing the views of the Gospel authors, knowledge of the stages of Gospel formation enables scholars to probe behind the written text for a glimpse of the historical Miriam. What they find is a first-century woman, probably unlettered, living in a rural village; a Jewish woman whose faith was shaped by the ancient Hebrew Scriptures and whose spirituality was centered on religious duties in the home, such as lighting the Sabbath candles[45]; the wife of Joseph and the mother of Jesus with a house full of at least six other children: James, Joses, Judas, Simon, and at least two of Jesus' sisters (unnamed as in the case of so many biblical women — see Mark 6:3)[46]; someone who did not at first understand her son's mission, but who, after the tragedy of his execution, was a member of the circle of disciples who believed in him. Elements of this historical picture enable scholars to construct an image of Mary as a woman of faith, an unconventional woman, a scandal, a member of the *'anawim,* a faithful disciple.[47]

Movements for Justice and Peace

The struggle for justice and peace is another important factor influencing contemporary thought about Mary. It yields a dynamic reading of the biblical picture of Mary as a woman of the people, one who shares in the sufferings, courage, and victories of the oppressed. A marginalized, peasant woman, she lives her life under the military rule of a foreign occupying power. Because of the decrees of the powerful State, she has to give birth in a stable far from home. She must flee with her child from the murderous intent of an evil king. Refusing to turn away from his prophetic ministry, her child is cruelly put to death by Roman soldiers.

Through it all, she clings to her God in hope, a stance expressed in the great song placed on her lips by Luke. Latin American liberation theology has virtually restored a critical reading of this hymn, the "Magnificat," to the consciousness of the world Church.[48] In this song, Mary prophetically announces the work of God who reverses the fortunes of the rich and poor, siding with the hungry in their need for food. She not only joyfully acclaims this, but embodies God's favor in her own life story. Carrying forward this reading, the *Pax Christi* litany addresses her as oppressed woman, marginalized woman, unwed mother, political refugee, seeker of sanctuary, woman centered in God, widowed mother, mother of a political prisoner, mother of an executed criminal. In each instance, she is claimed as *la compañera,* the companion. Her presence energizes those who hunger and thirst for justice, for it is precisely *this* kind of person for whom God has done great things, as symbol of the redemptive promise for all.

Feminist Theology

It does not escape the attention of feminist theologians that, through all of this, Mary lives her life precisely as a woman, that is, as a member of the group subordinated in every race and economic class. Mary shares with other women the fact that most of her historical story has not been remembered and that what has been preserved has been consistently shaped by the imagination of men. This imagination split her off from the company of women, making her rise over them as an unreachable ideal; even reaching it would ensure that they remain subordinate within a patriarchal system. In the face of this negative assessment of the Marian heritage as a whole, Christian feminism is engaged in searching for glimmers of light in the tradition which, when interpreted within the context of women's experience, will release a new, freeing understanding.[49]

A fundamental reshaping of the contours of Marian theology occurs as all the women in Jesus' circle of disciples are remembered and, in particular, the first apostolic witness of the resurrection, Mary Magdalene.[50] Within this circle, Mary of Nazareth's position as the mother of Jesus is recognized to be unique and, yet, as typical as any woman's. In contrast to the traditional emphasis on her motherhood, virginity, and humble obedience, her story is read so as to highlight her intelligence, initiative, independence, and personal identity within the framework of her historical vulnerability. It does not escape notice that, once Miriam of Nazareth gives her yes to God, she is never found at home again, according to biblical depiction.

In a particular way, feminist theology grapples with Mary's virginity and its ideological function in a system that has demeaned sexuality in general and female sexuality in particular. Mary's virginity has been used to exile women's sexual activity outside the realm of the sacred. But, is not sex the good creation of God and the way of holiness for most? Furthermore, the patriarchal imagination makes much of a woman's biological intactness, or lack thereof. But, why should a woman's identity be defined by her sexual relationship to a man? The stress on Mary's virginity itself betrays a sexist evaluation of women.

Drawing on critical biblical studies, feminist theology ponders the precise meaning of Mary's virginity. Since the infancy narratives of Matthew and Luke attest to the virginal conception of Jesus but not to Mary's *virginitas in partu* nor her perpetual virginity, subsequent and conflictual tradition must be consulted for the development of these beliefs. The Gospel infancy narratives themselves are literary constructions to such a degree that biblical scholars debate the proper interpretation of the virginal conception. Is it an historical fact, a theological symbol, or both?

The theologically important point of both these narratives is that Jesus is conceived by the overshadowing power of the Holy Spirit. This is the same Spirit who hovers over the primeval chaos at the creation of the world; who overshadows the Israelites in fire and cloud during their trek through the desert; and who descends to inspire the prophets. Biblically, the overshadowing of the Spirit always signals the creative power of God at work, healing, redeeming, liberating, making new beginnings. The theological significance of the virginal conception lies precisely here, in its witness that this child comes into the world thanks to God's free decision to be with the human race in a new, saving way. His life, in other words, is due to the creative presence of God. Whether the action of the Spirit excludes the normal biological manner of human conception is the point at issue, along with debate over whether, if there was a human father, it was Joseph, a Roman soldier, an unknown rapist.[51] The Gospel texts themselves bring forward what is of interest for faith: Mary's biological status as a religious symbol of the truth of her child's identity and the corresponding insight that her own faith was needed to recognize this. As a symbol, virginity points to an attitude, a disposition, an overture of the Spirit. Whatever the biological reality of history, Mary's virginity signifies her wholehearted centeredness in God, a stance that is exemplary for all disciples.

Feminist theology also critically appropriates Mary's representative function as type of the Church. Rather than typifying the "feminine" nature of the Church that receives grace from an active "masculine" God, Mary represents those subjugated people who have been lifted up by the emptying out of God's power in Jesus, being empowered to become self-actualizing persons in a new, redeemed community. As Rosemary Ruether writes:

> If Christ represents the emptying out of a divine power that puts itself at the service of others, then Mary, or the church, represents liberated humanity. Mary represents the 'person of the church' from the perspective of the conversion that has to go on

in history and between people to overcome dehumanizing power
and suppressed personhood.[52]

As the one whom all generations will call blessed, Mary heralds
a revolution in human relationships. The solidarity of sister-
hood with such a woman can turn oppressed women away from
their common denigrating lack of self-esteem and passive acceptance of marginalization. Instead of sapping and deflecting
the healthy anger of women, such a Mary can help to build a
genuine community of the discipleship of equals.

Popular Religion

A sympathetic analysis of popular religion is also contributing new insight. By no means restricted to theologically unso-
phisticated lay people, popular religion is a complex of
devotional expressions in particular cultures by cleric and lay
alike. Critics note that the Marian cult in popular religion ex-
hibits certain negative tendencies. It promotes a religious attitude that craves certainty, seeks tangible proof of the presence of
the divine, barters prayers for favors, is literal-minded and
emotionally intense, and, in its twentieth century form, often
expresses an apocalyptic, right-wing conservatism.[53] The positive experience of many who participate in the popular cult of
Mary, however, makes this, too, an ambiguous phenomenon.
Personal and corporate identity is enhanced, particularly in
groups under ethnic or cultural threat. Even in majority cultures, people find a spiritual link with the divine that is missing
from their experience of institutionalized Word and Sacrament.[54]

One phenomenon of popular religion deserves special mention in this regard, namely, apparitions or appearances of
Mary. These are puzzling phenomena to explain in ecumenical
dialogue; even to many Catholics their status is not clear. The
first key to their interpretation is the helpful theological distinction between public and private revelation. Public revelation is
the word of God communicated in the history of Israel and of
Jesus and his community, as set down in the Scriptures. Private
revelation, on the other hand, is insight granted to an individual person as a personal grace in the subsequent course of time.
Private revelation may serve as a gift for the Church, but it does
not require the belief or allegiance of the Church nor of any of
its members.

When ecclesial investigation results in approval of the appearance, and only a very small percentage are ever approved,
what this signifies is simply this: the message and practices asso-

ciated with the happening are in accord with the Gospel. Thus, the message and practices can be trusted not to lead persons astray. Conversion, prayer, work for peace, service to others — these are Gospel values and characterize the message of those apparitions that have received official approval. But, Church approval does not oblige Church members to direct their devotion toward the apparition, nor even to interest themselves in its story, for such matters belong to the sphere of private revelation and are not binding on the whole Church.

In a pastoral letter on Mary, the United States Catholic Bishops consider authenticated appearances, such as those at Lourdes or Fatima, to be "providential happenings [that] serve as reminders to us of the basic Christian themes: prayer, penance, and the necessity of the sacraments." In the context of this affirmation, these happenings are then put into proper perspective:

> Even when a private revelation has spread to the entire world, as in the case of Our Lady of Lourdes, and has been recognized in the liturgical calendar, the Church does not make mandatory the acceptance either of the original story or of particular forms of piety springing from it. With the Vatican Council we remind true lovers of Our Lady of the danger of superficial sentiment and vain credulity. Our faith does not seek new gospels, but leads us to know the excellence of the Mother of God and moves us to a filial love toward our Mother and to the imitation of her virtues. [55]

What is important is the Gospel, not a new invention. In the case of Mary, genuine honor is expressed by love that shows itself in following her example, imitation being the sincerest form of flattery.

There is no definitive Church teaching about what actually happens during an appearance. Theologians interpret the phenomenon in various ways. Such an occurrence is a manifestation of the charismatic element in the Church, a freely given moment in which the Spirit of God inspires the memory and imagination of a person to receive a message from God (Rahner). Or again, it is a hermeneutic of the nearness of God to people who are outside the normal official channels of access to divine power, such as the poor, the young, the non-ordained, the uneducated, rural folk, and women (Schillebeeckx). In particular circumstances, such a happening may be a sign of God's compassionate solidarity with defeated people, unleashing a new power of hope and human dignity (Elizondo on Guadalupe). [56] In any event, these phenomena are in the domain of private, not public, revelation, and, as with other devotional matters, individuals are free to participate or not, as the Spirit moves. Prudence would dictate that, in the case of current happenings that have not withstood critical scrutiny, care and caution be exercised. At the same time, these phenomena function in a prophetic way by calling attention to deficiencies in the way the official Church has opened access to the power and mercy of God through its institutional channels.

Ecumenical Dialogue

Clearing the ground of sixteenth century underbrush, ecumenical dialogue also contributes new directions for thought about Mary. It has uncovered a core of agreement among the divided Christian churches with regard to the biblical depictions of Mary and the Christological development that named her God-Bearer. It has also recognized that Christian people may fittingly honor Mary, along with other saints, for the grace God has given to her and for her faith-filled response. One surprise has been the discovery of the freedom Catholics enjoy with regard to any specific form of this honor. While the liturgy honors Mary and the saints and while individuals participate in this honoring insofar as they participate in the public prayer of the Church, there is no requirement that binds an individual's conscience to venerate Mary in private prayer or practices of piety.

Even granted this freedom, the practice of invocation, or calling upon Mary and other saints to "pray for us" to obtain spiritual or material favors, remains a problem for Protestant Christians. It seems to overshadow Christ's gracious role as sole Mediator, causing faith's trust to be displaced onto others. Although there is next to nothing written about this in the theological tradition, it can be answered that, just as Christians ask each other for prayer and help when alive, such prayer is not forbidden after death. Rather, within a rightly ordered faith, it can strengthen the bonds of friendship within the community of saints.

There remains the grave difficulty of the two modern Marian dogmas and their condemnations of those who do not believe in them, more offensive to Protestant Christians for their authoritative, conscience-binding character than for their content. One major dialogue to have tackled this so far, the Lutheran-Catholic Dialogue in the United States, has concluded that, if Lutherans do not condemn Catholics for believing these dogmas and if Catholics do not force Lutherans to accept them, then they need not be totally Church-dividing. The Church, it is argued, lived for centuries without them; they are not central to the hierarchy of truths; they were proclaimed during the period of division; and, unlike the situation where the pope in each case consulted the sense of the Catholic faithful before moving ahead, the sense of other Christian faithful was not consulted and, indeed, would have given a different answer.[57]

What ecumenism brings to a theology of the future, in addition to bracing critique, is a sober rootedness in the Gospel that sees Mary, in Luther's words, as "the foremost example of the grace of God."[58] Along with biblical studies, justice and peace insights, feminist theology, and new soundings in popular religion, it indicates roads *not* to be taken as well as a sense of new directions.

V. MARY IN THE CIRCLE OF DISCIPLES

Given the complexity of the Marian tradition and its interpretation; the implosion of traditional Mariology in the West after Vatican II; and the critical new shoots being put out by contemporary movements, whither a theology of Mary? While a full-fledged theology of Mary is perhaps premature, I propose to sketch a certain blueprint to draw disparate, but promising, elements into a new systematic order. This design is offered in the hope that it might ward off old excesses, conserve the best of the tradition, and bring it into contact with new insights, releasing a dynamism for the future.

In keeping with a major characteristic of all contemporary theology, the unifying theme of this design is a pressing concern for the well-being of persons, both individually and socially. Whether it be explicitly political, liberation, or feminist theology or more classic theology attuned now to human rights, justice and peace, a turn to praxis has occurred in our day, resulting in significant impact on the understanding of classical doctrines. These are being interpreted to yield their critical and productive force which challenges believers to become genuine disciples, following the suffering, liberating Messiah of God on a path which will inevitably bring them into the struggle for the good of all human beings.

Therefore, in the following series of theses I propose to examine the fundamental contours of a praxis-oriented theology of Mary, a theology that, in my judgment, will cohere with public concern for the good of others and be appropriate for the Church of the third millennium.

1. The correct theological locus for understanding Mary is the circle of disciples, the communion of saints.

This thesis presupposes that the central truths of Christian faith are solidly in place. There is only one loving God, neither male nor female but capable of being addressed as male or female, as Mother or Father. Divine mercy is poured out in Jesus the Christ whose Spirit dwells within each person, the community, and the world itself, renewing everything in the struggle of history toward the new creation. This thesis also assumes that criticisms from biblical and ecumenical studies and from the insights of women and the poor have registered, so that many elements of traditional Mariology will fade into insignificance. It presupposes, finally, the faith experience of large numbers of people in base community movements as well as in postmodern, Western culture. In this context and with these presumptions in place, Mary can be relieved of her compensatory functions (e.g., being the feminine face of God) and rejoin us in the community of believers.

2. Understanding Mary in the communion of saints accords with the pattern of biblical faith.

Just as Jesus surrounded himself with a community of disciples during his historical ministry, so too the risen Christ, who is not a vine without branches nor a head without a body. In Christian faith, Jesus Christ who alone is Savior is never found merely alone, but always surrounded by the company of his friends, both living and dead. Caught in the web of sinfulness, these people, "all the saints," receive God's graciousness into their lives and respond with love of their own. Known or unknown, they build up the world, tracing patterns of goodness in human history. Some do stand out for the risks that they took, and we remember them by name. The writer of the *Letter to the Hebrews* puts it this way:

> Now faith is the assurance of things hoped for, the conviction of things not seen. Indeed, by faith our ancestors received approval. By faith Abel offered to God a more acceptable sacrifice than Cain's. . . . By faith Noah respected God's warning and built an ark to save his household. . . . By faith Abraham obeyed when he was called to set out. . . . By faith Moses' parents hid him for three months after his birth. . . . By faith the people passed through the Red Sea as if it were dry land. . . . By faith Rahab the prostitute did not perish with those who were disobedient because she had received the spies in peace. . . . (Heb 11:1-40).

This magnificent litany comes to a crescendo with the encouraging words:

> Therefore, since we are surrounded by so great a cloud of witnesses, let us also lay aside every weight and the sin that clings so closely, and let us run with perseverance the race that is set before us, looking to Jesus, the pioneer and perfecter of our faith (Heb 12:1-2).

Just as faith in Christ creates a community of persons around the world despite geographical distance, so too it creates a unity of persons through time despite the distances of centuries.

The last Lukan depiction of Mary sees her gathered in prayer in the Upper Room along with the women and men disciples and the brothers of Jesus, all awaiting the coming of the Spirit (Acts 1:14). The last Johannine depiction of the mother of Jesus sees her bound in relationship to the disciple whom Jesus loved, forming one community born of the cross (John 19:25-27). In the biblical view, Mary is found within the great cloud of witnesses, in the circle of disciples, along with Mary Magdalene, the Samaritan woman, Peter, Andrew, Joanna, Susanna, Thomas, and so many others. She is one of our ancestors in the faith. Living out her conviction of things not seen, her life was a journey of faith, an adventure with its own rewards and terrors.[59] She gave herself to her God in the turmoil and darkness of human existence, walking by faith, not by sight. It is precisely this that commends and connects her to the community of disciples today.

3. Locating Mary within the communion of saints accords with the clear pattern chosen by Vatican II.

The Council's decision to include its teaching on Mary within the "Constitution on the Church" reveals a theological order of relationship basic to the subject. The Constitution opens with the affirmation that Jesus Christ is the light of the nations *(Lumen Gentium)*. Reflecting this light the way the moon does the light of the sun, the Church is the community of people who believe in Christ and witness him to the world. Subsequent chapters then treat of various groups within this pilgrim people: bishops and clergy, laity, religious. Knowing that death does not break the bonds that unite believers with Christ and thereby with each other, the Constitution does not end here. It goes on to speak of the faithful dead, those "friends and fellow heirs of Jesus Christ" with whom the pilgrim people on earth form one community.[60] Only within this context of the whole Church, earthly pilgrims and saints who are now forever alive in God,

does the Constitution then discuss Mary, that preeminent
member of the Church who is the faith-filled mother of Jesus.

4. Connecting Mary to the circle of disciples keeps her reality as a woman of our history firmly in view.

A first-century Jewish woman, known to have had an irregu-
lar pregnancy, married with children, taken up with the daily
routine of a village household, centered in God, taking unusual
journeys, suffering the execution of her first-born and joining
his circle of friends: this is the Mary of history. She is not a
goddess. She is not an archetype. She is not a principle. She is
not a "lady" nor a queen. She is not an ideal. She is a human
being, a village woman, her own self. She had her own life to
live:

> She struggled through, muddled too.
> In her years of prayerful pondering,
> grace was building on nature that had growing pains.
> Yes was successive, progressive.
> Mary advanced in the experience of age
> and the aging of experience.[61]

Historically, she has much more in common with average folk
than she has with the powerful, as she was excluded from posi-
tions of civil and religious headship. And, herein lies the power
of her story, for it is precisely *this* woman who hears the word of
God and acts upon it; precisely *this* woman to whom the gracious God has done great things, another remarkable instance
of the divine preferential love for the poor that creates the promise of a new order. If Mary is to be a symbol at all, a type of the
Church, then her historical reality must tether down this symbol at every point.

5. Locating Mary in the circle of disciples gives rise to the community model rather than the patronage model of relationship.

Both of these models of relationship to the saints and Mary
have occurred in history. The patronage model reflects a social
arrangement in which powerful persons can dispense favors to
those whom they wish. It seeks the saints with either petition for
their own blessings or with the request that they obtain blessings from the all-powerful God. One needs to have friends in
high places. This is reflected in the rather common idea that
Mary or one of the other saints has particular access to God or
Christ and, if prayed to correctly, can obtain a benefit for the
petitioner from an otherwise unaware or unwilling Almighty.

Arising from stress on personal neediness, this model approaches Mary as the most powerful heavenly intercessor.

The *communio* model, by contrast, structures relations among the redeemed in Christ along the lines of mutuality: all are companions in Christ. As early Christian writers describe it, other holy persons who are now with God are comrades, fellow disciples, pilgrims with us who follow after the one love. To use a spatial metaphor, the saints are not situated *between* Jesus Christ and believers, but are *with* their sisters and brothers in the one Spirit. It is not distance from Jesus Christ, nor fear of his judgment, nor impression of his cold disinterest, nor need for grace given only in small portions, nor any other such motivation sometimes found in the patron-petitioner model, which impel one to honor Mary or the other saints. Rather, gratitude and delight in this cloud of witnesses with whom we share a common humanity, a common struggle, and a common faith commend their memory to our interest.

This is not to say that there is no difference between pilgrims on earth and saints now blessedly with God in heaven. But, it is to emphasize that, in the light of salvation by God in Jesus Christ, the relationship among all of the redeemed is fundamentally mutual and collegial. In this model, Mary is approached as our *campañera,* our friend. She is, in the words of Paul VI, "truly our sister, who as a poor and humble woman fully shared our lot."[62] Drawing courage from her example, we pray *with* her more often than we pray to her, realizing our common stance before God.

6. The categories of memory, narrative, and solidarity express theological understanding of Mary in the circle of disciples.

These conceptual tools are not decorative notions brought in to adorn a Christian proclamation that can be better understood by more abstract thought processes. Rather, they are basic categories of human historical consciousness which are important to doing the truth in love in the midst of a conflictual world. What was expressed in classical theology of Mary receives new meaning in these categories.[63]

Solidarity, in addition to expressing the living *koinonia* of God's people, also connotes a vital union of interests in a group, usually in the face of opposition. Besides common feeling for people like ourselves, it involves partnership with those unlike ourselves, particularly with those in need, perhaps causing us loss. When used with reference to all the saints, this category

signifies a vital community in God between the living and the
dead in the face of the powers of evil. In a particular way, it
evokes alliance with the victims of history, those who have been
defeated and overcome. The living do not go on as if these persons are unimportant, but witness to their lasting value before
God. In solidarity with Mary who suffered the loss of her child
due to an unjust exercise of State power, for example, Latin
American women whose children have been disappeared demand their return. Solidarity is thus a category of help, support, and challenge by means of which the dead are affirmed as
having a future and the living are strengthened to put their
shoulders to the wheel of the unfinished agenda of justice. It
brings critical, productive power to the conciliar community
model of Mary and the saints.

In spite of the persistence of human imagination that, with a
kind of naive realism, pictures Mary in heaven in earthly terms,
her transformed situation is more unlike than like ordinary human existence. For this reason, solidarity is activated primarily
through narrative memory, a remembrance that makes power-
fully present the effectiveness of her life.

Narrative remembrance tells the story of past sufferings and
victories in order to break the stranglehold of present oppression. It calls the present into question. By lifting up promises
that still go unrealized, it galvanizes hope that new possibilities
can become reality now, at last. By imagining a better future, it
paves the way to protest and resistance, startling those who are
despondent into movement. The future is opened up in a new
way by the surplus of meaning carried in the act of remember-
ing.

At the heart of Christian faith is *the* dangerous memory of the
passion, death, and resurrection of Jesus, that carries the
pledge of a future for all. As noted repeatedly in the liturgy and
in conciliar documents, the Church "venerates the memory" of
the saints and Mary whose stories are woven in with his.[64] This
action evokes the challenge of their lives and sets the community
on the path of resistance, celebration, and hope in God. Within
the circle of disciples, narrative remembrance of Mary carries
this critical, prophetic, life-releasing edge. We remember her;
we tell her story; we find ourselves in a graced circle of love with
her before God; our lives enact the critical dream of God for the
world.

7. Within the circle of disciples Mary, along with others in differing ways, assumes a symbolic function, signifying to the community something of the best of its own truth and aspirations.

This symbolization is a process that takes place in the imagination of every community as it seeks exemplars and inspiring personifications of its own ideal identity. In the Christian community, all the saints are concrete persons in whom the grace of God has become victorious in this world in such a way that others can actually recognize their own calling. As both redeemed sinners themselves and creative models of holiness for others, they are a vital part of the history of grace in the world. In her own particular way, St. Mary carries out this vocation of the saint.[65] In God's favor to her and the pattern of her faith-filled life, the mystery of victorious grace is made uniquely manifest to the people called Church who are similarly called through grace to ultimate glory.

In this context, the ancient doctrines of Mary's motherhood and virginity point evocatively to the call of all disciples to give birth to Christ with free, wholehearted dedication.[66] The modern Marian dogmas of the Immaculate Conception and Assumption can also be interpreted as "not isolated privileges but mysteries filled with meaning for the whole Church."[67] Insofar as the absence of sin signals the presence of grace, the former testifies to the graciousness of God that surrounds her life from its beginning, symbol of God's free offer of grace to every human life born into the world. The latter points to that redeemed future promised to all people in the completeness of their embodied identity. Mary's own journey of faith gives a particular shape to the articulation of these doctrines, but the truth of grace and glory to which they point is universal.

*   *   *   *   *

Each of the above theses clarifies the design proposed here for a Marian theology of the future, whose unifying vision lies in the idea that the correct theological locus for understanding Mary is the circle of disciples, the communion of saints.

CONCLUSION

This essay has traversed much terrain, scouting a theology of Mary past, present, and future. Much more remains to be done. My own recommendation of a *communio* pattern to Marian theology is motivated as much by its coherence with biblical and conciliar models as it is by its value for a credible, living faith today. Daily headlines bear out the rampant individualism

that characterizes the public culture of the late twentieth century capitalist West, living as we do without "habits of the heart"
that cherish community. The tradition of the saints, with St.
Mary in the circle of disciples, is a resource for developing these
habits, needed for ecclesial as well as for civic life. Participating
with the living dead in the Spirit of Christ expands consciousness as we acknowledge the graced lives of this cloud of witnesses, thank God for their victory, learn from their example,
and share their friendship on the road of discipleship. This, in
turn, orients us toward others in the struggle for freedom and
justice on our conflictual earth.

A story told by one of my former students illustrates the
power of the Marian tradition when understood in this way.[68]
Shortly after arriving in the Philippines, he noticed that an old
woman remained after daily morning Mass to make the Stations of the Cross. While impressed by her piety, he nevertheless found it odd that she performed this devotion backwards,
starting at the last station and walking around to the first. When
he finally got to know her better, he gently inquired about this
practice, asking whether she knew she was going in reverse.
Her reply was stunning. She knew very well what she was doing, she said, and made the Stations that way so that "Mary
would not have to walk home alone." So much is carried in this
reply: a sense of solidarity with those who suffer, a willing compassion that accompanies them so that at least they have the
solace of another human presence, and a vision of Mary within
this circle.

Upon his return to his own Milwaukee parish, this priest invited all who had lost a loved one to death in the past year to
gather for evening prayer on the feast of All Souls. The prayer
service was designed in accord with his Philippines encounter,
emphasizing in music, scripture, readings, homily, litany, and
prayers that, just as Mary received the support of God through
her community, so she walks with us as friend and companion
in our troubles; in her company, along with others around Jesus
Christ, we need never be alone. At the end, following the greeting of peace, all the people linked arms and walked out of the
church together, moving to the hall where they shared refresh-
ments and mutual companionship.

The closing prayer of this service sums up the significance of
the discipleship model:

> Good and gracious God, we thank you for our sister Mary, full
> of your grace and love, who walks with us as a living reminder of
> your enduring presence among us. May we all journey together,
> keeping faith with those who suffer, until one day when we are at

our eternal home to live with you forever. We pray this through her son, Jesus Christ the Lord. Amen.

What we have here, I suggest, is the beginning of the theology of Mary that we seek for the future.

NOTES

[1]See the foundational discussion by David Tracy, *Plurality and Ambiguity: Hermeneutics, Religion, Hope* (San Francisco: Harper and Row, 1987).

[2]Hilda Graef, *Mary, A History of Doctrine and Devotion* (Westminster, MD: Christian Classics, 1985); and Walter Delius, *Geschichte der Marienverehrung* (Munich: Reinhardt Verlag, 1963).

[3]Irenaeus, *Adversus Haereses* 1.7, 2; see 3.11, 3.

[4]Walter Burghardt, "Mary in Western Patristic Thought," in Juniper Carol, ed., *Mariology* (Milwaukee: Bruce, 1957), I: 109-55; and "Mary in Eastern Patristic Thought," ibid., II: 88-153.

[5]"The Protoevangelium of James," in Wilhelm Schneemelcher, ed., *New Testament Apocrypha* (Philadelphia: Westminster, 1963), I:370-88.

[6]Jaroslav Pelikan, *The Growth of Medieval Theology (600-1300)* (Chicago: Chicago University Press, 1978), 158-74; Etienne Dalaruelle, *La piété populaire au moyen âge* (Torino: Bottege d'Erasmo, 1975), 529-45; Heiko Oberman, *The Harvest of Medieval Theology* (Cambridge, MA: Harvard University Press, 1963), 281-322; Elizabeth Johnson, "Marian Devotion in the Western Church," in Jill Raitt, ed., *Christian Spirituality: High Middle Ages and Reformation* (NY: Crossroad, 1987), 392-414. For background, see Clarissa Atkinson, *The Oldest Vocation: Christian Motherhood in the Middle Ages* (Ithaca: Cornell University Press, 1991), especially 101-43.

[7]Peter Damien (*PL* 144:761); in Graef, 207.

[8]". . . sic est voluntas eius, qui totum nos habere voluit per Mariam," in "Sermo in Nativitate B.V. Mariae (De aquaeductu)," *PL* 183:441 (whole sermon, cols. 437-48). This line was quoted in the Marian teaching of later Popes and became a classic axiom in the literature of Mariology.

[9]Influential sermon by an unknown author, thought until the twentieth century to be Bonaventure; Graef, 289.

[10]Bernardine of Siena, "Sermo 5 de nativitate B.M.V.," ch. 8, *Opera Omnia* (Lugduni, 1650), Vol 4:96.

[11]René Laurentin, *Queen of Heaven: A Short Treatise on Marian Theology* (London: Burns, Oates & Washbourne, 1956), 60.

[12]The term was coined by P. Nigido in his treatise, *Summa sacrae Mariologiae pars prima* (Panhormi, 1602), which split reflection on Mary off from other theological tracts. The maximalism associated with this word explains today's preference for "theology of Mary"-Donal Flanagan, *The Theology of Mary* (Hales Corner, WI: Clergy Book Service, 1976).

[13]Jean Daniélou, "Le culte marial et le paganisme," in D'Hubert du Manoir, ed., *Maria: Etudes sur la Sainte Vierge* (Paris: Beauchesne et ses

Fils, 1949), 159-81; J. Salgado, "Le culte marial dans le bassin de la Méditerranée, des origines au début du IV siècle," *Marianum* 34 (1972): 1-41; R.E. Witt, "The Great Forerunner," in *Isis in the Graeco-Roman World* (Ithaca, N.Y.: Cornell University Press, 1971), 269-81; and Elizabeth Johnson, "Mary and the Female Face of God," *Theological Studies* 50 (1989): 500-26.

[14]Geoffrey Ashe, *The Virgin* (London: Routledge & Kegan Paul, 1976).

[15]Peter Brown, *The Cult of the Saints: Its Rise in Latin Christianity* (Chicago: University of Chicago Press, 1981).

[16]Benedicta Ward, *Miracles and the Medieval Mind: Theory, Record, and Event, 1000-1215* (Philadelphia: University of Pennsylvania Press, 1982), 136-37.

[17]For political images of Mary, see Thomas Kselman, *Miracles and Prophecies in Nineteenth-Century France* (New Brunswick: Rutgers University Press, 1983).

[18]Michael Carroll, *The Cult of the Virgin Mary: Psychological Origins* (Princeton: Princeton University Press, 1986).

[19]C.G. Jung, *The Collected Works,* ed. Herbert Read et al. (Princeton, NJ: Princeton University Press, 1969), Vol. 11: 107-200 and 355-470.

[20]Joan Chamberlain Engelsman, *The Feminine Dimension of the Divine* (Philadelphia: Westminster, 1979), 132. See Ann Belford Ulanov, *The Feminine: In Jungian Psychology and in Christian Theology* (Evanston, IL: Northwestern University Press, 1971), espec. 314-34.

[21]Yves Congar, *Christ, Our Lady and the Church,* trans. Henry St. John (London: Longmans, Green & Co., 1956), 68-77. See René Laurentin, "Mary in the Liturgy and in Catholic Devotion," *The Furrow* 17 (1966), 347, who also points out the way Marian Devotion took on "the character of a compensation of life and of the heart." For background, consult Anthony Tambasco, *What Are They Saying about Mary?* (NY: Paulist, 1984).

[22]Heribert Mühlen, *L'Esprit dans l'Église* (Paris: Editions du Cerf, 1969); and Yves Congar, *I Believe in the Holy Spirit* (NY: Seabury, 1983), I:159-66 and III:155-64.

[23]Michael Schmaus, *Der Glaube der Kirche: Handbuch katholischer Dogmatik* (Munich: Max Hueber Verlag, 1970), II:693.

[24]Karl Rahner, "One Mediator and Many Mediations," *Theological Investigations* (NY: Seabury Press, n.d.), 9:172-73 and n.21.

[25]Karl Barth, *Church Dogmatics* I/2: *The Doctrine of the Word of God* (Edinburgh: T&T Clark, 1956), 143.

[26]Ibid., 139.

[27]George Anderson et al., eds., *The One Mediator, The Saints, and Mary: Lutherans and Catholics in Dialogue* (Minneapolis: Augsburg Fortress, 1992), especially 35-41, 49-59.

[28]Leonardo Boff, *The Maternal Face of God* (San Francisco: Harper and Row, 1987); see also Ivone Gebara and Maria Clara Bingemer, *Mary, Mother of God, Mother of the Poor* (Maryknoll, NY: Orbis, 1987).

[29]Virgil Elizondo, "Mary and the Poor: A Model of Evangelizing," in Hans Küng and Jürgen Moltmann, eds., *Mary in the Churches (Con-*

cilium 168) (NY: Seabury, 1983), 64. Whether this understanding in itself is helpful to the liberation of women is a disputed point; see Evelyn Stevens, "Marianismo: The Other Face of Machismo in Latin America," in *Male and Female in Latin America,* ed. Ann Pescatello (Pittsburgh: University of Pittsburgh Press, 1973), 90-100; and Mary DeCock, "Our Lady of Guadalupe: Symbol of Liberation?," in Carol Frances Jegen, *Mary According to Women* (Kansas City, MO: Leaven Press, 1985), 113-41.

[30]Marina Warner, *Alone of All Her Sex: The Myth and The Cult of the Virgin Mary* (NY: Knopf, 1976). See Kari Borresen, "Mary in Catholic Theology," in *Mary in the Churches,* 48-56; Catharina Halkes, "Mary and Women," ibid., 66-73; Elizabeth Johnson, "The Marian Tradition and the Reality of Women," *Horizons* 12 (1985): 116-35.

[31]John Paul II, *Redemptoris Mater;* E.T., *Mother of the Redeemer, Origins* 16:43 (April 9, 1987), #26.

[32]Ibid., #46.

[33]Rosemary Radford Ruether, "Mistress of Heaven: The Meaning of Mariology," in *New Woman, New Earth: Sexist Ideologies and Human Liberation* (San Francisco: Harper and Row, 1975), 50. Ruether probes the notion of the patriarchal feminine in "The Female Nature of God: A Problem in Contemporary Religious Life," in *God as Father? (Concilium* 143), Johannes B. Metz and Edward Schillebeeckx, eds. (NY: Seabury, 1981), 61-66; see also her *Sexism and God-Talk: Toward a Feminist Theology* (Boston: Beacon, 1983), 139-58.

[34]Mary Daly, *Beyond God the Father: Toward A Philosophy of Women's Liberation* (Boston: Beacon, 1973), 82-92; Barbara Corrado Pope, "Immaculate and Powerful: The Marian Revival in the Nineteenth Century," in C. Atkinson, C. Buchanan, and M. Miles, eds., *Immaculate and Powerful: The Female in Sacred Image and Social Reality* (Boston: Beacon, 1985), 173-200.

[35]"Dogmatic Constitution on the Church," in *The Documents of Vatican II,* ed. Walter Abbott (NY: America Press, 1966); hereafter cited as *LG* from its Latin title, *Lumen Gentium.*

See Otto Semmelroth, "Dogmatic Constitution on the Church, chap. 8," in Herbert Vorgrimler, ed., *Commentary on the Documents of Vatican II* (NY: Herder & Herder, 1967), 285-96; Karl Rahner, "Zur konziliaren Mariologie," *Stimmen der Zeit* 174 (1964): 87-101; René Laurentin, *La Vierge au Concile* (Paris: Lethielleux, 1965); and Elizabeth Johnson, "Mary as Mediatrix: History and Interpretation," in George Anderson et al., eds., *The One Mediator, the Saints, and Mary: Lutherans and Catholics in Dialogue,* Vol. VIII (Minneapolis: Augsburg Fortress, 1992), 311-26.

[36]Stefano de Fiores, "Mary in Postconciliar Theology," in René Latourelle, ed., *Vatican II: Assessment and Perspectives* (NY: Paulist Press, 1988), I:469-539. De Fiores points out the shortcoming that "not one of the postconciliar mariological manuals adopts the methodology indicated by the Council," p. 478.

[37]The Apostolic Exhortation, *Marialis Cultus,* issued 2/2/74, E.T., *True Devotion to the Blessed Virgin Mary* (Washington, DC: USCC, 1974). For what follows, see especially #25-39.

[38]John Mbiti, *New Testament Eschatology in an African Background* (Oxford: University Press, 1971); Edward Fasholé-Luke, "Ancestor Veneration and the Communion of Saints," in *New Testament Christianity for Africa and the World,* ed. M. Glasswell and E. Fasholé-Luke (London: SPCK, 1974), 209-21.

[39]K. Rahner, "The Spirituality of the Church of the Future," *Theological Investigations* (NY: Crossroad, 1981), 20:143-53; C. Fitzgerald, "Impasse and Dark Night," in Tilden Edwards, ed., *Living with Apocalypse: Spiritual Resources for Social Compassion* (NY: Harper & Row, 1984), 93-116; M. Marty, *A Cry of Absence: Reflections for the Winter of the Heart* (San Francisco: Harper and Row, 1983); M.Buber, *The Eclipse of God* (NY: Harper & Row, 1952); M. Buckley, "Atheism and Contemplation," *Theological Studies* 40 (1979): 680-99.

[40]William J. Hill, *Knowing the Unknown God* (NY: Philosophical Library, 1971), and *In Search of the Absent God,* ed. Mary Catherine Hilkert (NY: Crossroad, 1992).

[41]David Griffin, ed., *Spirituality and Society: Postmodern Visions* (Albany: State University of New York, 1988).

[42]Karl Rahner, "Why and How Can We Venerate the Saints?," *Theological Investigations* (NY: Herder & Herder, 1971), 8:7; and "The Life of the Dead," *Theological Investigations* (NY: Seabury, 1974), 4:347-54.

[43]Robert Bellah et al., *Habits of the Heart: Individualism and Commitment in American Life* (San Francisco: Harper and Row, 1985).

[44]Raymond Brown et al., *Mary in the New Testament* (Philadelphia: Fortress, and NY: Paulist, 1978).

[45]David Flusser, "Mary and Israel," in Jaroslav Pelikan et al., *Mary: Images of the Mother of Jesus in Jewish and Christian Perspective* (Philadelphia: Fortress, 1986), 7-16.

[46]John Meier, *A Marginal Jew: Rethinking the Historical Jesus* (NY: Doubleday, 1991), 316-32.

[47]Anne Carr, "Mary: Model of Faith," 7-24; Donald Senior, "Gospel Portrait of Mary: Images and Symbols from the Synoptic Tradition," 92-108; Richard Sklba, "Mary and the 'Anawim," 123-32; in Doris Donnelly, ed., *Mary, Woman of Nazareth* (NY: Paulist, 1989); Bertrand Buby, *Mary, The Faithful Disciple* (NY: Paulist, 1985).

[48]Leonardo Boff, *The Maternal Face of God,* 188-203; Mary Donahey, "Mary, Mirror of Justice," 71-90, and Mary L. Lifka, "Mary of Nazareth: Paradigm of a Peacemaker," 91-112, in C. Jegen, ed., *Mary According to Women.*

[49]Els Maeckelberghe, *Desperately Seeking Mary: A Feminist Appropriation of a Traditional Religious Symbol* (Kamoen, The Netherlands: Pharos, 1991), describes eleven feminist interpretations, and there are even more.

[50]Elisabeth Moltmann-Wendel, *The Women around Jesus* (NY: Crossroad, 1986); Elisabeth Schüssler Fiorenza, "Mary of Magdala: Re-

membering the Past," in her *But SHE Said: Feminist Practices of Biblical Interpretation* (Boston: Beacon, 1992), 79-101.

[51]In addition to *Mary in the New Testament,* see Raymond Brown, *The Virginal Conception and the Bodily Resurrection of Jesus* (NY: Paulist, 1973), 21-68; Raymond Brown, *The Birth of the Messiah* (NY: Doubleday, 1977), 122-64, 286-329, 517-42; Jane Schaberg, *The Illegitimacy of Jesus* (NY: Crossroad, 1990); Ute Ranke-Heinemann, *Eunuchs for the Kingdom of Heaven* (NY: Doubleday, 1990), 27-45, 340-48. Joseph Ratzinger notes that the doctrine of Jesus' divinity would not be affected if Jesus had been the product of a normal human marriage, *Introduction to Christianity* (NY: Seabury, 1968), 207-208.

[52]R. Ruether, *Mary, The Feminine Face of the Church* (Philadelphia: Westminster, 1977), 86. For other constructive suggestions, see Anne Carr, *Transforming Grace: Christian Tradition and Women's Experience* (San Francisco: Harper and Row, 1988), 180-200; Mary Jo Weaver, *New Catholic Women* (San Francisco: Harper and Row, 1985), 201-13; Mary Grey, "Reclaiming Mary: A Task for Feminist Theology," *The Way* 29 (1989): 334-40; and a South African perspective by Megan Walker, "Mary of Nazareth in Feminist Perspective: Towards a Liberating Mariology," in Denise Ackermann et al., eds., *Women Hold Up Half the Sky* (Pietermaritzburg: Cluster Pub., 1991), 145-60.

[53]John Shinners, "Mary and the People: The Cult of Mary and Popular Belief," in D. Donnelly, ed., *Mary, Woman of Nazareth,* 161-86.

[54]For modern trends in the study of popular religion, see Robert Schreiter, *Constructing Local Theologies* (Maryknoll, NY: Orbis, 1985); also Orlando Espin, "Tradition and Popular Religion: An Understanding of the *Sensus Fidelium,*" in Allan Figueroa Deck, *Frontiers of Hispanic Theology in the United States* (Maryknoll, NY: Orbis, 1992), 62-87. Regarding Mary, see Sandra Zimdars-Swartz, *Encountering Mary: From LaSalette to Medjugorje* (Princeton: Princeton University Press, 1991).

[55]National Conference of Catholic Bishops, *Behold Your Mother: Woman of Faith, Catholic Mind* 72 (1974), 26-64, quote at 51, #100.

[56]Karl Rahner, *Visions and Prophecies* (NY: Herder & Herder, 1963); Edward Schillebeeckx, *Mary, Mother of the Redemption* (NY: Sheed & Ward, 1964), 131-75; Virgil Elizondo, "Our Lady of Guadalupe as a Cultural Symbol: The Power of the Powerless," in H. Schmidt and D. Power, eds., *Liturgy and Cultural Religious Traditions* (NY: Seabury, 1977), 25-33.

[57]Anderson, ed., *The One Mediator, The Saints, and Mary,* 55-62; William Henn, "Interpreting Marian Doctrine," *Gregorianum* 70 (1989): 413-37.

[58]Martin Luther, *Commentary on the Magnificat,* in *Luther's Works* (American Edition, Philadelphia: Fortress, 1955-), 21:323. See Alberic Stacpoole, ed., *Mary's Place in Christian Dialogue* (Middlegrcen, Slough, England: St. Paul Pub., 1982); John Macquarrie, *Mary for All Christians* (Grand Rapids, MI: Eerdmans, 1990); and Wolfgang Beinert, "Maria in der Deutschen Protestantischen Theologie der Gegenwart," *Catholica* 45 (1991): 1-35.

[59]*LG* 58.

[60]*LG* 50; Elizabeth Johnson, "Saints and Mary," in Francis Schüssler Fiorenza and John Galvin, eds., *Systematic Theology: Roman Catholic Perspectives* (Minneapolis: Fortress, 1991), 143-77.

[61]Mary Lou Sleevi, *Women of the Word* (Notre Dame, IN: Ave Maria Press, 1989), 76.

[62]*Marialis Cultus,* #56.

[63]For solidarity, see Matthew Lamb, *Solidarity with Victims* (NY: Crossroad, 1982). For narrative memory, see Johannes Baptist Metz, *Faith in History and Society* (NY: Seabury, 1980); Stephen Crites, "The Narrative Quality of Experience," *Journal of the American Academy of Religion* 39 (1971): 291-311; Gary Comstock, "Two Types of Narrative Theology," *Journal of the American Academy of Religion* 55 (1987): 687-717. For Mary, see Walter Brennan, *The Sacred Memory of Mary* (NY: Paulist, 1988); and Elizabeth Johnson, "Reconstructing a Theology of Mary," in D. Donnelly, ed., *Mary, Woman of Nazareth,* 69-91.

[64]*LG* 50; also Vatican II, "Constitution on the Sacred Liturgy" #8, #104; as well as actual liturgical texts, such as the solemn blessing of the eucharistic liturgy for the feast of All Saints.

[65]Karl Rahner, "The Church of the Saints," *Theological Investigations* (Baltimore: Helicon, 1967), 3:91-104; ibid., *Mary, Mother of the Lord* (NY: Herder & Herder, 1963); Max Thurian, *Mary, Mother of the Lord, Figure of the Church* (London: Faith Press, 1963).

[66]*LG* 63-65; John Shea, "Giving Birth to Christ," *Church* 6 (Winter, 1990): 5-10.

[67]NCCB, "Behold Your Mother, Woman of Faith," #102.

[68]Rev. Jack Kerns, Summer Institute of Boston College, 1990.

Images of Mary in the Christian Scriptures

Alice L. Laffey

I. INTRODUCTION: THE BIBLICAL TEXTS

Of the twenty-seven books which compose the New Testament only six mention Mary, the mother of Jesus. These include the letter to the Galatians, attributed to Paul, each of the four Gospels, and the Acts of the Apostles, whose authorship is attributed to the evangelist Luke. Even in these books mention of Mary is minimal. She is nameless in Galatians which says only, "But when the time had fully come, God sent forth his Son, born of woman, born under the law" (4:4).[1] The text makes explicit that Jesus was a Jew, with a *human* mother and *God* as his father.[2]

The Gospel of Mark contains two references to the mother of Jesus.[3] In the first she is again unnamed. This time the reference functions, not to delineate Jesus, but to delineate his followers. The crowd sitting with Jesus tells him that his mother and brothers are outside asking for him. This scene occasions Jesus' teaching about the identity of his disciples. He asks, "Who are my mother and my brothers?" and then himself gives answer, "Whoever does the will of God is my brother and sister and mother" (Mk. 3:31-35). Jesus claims *familial intimacy* with any who do the will of God.[4]

In the second Markan reference to Mary, although she is here, for the first time, referred to by name, the text is again not about her but, this time, about Jesus. It functions, in the mouths of fellow natives of Nazareth, as an attempt to diminish Jesus' power and authority: "Is not this the carpenter, the son of Mary and brother of James and Joses and Judas and Simon, and are not his sisters here with us?" (6:3). In other words, since his occupation, his human origins, and the members of his family are well known to us, he cannot possibly be so wise and so powerful as his teachings suggest.

When one turns to the Gospel of Matthew, one finds six references to Mary. In four of these she is named (1:16, 18-25; 2:11; 13:55). The first two references appear in chapter 1. An extensive genealogy, identified as "the genealogy of Jesus Christ, the son of David, the son of Abraham" (vs. 1), concludes with "and Jacob the father of Joseph the husband of Mary, of whom Jesus was born, who is called the Messiah" (vs. 16). The verse tells us four things: Jesus is called the Messiah; Jesus was born of Mary; Joseph was the husband of Mary; Jacob was the father of Joseph. Mary is here identified in traditional patriarchal fashion, by the husband to whom she belongs and by the son whom she has borne.[5] According to custom, however, Mary might be expected to be identified as *the wife of* Joseph.

Chapter 1 of Matthew's Gospel also mentions Mary in its attempt to explain the way the birth of Jesus came about. The text reads:

> . . . When his mother Mary had been engaged to Joseph, but before they lived together, she was found to be with child from the Holy Spirit. Her husband Joseph, being a righteous man and unwilling to expose her to public disgrace, planned to dismiss her quietly. But just when he had resolved to do this, an angel of the Lord appeared to him in a dream and said,
> "Joseph, son of David, do not be afraid to take Mary as your wife, for the child conceived in her is from the Holy Spirit. She will bear a son, and you are to name him Jesus, for he will save his people from their sins."
> All this took place to fulfill what had been spoken by the Lord through the prophet:
> "Look, the virgin shall conceive and bear a son, and they shall name him Emmanuel,"
> which means, "God is with us."
> When Joseph awoke from sleep, he did as the angel of the Lord commanded him; he took her as his wife, but had no marital relations with her until she had borne a son; and he named him Jesus (vv. 18-25).[6]

Just as the references to Mary in Galatians and the Gospel of Mark, this text also *uses* Mary in its explication of Jesus; in it, an angel of the Lord assures Joseph that he can take his betrothed into his home as his wife, despite her pregnant state, because the child she is bearing is of the Holy Spirit. It is *the child* that legitimates such extraordinary behavior on Joseph's part; it is *the child* who is extraordinary.[7] Mary is the passive recipient of the act of the Holy Spirit.

The third and fourth references to Mary in the Gospel of Matthew occur in chapter 2. The third reference is occasioned by the visit of the wise men or astrologers to Jesus. When they enter the house, they see the child with Mary his mother, and they prostrate themselves and pay homage. The text merely asserts that the child — the "king of the Jews" whom they sought — was with his mother (vs. 11; cf. vs. 2).

The fourth reference, in which Mary is again unnamed, follows almost immediately. After the wise men had departed, an angel appeared to Joseph in a dream with a warning that King Herod was seeking to kill Jesus; the angel instructed Joseph to take the child and his mother to Egypt where they were to remain until further notice (vs. 13). Joseph obeyed. Then, after Herod's death, the angel again appeared to Joseph, this time telling him to take the child and his mother to the land of Israel (vs. 20). This word, also, Joseph obeyed. In three of the first four Matthean texts, Mary's identity is as mother, in relation to her son.

The fifth Matthean reference to Mary, occurring in 12:46-50, is a passage parallel to the one found in Mark 3:31-35. The literary unit affirms that intimacy and familial relationship are not dependent on blood, but on doing the will of Jesus' Father in heaven. Those who do so are Jesus' mother and brother and sister.

The sixth and final Matthean reference, 13:55, parallels, with slight variation, Mk. 6:3. Since the people of Nazareth know the carpenter (presumably Jesus' father, Joseph) and his mother Mary and several other named members of Jesus' family, they take offense at his wisdom and mighty deeds. In this, as in all other texts we have seen so far, the mention of Mary is not on her own behalf, but on behalf of another, whether that be in an attempt to identify Jesus, to describe the marvellous circumstances surrounding his birth, or to compare the close relationship Jesus has with those who do God's will.

When one turns to the Gospel of Luke, one finds seven references to Mary.[8] Six are unique to Luke's Gospel, and, in four of these, Mary is named; the other reference is a parallel, with variation, to Mk. 3:31-35 and Matt. 12:46-50. The first two Marian references in Luke occur in chapter one. The first of the two reads as follows:

> In the sixth month the angel Gabriel was sent by God to a town in Galilee called Nazareth, to a virgin engaged to a man whose name was Joseph, of the house of David. The virgin's name was Mary. And he came to her and said,
> "Greetings, favored one! The Lord is with you."

But she was much perplexed by his words and pondered what sort of greeting this might be. The angel said to her,

"Do not be afraid, Mary, for you have found favor with God. And now, you will conceive in your womb and bear a son, and you will name him Jesus. He will be great, and will be called the Son of the Most High, and the Lord God will give to him the throne of his father David. He will reign over the house of Jacob forever, and of his kingdom there will be no end."

Mary said to the angel,

"How can this be, since I am a virgin?"

The angel said to her,

"The Holy Spirit will come upon you, and the power of the Most High will overshadow you; therefore the child to be born will be holy; he will be called Son of God. And now, your relative Elizabeth in her old age has also conceived a son; and this is the sixth month for her who was said to be barren. For nothing will be impossible with God."

Then Mary said,

"Here am I, the servant of the Lord; let it be with me according to your word."

Then the angel departed from her (1:26-38).

The second reference to Mary in the Gospel of Luke follows immediately on the first and records her visit to Elizabeth:

In those days Mary set out and went with haste to a Judean town in the hill country, where she entered the house of Zechariah and greeted Elizabeth. When Elizabeth heard Mary's greeting, the child leaped in her womb. And Elizabeth was filled with the Holy Spirit and exclaimed with a loud cry,

"Blessed are you among women, and blessed is the fruit of your womb. And why has this happened to me, that the mother of my Lord comes to me? For as soon as I heard the sound of your greeting, the child in my womb leaped for joy. And blessed is she who believed that there would be a fulfillment of what was spoken to her by the Lord."

And Mary said,

"My soul magnifies the Lord,
    and my spirit rejoices in God my Savior.
For he has looked with favor on the lowliness
    of his servant.
Surely, from now on all generations will
    call me blessed;
For the Mighty One has done great things for me,
    and holy is his name.
His mercy is for those who fear him
    from generation to generation.
He has shown strength with his arm,
    he has scattered the proud in the thoughts of their hearts.
He has brought down the powerful from their thrones,

> but lifted up the lowly;
>> he has filled the hungry with good things,
>>> and sent the rich away empty.
>> He has helped his servant Israel,
>>> in remembrance of his mercy,
>> according to the promise he made to our fathers,
>>> to Abraham and to his descendants forever" (vv. 39-55).[9]

The narrator concludes the scene with the comment that "Mary remained with her three months and then returned to her home" (vs. 56).

These two scenes differ greatly from the preceding texts which refer to Mary. While both focus on her role as mother and the identity of her offspring, still, the angel appears to her, not to a man. She speaks, questioning the Lord's messenger. He replies with an answer sufficiently satisfactory to her that she agrees to his word.

In the second scene, Mary takes the initiative. Having been informed that her elderly cousin Elizabeth is pregnant, she decides to visit her. When Elizabeth tells Mary that she knows of Mary's pregnancy and the identity of the child she is bearing, Mary responds with a prayer of praise to the Lord who acts through the lowly.[10]

Three references to Mary occur in Luke 2. The first is embedded in Luke's account of the birth of Jesus. Joseph obeys the decree of Caesar Augustus that he and his family be registered; he therefore goes, "with Mary to whom he was engaged and who was expecting a child," from the town of Nazareth in Galilee to Judea, to the city of David called Bethlehem, because he was descended from the house and family of David. While they were there, she gave birth to her firstborn son, and wrapped him in bands of cloth, and laid him in a manger (vv. 1-7). Soon after, the shepherds, heeding the words of the angels, "went with haste and found Mary and Joseph, and the child lying in the manger" (vs. 16). Mary's response, when the shepherds made known what had been told them about the child, was to share the amazement of all who heard what the shepherds told them (vs. 18) and to treasure their words and ponder them in her heart (vs. 19).

In this passage, Mary does not speak; she is the recipient of others' words. The words spoken are not about her, but about her son. Nevertheless, she responds to those words — with the amazement experienced by all who heard the shepherds' words — but, in addition, with an appreciation of their import, and with reflection.

Luke's next reference to Mary occurs at the time of Jesus' presentation in the temple. "They (implying his parents) took him up to Jerusalem to present him to the Lord" (2:22). ". . . When *the parents* brought in the child Jesus, to do for him what was customary under the law, Simeon took him in his arms and praised God . . ." (vv. 27-28). After Simeon's blessing, the narrator reports that "the child's father and mother were amazed at what was said about him" (vs. 33). The narrator continues with the assertion that Simeon blessed them, that is, Jesus' parents, and said to Mary, his mother, "This child is destined for the falling and the rising of many in Israel, and to be a sign of contradiction that will be opposed so that the inner thoughts of many will be revealed — and a sword will pierce your own soul too" (vv. 34-35).

In this passage, Joseph and Mary appear in their role as parents. Their response to Simeon's words — like the response of all those who heard the words of the shepherds at Jesus' birth — is one of amazement. But, this text goes further. It singles Mary out — not just to indicate her *response* to words about her son, but to make her the recipient of words directed especially to her. Simeon speaks not only about Mary's son, but about Mary as well. He tells her that a sword will pierce her soul. Unfortunately, the narrator deprives us of Mary's response to these words.

The third reference to Mary in Luke 2 occurs within the context of Jesus' parents going to Jerusalem for the festival of Passover when Jesus was twelve (vv. 41-42):

> When the festival was ended and they started to return, the boy Jesus stayed behind in Jerusalem, but his parents did not know it. Assuming that he was in the group of travelers, they went a day's journey. Then they started to look for him among their relatives and friends.
>
> When they did not find him, they returned to Jerusalem to search for him. After three days they found him in the temple, sitting among the teachers, listening to them and asking them questions. . . .
>
> When his parents saw him they were astonished; and his mother said to him, "Child, why have you treated us like this? Look, your father and I have been searching for you in great anxiety."
>
> He said to them, "Why were you searching for me? Did you not know that I must be in my Father's house?"
>
> But they did not understand what he said to them. . . . His mother treasured all these things in her heart (vv. 43-51).

In this passage, also, Mary and Joseph appear in their role as parents. However, in this passage, Mary speaks. Jesus' behavior had astonished his parents. (In the previous two episodes of chapter 2, the words of the shepherds, and then the words of Simeon, had amazed them.) Mary speaks for the first time in the chapter. She who had been amazed (vs. 18 and vs. 33) and astonished (vs. 48) now asks Jesus the reason he has treated his parents as he has. Jesus' response is to ask his parents the reason they were searching for him (and why they were anxious?). They did not understand, and he, seemingly from his questions, did not understand that they had not understood. The narrative closes with a report that Mary "treasured" all these things in her heart. She who "treasured" the shepherds' words about her son (vs. 19) is now reported to "treasure," implicitly, the words of Simeon to her and the actions and words of her son.

The three references to Mary in Luke 2 are references to the woman who is the mother of Jesus, to the mother of the one who is "a Savior, who is the Messiah, the Lord" (vs. 11), of the one who is "the light for revelation to the Gentiles and for glory to the Lord's people Israel" (vs. 32), and of the one who "must be in my (his) Father's house" (vs. 49). As mother, within these three texts contained in Luke 2, she is spoken to about her son and by her son; once she even speaks to her son.

The sixth reference to Mary in the Gospel of Luke, 8:19-21, is a slightly abbreviated parallel to Mk. 3:31-35 and Matt. 12:46-50. Those who hear the word of God and act on it were those whom Jesus identifies as his mother and brothers.

A few chapters later, in 11:27-28, the seventh and final reference to Mary in the Gospel, the same message is brought home. This time a woman from the crowd, wishing to acknowledge the wonder of Jesus, extols the womb that carried him and the breasts at which he nursed. Jesus responds by extending this intimacy to "those who hear the word of God and observe it," not necessarily diminishing his mother, but intending to embrace many more than her.

In the Gospel of Luke, as in Galatians and the Gospels of Mark and Matthew, Mary is portrayed in typical patriarchal fashion, that is, in a manner which derives her identity and her importance from the male members of her family — in this case, Mary's son.[11]

A final reference to Mary attributed to Luke occurs in the first chapter of the Acts of the Apostles.[12] The reference is brief, the narrator's description of those who returned to Jerusalem after Jesus' ascension into heaven. The text reads:

> When they had entered the city, they went to the room upstairs
> where they were staying, Peter, and John, and James, and An-
> drew, Philip and Thomas, Bartholomew and Matthew, James
> son of Alphaeus, and Simon the Zealot, and Judas son of James.
> All these were constantly devoting themselves to prayer, together
> with certain women, including Mary the mother of Jesus, as
> well as his brothers (1:13-14).

Although the text names Mary, she does not speak. She joins
the others in prayer. The list of those who form this community
of believers includes those elsewhere named as Jesus' apostles as
well as his mother. Is this naming of Mary with the apostles an
attempt to raise her to their status and/or to indicate that Mary
travelled with Jesus throughout his public ministry? Is Luke's
intention here to incarnate what Jesus asserts in Lk 8:19-21 and
the parallels, that is, that the community of those who hear the
word of God and do it are his mother and brothers?

When one turns one's attention to the Gospel of John, one
discovers that, just as the Matthean Gospel contains references
to Mary not present in either the Markan or Lukan materials
and just as Luke's Gospel contains scenes involving Mary not
present in either the Markan or Matthean materials, so the
Gospel produced by the Johannine community contains two
scenes unique to it.[13] In these scenes, Mary is a central character. Yet, they are the only scenes in the entire Gospel in which
she does appear; and, although Mary speaks in one of them,
she is not spoken of by name in either one of them.

The first scene occurs in chapter 2 of the Gospel.[14] The text
reads:

> On the third day there was a wedding in Cana of Galilee, and
> the mother of Jesus was there. Jesus and his disciples had also
> been invited to the wedding. When the wine gave out, the
> mother of Jesus said to him,
> "They have no wine."
> And Jesus said to her,
> "Woman, what concern is that to you and to me?
> My hour has not yet come."
> His mother said to the servants,
> "Do whatever he tells you."
> Now standing there were six stone water jars for the Jewish
> rites of purification, each holding twenty or thirty gallons. Jesus
> said to them,
> "Fill the jars with water."
> And they filled them up to the brim. He said to them,
> "Now draw some out, and take it to the chief steward."
> So they took it. When the steward tasted the water that had
> become wine, and did not know where it came from (though the

servants who had drawn the water knew), the steward called the
bridegroom and said to him,
    "Everyone serves the good wine first, and then the inferior
wine after the guests have become drunk. But you have kept the
good wine until now."
    Jesus did this, the first of his signs, in Cana of Galilee, and
revealed his glory; and his disciples believed in him (vv. 1-11).

The narrator concludes that "after this, he (Jesus) went down to
Capernaum with his mother, his brothers, and his disciples;
and they remained there a few days" (vs. 12).

    This text departs significantly from the Synoptic tradition in
its depiction of Mary. Although it identifies her as the mother of
Jesus (vs. 1), in this scene Mary speaks, first to her son and then
to the servers. She does not tell her son what to do, but she
intuits that he will do something, for which reason she tells the
servers to do whatever he tells them. She travels with Jesus to
Cana, which turns out to be the site of his first miracle, and it is
at least partially due to her intervention that the miracle takes
place.[15]

    Much has been said and written about Jesus' addressing his
mother here as "woman." Since almost the only attention paid to
Mary elsewhere has been to her role as mother, might not one
suggest that this late Gospel wishes to grant her, not the physical
intimacy of natural motherhood, but the intimacy of "those who
hear the word of God and do it"?[16] In the final verse, the narrator reports that Mary travels with Jesus, his disciples and brothers, from Cana to Capernaum. One may ask whether the
Johannine community intends to imply that Mary accompanied Jesus throughout his entire public ministry (see also Acts
1:13-14 above).

    The second and final reference to Mary in the Gospel of John
occurs in the scene of Jesus' crucifixion.[17] The text reads:

    . . . Meanwhile, standing near the cross of Jesus were his
mother, and his mother's sister, Mary, the wife of Clopas, and
Mary Magdalene. When Jesus saw his mother and the disciple
whom he loved standing beside her, he said to his mother,
    "Woman, here is your son."
    Then he said to the disciple,
    "Here is your mother."
    And from that hour the disciple took her into his own home
(19:25-27).

In this final reference, Mary does not speak. Jesus speaks to her
and to "the disciple whom he loves." Nevertheless, the reader
may conclude from the narrator's comment that both Mary and
the disciple accepted Jesus' words to them. Jesus' physical

mother and his beloved disciple effect the intimate relationship Jesus wishes for all believers. Jesus' "hour" (cf. 2:4) produced Jesus' first miracle and has now produced the community eventually called Church.

Taking each text separately, including the parallels, one finds nineteen references to Mary in the New Testament.[18] In virtually every one of these texts, Mary's role as mother is specified. When one asks, then, what *image* of Mary can be derived from the New Testament, the obvious answer is that of "mother."

II. IMAGES OF MARY IN THE NEW TESTAMENT

A. Mary as Mother

In patriarchal cultures generally, a woman is identified by her father, and then by her husband, and then by the sons whom she bears. If one or another of these males is particularly outstanding — whether father, husband, or son, she is identified primarily by that male. The Jewish culture to which Joseph and Mary belonged was certainly no exception. Much has been written to justify the origins of patriarchy — the need to protect women as childbearers and to exalt the role of motherhood in a society whose very survival was threatened by high infant mortality, by multiple types of deadly disease, and by various human enemies struggling to dominate limited resources; however, much has also been written, predominantly by women it is true, to denounce patriarchy as a social system which categorically extols the male and denigrates the female. That Mary is portrayed in the New Testament predominantly as mother is both consistent with patriarchy and consistent with later Christian tradition which has viewed her almost solely in light of the particular son whom she bore. After all, is Mary not the mother *of God?*[19]

Because Mary's identity was so closely allied to her role as mother by those who produced the biblical texts, interpreters could and did readily describe her words and manner, especially in Lk. 1:26-38, as submissive. Patriarchal cultures presume and expect that females will be submissive to males. Traditional interpretation has, then, extolled Mary both for her role as mother of Jesus and also for her submissive behavior, expected of women under patriarchy.

B. Mary as Faithful Disciple

At least five of the New Testament texts which refer to Mary have been interpreted as understanding her in relation to Jesus' faithful followers.[20] Four times, in the mouth of Jesus himself, we hear that those who hear and do the word of God are his mother and sister and brother. Mary had heard the word of God, explicitly in Luke's account of the message of Gabriel, but only implicitly in Mark and Matthew, and had acted accordingly. She had borne Jesus, and her obedience became the model for all believers in Jesus; her motherhood was her faithfulness.[21] While those who hear and do the word of God are likened to Jesus' mother and brother and sister, they are never likened to Jesus' father. The obvious explanation for that omission is that Jesus' father is God. A corollary explanation, though one often overlooked, is that fathers are chiefs in patriarchal cultures, and, as such, they are not typically and appropriately placed in a subordinate position.

In the Gospel of John, not only does Mary travel with Jesus to Cana and to Capernaum (chap. 2), but she also becomes, symbolically, the mother of his beloved disciple, and, as such, of "all disciples," when Jesus identifies his beloved disciple as her son and identifies her as the beloved disciple's mother. Mary thus becomes the mother of all disciples, just as she had become the mother of Jesus. The text would suggest that Mary is again appropriately submissive: she hears the word of her son who is son of God and does accordingly.[22]

So much for traditional interpretations of Mary in the New Testament. They yield images of Mary as mother, the mother of Jesus, and of Mary, the model of true discipleship, with Mary's roles of mother and disciple closely intertwined. More recently, however, less traditional images of the way Mary is depicted in the New Testament have been suggested.

C. Mary as Unconventional Woman

The image of Mary as "an unconventional woman" has been put forth by Donald Senior, with the help of certain feminist and liberation theologians.[23] Building on Jane Schaberg's analysis of the Matthew infancy narrative, Senior concludes that Mary is a "scandal" in the Gospel of Matthew. When Joseph discovers that Mary is pregnant, as you will recall the text, he wishes to put her away quietly. However, an angel intervenes, assuring him that "that which is conceived in her is of the Holy Spirit" (1: 20). Though this text has usually been interpreted as indicating the extraordinary character of the child whom Mary was bearing, it is possible to interpret the verse, as Jane Schaberg has done, as a reference to the fact that Jesus was illegitimately conceived, either through seduction or rape.[24] If this is the case, then, according to Senior, the physical illegitimacy of

Jesus supports the theology which pervades Matthew's Gospel, that the God of Israel and the God of Jesus sides with the outcast.

Senior also concludes that Mary is unconventional because of the way she is portrayed in the Gospel of Luke. She is depicted there as what he calls an "unfulfilled promise." In the text, Mary herself queries the angel, who has just told her that she will bear a son, as to how this can happen since she does not know man (1:34). She, like Elizabeth — in Elizabeth's case, because of old age, and in Mary's, because of her present situation of lacking a husband — is not a likely subject for pregnancy. Yet, the angel assures her — with herself no less than with Elizabeth — that God can do the impossible. She, who cannot bring about God's will with natural recourse to intercourse, will be provided for by the Holy Spirit. Senior concludes, then, that by either measure — as the mother of an illegitimate son or as a young woman without a sexual partner — Mary's image is that of an unconventional woman.

The remainder of this essay will pursue some additional images of Mary as, I believe, she is presented in the New Testament. They are less traditional images; however, they too, like the image of "unconventional woman," are dependent on a liberationist/feminist perspective. Let me speak first to this perspective and acknowledge my presuppositions.

A feminist perspective presumes that the biblical texts, in this case, Galatians, each of the four Gospels and the book of Acts, were produced in a predominantly patriarchal culture, that men dominated the communities which produced these particular texts, that the texts were written by men, and that the texts have continued, until very recently, to be interpreted in a patriarchal culture and mostly by men. Patriarchal culture depicts women as inferior to men and as deriving their value relative to the men with whom they are associated — their fathers, their husbands, and their sons. In Mary's case, she is depicted predominantly in relation to the Son whom she bore, Jesus.

A feminist perspective employs a hermeneutics of suspicion as it seeks to interpret texts produced by men in a patriarchal culture. It suspects male bias and seeks to compensate by reading between the lines, paying almost as much attention to what is not said as to what is said. Further, because it assumes that women are equal to men, it looks for hints in the text which give indication of a woman's character and identity independent of the men with whom she was associated — her words, her deeds, et cetera — and seeks ways of interpreting these which may have been overlooked or discounted because of male presumption. It is such a perspective which has allowed Jane Schaberg, for example, to pose the question of the identity of Jesus' biological father, presuming that the patriarchal culture of Jesus' day and the patriarchal culture which has followed would have wished to suppress the idea that the Messiah's father had acted inappropriately — that he might even have been a rapist — and that, in any case, the Messiah's lineage was questionable.

That same feminist perspective allows me now to move from the images of Mary as mother and Mary as faithful disciple of Jesus, and even from Mary as "unconventional woman," to images of her as Prophet, as Queen, as Queen Mother, and as Matriarch.

D. Mary as Prophet

A prophet is one who speaks on behalf of and/or does the word, the will, of God. Though the English word "prophet" is derived from the two Greek words, "pro" and "femi," which mean "to speak in behalf of," the words *dibbēr* and *dābār* in Hebrew better identify the role of a *nābî,* a Hebrew prophet.[25] *Dibbēr* means to speak *or* to do (or to speak *and* to do), while *dābār* refers to the word spoken and/or the deed done. I would like to suggest that that which defines a prophet and that which is constitutive of biblical personages identified as prophets are also possessed by Mary.[26]

1. Like Abraham and like Gideon

Abraham, when spoken to by God, does the will of God; he obeys. Gen. 12:1-4 reads:

> Go from your country and
>   your kindred and
>   your father's house
>   to the land that I will show you.
> I will make of you a great nation, and
> I will bless you, and
>   make your name great, so that
> you will be a blessing.
> I will bless those who bless you, and
>   the one who curses you
> I will curse; and in you
> all the communities of the earth
> shall be blessed.
> So Abraham went as the Lord had told him. . . .

In the same way, when the angel Gabriel told Mary

> that God had favored her,
> that she was about to conceive in her womb and bear
> a Son whom she should name Jesus,
> a Son who would be great and be called
> the Son of the Most High,
> a Son to whom the Lord God would give
>   the throne of David his father,
> a Son who would rule over the house of Jacob forever,
> a Son whose kingdom would not end,

she responded that she was the handmaid of the Lord. Mary consented, allowing God's word through the angel to be fulfilled in her. In other words, she obeyed (1:28-38). Whereas the biblical text explicitly claims for Abraham the role of prophet (Gen. 20:7), no such explicit designation is given to Mary.

The biblical text seems also to identify Gideon as a prophet (Jdgs. 6:7). According to the account in Judges 6, when the Israelites cried out to the Lord on account of the Midianites, the Lord sent to them a prophet (vs. 7). The Lord called Gideon to "save Israel from the power of Midian" (vs. 14). Once Gideon realized that it was the Lord who had commissioned him, he obeyed.

In addition to the Lord's word to both Abraham and Gideon, and their obedience, another similarity exists between these two prophets and Mary, a linguistic one. When the Lord made a covenant with Abram, promising to give the land to his descendants and assuring him that he should "fear not" (Gen. 15:1), that the Lord was his shield, Abram lamented to God that he was childless, indicating that the inheritance would fall to an unrelated member of his household. A few chapters later, however, when the Lord again appeared to Abraham, this time by the oaks of Mamre in the form of three messengers, Abraham addressed the guests with this request, "My Lord, if I have found favor in your sight, do not pass by your servant" (Gen. 18:3, *RSV*). That very scene includes the promise to Abraham that Sarah will bear a son. Abraham had indeed found favor with God and should not be anxious over the present lack of a future heir.

The same juxtaposition of a prophet's responding to a messenger from the Lord with the request, "if I have found favor with you," and the Lord's assurance to the prophet to "fear not," occurs in connection with the prophet/judge Gideon. When Gideon is commissioned/called by the Lord to deliver Israel from the hand of the Midianites, he requests that he might receive a sign, some indication that will convince him that it is truly the Lord who is calling him (Jdgs. 6:17). A few verses later, God assures Gideon that his encounter with God will not result in Gideon's death; he has no reason to fear (vs. 23). Gideon, like Abraham, had indeed found favor with the Lord and should not be anxious over the outcome of the battle.

The linguistic juxtaposition of the imperative, "fear not," and the dependent clause about "finding favor with" God, might be considered merely coincidental, except for the fact that both phrases appear together only in relation to these two Old Testament personages, both of whom are identified as prophets.

These two phrases occur in the New Testament only in relation to one personage, and that is Mary. Gabriel tells her, "do not fear"; he then assures her that she has in fact "found favor with" God. With both Abraham and Mary, the favor results in a child; for Abraham, he is the heir of the covenant; for Mary, he is the offspring who will inaugurate a new covenant. With both Gideon and Mary, the favor results in deliverance/salvation; for Gideon, Israelite victory over the Midianites; for Mary, her son's victory over sin and death.[27]

2. Like Miriam (and Deborah and Hannah and Anna)

Exod. 15:1-21 contains a victory song associated with the Hebrews' defeat of the Egyptians at the Red Sea. In verse 20, the narrator reports that the prophet Miriam led the women in singing the victory refrain.[28] The verses read as follows:

> Then the prophet Miriam, Aaron's sister, took a tambourine in her hand; and all the women went out after her with tambourines and with dancing. And Miriam sang to them:
> "Sing to the Lord, for he has triumphed gloriously; horse and rider he has thrown into the sea" (vv. 20-21).

Miriam communicates the revelation, the reminder, that the victory is the Lord's.

Deborah, in Judges 4-5, is also identified as a prophet. She, too, sings a victory song; this time, after the Israelites' victory over the Midianites. She chants:

> That the leaders took the lead in Israel,
> that the people offered themselves willingly,
> bless the Lord! (vs. 2, *RSV*)

and concludes with the affirmation:

> So perish all thine enemies, O Lord!
> But thy friends be like the sun
> As he rises in his might! (vs. 31).

One other woman sings a victory song in the Old Testament, a song this time, not of victory over the people's enemies, in battle, but over her own enemy, barrenness. She is Hannah. After offering her son Samuel to God, "she worshipped the Lord," concluding her victory song with the following declaration:

> The Lord kills and brings to life;
>   he brings down to Sheol and raises up.
> The Lord makes poor and makes rich;
>   he brings low, he also exalts.
> He raises up the poor from the dust;
>   he lifts the needy from the ash heap,
>   to make them sit with princes
>   and inherit a seat of honor.
> For the pillars of the earth are the Lord's,
>   and on them he has set the world.
> He will guard the feet of his faithful ones,
>   but the wicked shall be cut off in darkness;
>   for not by might does one prevail.
> The Lord! His adversaries shall be shattered;
>   the Most High will thunder in heaven.
> The Lord will judge the ends of the earth;
>   he will give strength to his king,
>   and exalt the power of his anointed (I Sam. 2:6-10).

Though Hannah is never explicitly called a "prophet" in I Samuel, she is so named in *Tarqum Jonathan of the Former Prophets,* which suggests that, by the first century of the common era, she had become identified as a prophet.[29]

Similar to the prophet Miriam, and to the prophet Deborah, and to the prophet Hannah, Mary, after Elizabeth's confirmation of the victory wrought in her, proclaims:

> . . . He has shown strength with his arm;
>   he has scattered the proud in the thoughts
>   of their hearts.
> He has brought down the powerful from their thrones,
>   and lifted up the lowly;
> He has filled the hungry with good things,
>   and sent the rich away empty.
> He has helped his servant Israel,
>   in remembrance of his mercy,
>   according to the promise he made
>   to our fathers,
>   to Abraham and to his descendants forever (Lk. 1:51-55).

One woman in the New Testament, Anna, is explicitly identified as a prophet. After her husband died, the text recounts that she "never left the temple but worshipped there with fasting and prayer night and day" (Lk. 2:37). At the time Jesus was being presented in the temple, she came forward and "began to praise God and to speak about the child to all who were looking for the redemption of Jerusalem" (vs. 38).

Mary does what the prophet Miriam did: she sings a victory song in praise of the awesome accomplishments of God; and Mary does what the prophet Deborah did: she rejoices in God who has helped his servant Israel; and Mary does what (the prophet) Hannah did: she praises the Lord who brings down the powerful and lifts the lowly. Finally, Mary does what the prophet Anna did: she, too, praises God for the child who will redeem Israel.

3. Like Moses

But, Mary's prophetic role is not limited to the obedience of an Abraham, or the victory proclamation of a Miriam or a Deborah or a Hannah or an Anna; rather, Mary also shares the prophetic call of Moses. Recall Moses' first encounter with God on Horeb. Moses caught sight of the burning bush, drew near, and heard God's declaration that he had witnessed his people's affliction in Egypt, that he had heard their cry, and that he had decided to rescue them and lead them into a good and spacious land. The Lord then said to Moses,

> . . . come, I will send you to Pharaoh to bring
> my people, the Israelites, out of Egypt (Exod. 3:10).

Moses answered the Lord with a question,

> Who am I that I should go to Pharaoh, and
> bring the Israelites out of Egypt? (vs. 11).

God replied that he would be with Moses and that, as a sign that the Lord would be with him, God promised Moses that he would worship on Horeb after he had brought the people out of Egypt.

Moses replied to God with another question,

> . . . If I come to the Israelites and say to them,
>   "The God of your fathers has sent me to you,"
>   and they ask me,
>   "What is his name?"
>   what shall I say to them? (vs. 13).

To this question also, God provided a reply: I am/I will be who I am/who I will be. He is Yahweh (3:14).

Again, Moses questioned God, ". . . But suppose they do not believe me, or listen to me?" (4:1); in response to which God gave Moses the power to transform a rod into a snake and then

back into a rod again (vv. 2-4). Surely the people would take
seriously the word of one who could do such a thing.

When Moses questioned God again, asking the reason Phar-
aoh would listen to him (6:30) since he was a poor speaker, the
Lord answered his question by appointing Aaron to be the
spokesperson of Moses. In spite of Moses' many questions to
the Lord and his uncertainty about his ability to carry out the
Lord's will, the Lord assured him that he would be with him
and that his word is (and will be) effective.

When Mary encounters the angel of the Lord who declares to
her that she will conceive and bear a son, she too raises a question:

> How shall this be since I have no relations
> with a man? (Lk. 1:34, NAB).

The angel's reply to Mary is three fold:
1) that the Holy Spirit will come upon her and the power of
   the Most High will overshadow her, because of which the
   child to be born will be called the Son of God;
2) that her cousin Elizabeth has conceived a child in her old
   age, and
3) that nothing is impossible with God.

The reply satisfies her. She consents to become the child's
mother.

The structure of the text would suggest that Elizabeth's pregnancy functions in a manner similar to the signs God promised
Moses. Prophetic word which is true is of God and comes to
pass (cf. Deut. 18); the pregnancy of a barren old woman is also
of God. When their questions are answered, both Moses and
Mary embrace the tasks to which God has called them. Yet, in
contrast to Moses who identifies himself as God's prophet when
he tells the Israelites that they should listen to the prophet like
himself whom the Lord will raise up for them (Deut. 18:15) and
whom the narrator describes as unlike any other prophet whom
the Lord raised up either before or after him, whom the Lord
knew face to face (34:10), Mary is deprived of the designation
prophet.

4. Like Elijah and Elisha

The accounts regarding Elijah and Elisha contained in 1-2
Kings make clear their prophetic identity. Not only do they
speak the word of God, a word which the editors take great pains
to assure us is fulfilled, but they also *act* with the power of God to
do the work of God. As Moses' rod split the sea in two, that the
Israelites might pass through it on dry land (Exod. 14:16), so

Elijah saw to it that, despite the drought and famine, neither the widow's jar of flour nor her jug of oil went empty (1 Kgs. 17:7-16) and Elisha raised back to life the Shunammite's son (2 Kgs. 4:8-37). In the same way, acting with the power of God to do the work of God, the young woman Mary, who confessed to not having had sexual relations, becomes the mother of Jesus. Elijah and Elisha, like Moses and Mary, bear witness to the fact that "nothing is impossible with God" (Lk. 1:37).

5. Like Hosea, and Jeremiah, and Ezekiel

When most of us think of the Old Testament prophets, we think of the men after whom books of the Bible are named, i.e., Hosea, Jeremiah, Ezekiel, and the like. While we may think of Moses as a prophet because he speaks and does the word of God, he is more frequently identified as Israel's lawgiver. We are even less inclined to think of Abraham, Miriam, and Deborah as important prophets. Yet, the biblical texts do identify them as such, and they do conform to what a prophet is understood to be: they say and do the will, the word, of God. Nevertheless, let us turn our attention now to the writing prophets.

Mary has at least one thing in common with three of the writing prophets, and that is her sexuality. No, it is not likely that Hosea, Jeremiah, and Ezekiel were women. In fact, quite unlikely. Nevertheless, these three prophets use their own sexual circumstances as symbolic of Yahweh's relationship with Israel.

The prophet Hosea uses his marriage to a promiscuous wife Gomer as a metaphor for Yahweh's covenant with unfaithful Israel (Hos. 1-3). Gomer's three children bear names depicting Yahweh's alienation from the people — "Not My People," "I will no longer have compassion," and "Jezreel" (the valley of judgment).[30]

In contrast to Hosea, Jeremiah is instructed by the Lord neither to marry nor to beget offspring. Such celibacy for a Hebrew male would be extraordinary in Israel's patriarchal culture (Jer. 16). Yet, the word of the Lord indicates that Jeremiah's sexual deprivation is to prevent his sons and daughters from suffering the fate that would soon come to other sons and daughters of Judah — death either by the sword or disease, with no one available to mourn or to bury them, or else participation in the death of the nation through exile.

Finally, Ezekiel is told that he will become a widower, that the Lord will deprive him of "the delight of his eyes," but that he is not to mourn his loss after his wife's death (Ezek. 24). This event is to symbolize the profanation of the sanctuary and the fate of the soon to be exiled Judah. In each of these texts, the prophet's body incorporates into itself the fate of the nation.

The comparison with Mary should be obvious. Just as God had directed the marital relationships, the sexual behavior, and/ or the offspring of each of the three prophets in relation to the nation, so God directed the marital relationship, the sexual behavior, and the offspring of Mary in relation to the nation. In the same way, Mary's body expresses more than herself; it comes to symbolize the new life of the people of the new Israel. Her familial intimacy with Jesus incarnates the familial intimacy of all believers.

6. Conclusion

One must now ask, "Why did the evangelists not identify Mary as a prophet since both what she says and what she does clearly delineate her as possessing such a role?" A feminist hermeneutics of suspicion would suggest that it is precisely Mary's role as mother which has prevented her from being considered a prophet. Whereas Miriam and Deborah, both of whom sang victory songs, could be called "prophets," they sang of military victory, not fertility victory. That may explain the reason — even though Hannah exclaims quite explicitly that the Lord has swallowed up her enemies, that the Lord's adversaries will be shattered, and that the Lord will judge the ends of the earth, the biblical text does not name her a prophet.

Not only the writers of the biblical text, but also its interpreters, have been blinded by Mary's role as mother. Why is it that we speak of "prophetic calls," but of "annunciation" or "announcement" scenes?[31] I deliberately detailed the call of Moses, but I might also have detailed the calls of Jeremiah (Jer. 1), or Samuel (1 Sam. 3), or Isaiah (Isa. 6), each of whom is called by God to a task.

Abraham is called to go forth from his family's land to a land the Lord will show him (Gen. 12:1); Moses is called to lead his people out of bondage in Egypt to a fertile land (Exod. 3:10); Samuel is called to initiate Israel's monarchy (1 Sam. 3:13); Isaiah is called to go and speak the Lord's word to the people (Isa. 6:9); Jeremiah is called to speak the Lord's word, "to root up and tear down, to destroy and to demolish, to build and to plant" nations and kingdoms (Jer. 1:10). Is not the literary structure of God's call of Mary to become the mother of Jesus similar? The angel Gabriel declares to her the Lord's will, and she consents; in a manner similar to Moses, Jeremiah, and the others, her obedience changes not only her own life, but the life of God's people.

But, you might ask, "Why is it important to establish Mary's role as a prophet?" To that query I answer, "Separate but equal" is most insidious indeed. Extolling Mary's role as mother, but excluding her from sharing other roles, have resulted in associating women, in the Christian tradition, principally (if not exclusively) with a role of mothering. Though the origins of exalting the value of motherhood can be traced to survival needs from earliest times, to look at women's contribution only in terms of motherhood is to deprive all women, including Mary, of roles which I contend she was, and other women have been and continue to be, called to play in Church and society.

E. Mary as Queen

When one reads 2 Samuel 7:12-14, one notes the Lord speaking to King David through his prophet Nathan; included in his message is the following:

> When your days are fulfilled
> and you lie down with your fathers,
> I will raise up your offspring after you,
> who shall come forth from your body,
> and I will establish his kingdom. . . .
> I will establish the throne of his kingdom forever.
> I will be a father to him,
> and he shall be a son to me (vv. 12-14).

When one reads the first chapter of Luke's Gospel, verses 31-33, one hears the Lord speaking through the angel Gabriel to Mary; included in his message is the following:

> . . . And now, you will conceive in your womb
> and bear a son, and you will name him Jesus.
> He will be great, and
>   will be called the son of the Most High, and
> the Lord God will give to him
>   the throne of his father David.
> He will reign over the house of Jacob forever,
>   and of his kingdom there will be no end (vv. 31-33).

Do the two texts sound similar? What is declared to King David is declared also to (Queen) Mary.[32] And, both respond to the Lord, identifying themselves as the Lord's servant, i.e., references by David in 2 Sam. 7:19,21,26, and 29 (2x), and by Mary in Lk. 1:38. While both the *RSV* and the *NAB* translate *doule* as "handmaid," the *NRSV* translates the term as "servant." Accordingly, Lk. 1:38 reads as follows: "Then Mary said, 'Here

I am, the servant of the Lord; let it be to me according to your word' . . ."[33] Historical critics, examining what the original author(s) of 2 Samuel 7 intended, suggest that the verses legitimate a dynasty for David; the offspring who will come forth from David's loins is divinely sanctioned; in fact, God will be his father.[34] At a time that power struggles in the form of conspirators at the court or other contenders to the throne flourished, the text served to strengthen the claim of David's son, Solomon, to the throne.

Yet, whatever the intention of the original author(s) of 2 Samuel 7, it seems clear that the Lukan community deliberately adapted the text and used it for its own purpose: the promise to David of a dynasty is now being fulfilled in the person of Jesus. That which was said of old to King David is reiterated anew to "Queen" Mary.

It is unfortunate, however, that there is no precedent in the Old Testament texts for referring to Mary as a queen. The patriarchal culture of ancient Israel deprived all Israelite wives of kings, except Esther, of that title.[35]

F. Mary as Queen Mother

Jesus is understood to be king. The wise men of Matthew's Gospel come from the East to Jerusalem, asking, "Where is the child who has been born king of the Jews?" (2:2). Nathanael declares to Jesus, ". . . You are the Son of God! you are the King of Israel" (Jn. 1:49). In the Johannine account, after Jesus had multiplied the loaves and fish and fed about five thousand, the narrator reports that Jesus retreated to the mountain by himself because he realized that they were about to come and take him by force to make him king (Jn. 6:15).

Both the Matthean and Johannine Gospels indicate that Jesus' entry into Jerusalem fulfilled Zech. 9:9. It is Zion's king, the king of Israel, who enters Jerusalem. Matthew 21:5 adapts Zech. 9:9 to read:

> Tell the daughter of Zion,
> Look, your king is coming to you,
> humble, and mounted on a donkey,
> and on a colt, the foal of a donkey.

Jn. 12-13, 15 adapts Zech. 9:9 to read:

> . . . Hosanna!
> Blessed is the one who comes
>   in the name of the Lord —
>   the King of Israel! . . .

> Do not be afraid, daughter of Zion,
> Look, your king is coming,
>   sitting on a donkey's colt.

The author of Luke's Gospel places in the mouths of those acknowledging Jesus' entry into Jerusalem an adaptation of Ps.
118:26: "Blessed is the king who comes in the name of the
Lord. . . ."

According to each of the Gospels, Jesus' identity as "king of
the Jews" or "king of Israel" is central to his crucifixion. When
Jesus was brought before Pilate, it was with the accusation that
he was saying that he himself was a Messiah, a king (Lk. 23:3);
Pilate asked Jesus, "Are you the King of the Jews?" (Matt.
27:11; Mk. 15:2; Lk. 23:3; Jn. 18:33; cf. vs. 37); the soldiers
mocked Jesus, saying, "Hail, king of the Jews!" (Matt. 27:29;
Mk. 15:18; Jn. 19:3); Pilate, referring to Jesus, asked the
crowds, "Do you want me to release for you the King of the
Jews?" (Mk. 15:9; Jn. 18:39; cf. Mk. 15:32; Jn. 19:14); while
Jesus hung on the cross, soldiers taunted him, saying, ". . . He
is the King of Israel; let him come down from the cross now, and
we will believe in him" (Matt. 27:42; cf. Mk. 15:26), or, "If you
are the King of the Jews, save yourself!" (Lk. 23:37); finally,
over Jesus' head on the cross, they placed an inscription which
read, "(This is) the King of the Jews" (Matt. 27:37; Mk. 15:26;
Lk. 23:38; cf. Jn. 19:19,21).

Though Jesus never admits to being king, that is, he never
names himself as king, he does assert that he has come to bring
the kingdom of God (Matt. 4:17), and he even refers to his kingdom (Lk. 22:30; Jn. 18:36; cf. Matt. 20:21).[36] If Jesus is recognized as the Son of the Most High, as the one who would accede
to King David's throne and rule over Jacob's house; if he is addressed as Son of David and identified as king of Israel, as king
of the Jews — no matter what form his rule and kingship might
take, including merciful healing and kingly meekness, even
crucifixion — why is Mary never identified in any of the Gospels as a Queen Mother? Does not the Lukan text portray her as
functioning in a manner similar to David, with both receiving
the promise regarding the future of their respective sons? Will
not her son *rule* over the house of Israel? Is he not identified as a
king? Does he not identify himself as issuing in a *kingdom?*

Furthermore, in each of the three Synoptic Gospels, Jesus is
addressed and/or referred to as "Son of David." Blind men cry
out to him, "Have mercy on us, Son of David (Matt. 9:27;
20:30-31; Mk. 10:47-48; Lk. 10:38-39); a Canaanite woman
whose daughter is tormented by a demon does likewise (Matt.
15:22); finally, when Jesus enters triumphantly into Jerusalem,

the crowds call to him, "Hosanna to the Son of David! Blessed is the one who comes in the name of the Lord" (Matt. 21:9).[37]

The patriarchal culture of ancient Israel deprived most mothers of Israelite kings of the title, "queen mother." In fact, only three are explicitly accorded the title: Maacah (1 Kgs. 15:13; 2 Chron. 15:16), Athaliah (2 Kgs. 10:13), and Nehushta (Jer. 29:2). Maacah and Athaliah are both judged to be evil. According to the text, Maacah made an abominable image for Asherah, for which reason her son Asa removed her from being queen mother. Athaliah, who was a granddaughter of Omri, king of Israel, killed the royal family and was herself killed. Nehushta was taken into exile in Babylon with her son Jeconiah/ Jehoachin and others.

What I am suggesting is that, in the same way that the patriarchal culture deprived most mothers of kings of the title queen mother and of the recognition that might have accompanied such a title, the patriarchal culture of first century Palestine deprived Mary of being imaged as queen mother or as queen. By so doing, the New Testament texts deprive Mary of changing the image of queen and queen mother as her son Jesus changed the image of king and kingship.[38] Jesus' triumphal entry into Jerusalem was as one meek, humble, riding a donkey (Matt. 21:5; Jn. 12:13,15); so also (Queen) Mary, in contrast to the wealth and power associated with queens and queen mothers, wrapped her child in swaddling clothes and lay him in a manger (Lk. 2:7,12,16).[39] By failing to attribute the titles either of queen or of queen mother to Mary, the authors deflected attention away from her and to the others, especially, but by no means exclusively, to the Son whom she bore.

G. Mary as Matriarch

In the sections which precede, I deliberately changed the *New Revised Standard Version* translation "ancestors" back to the literal rendering of the Hebrew, "fathers." When the biblical text is proclaimed in prayer for a contemporary believing community, by all means inclusive language should be used. However, when it was written, its authors were not intending to include women, and their exclusion is part of the history that needs to be written back into the biblical text.[40] Sometimes this can be done by the use of inclusive language. However, at other times, other means are necessary.[41] It is to this end that I propose the image of Mary as Matriarch.

The word "patriarch" never occurs in the Old Testament, though the term is frequently used in Old Testament studies to refer to Abraham, Isaac, and Jacob. Rather, the term "fathers," referring to Abraham, Isaac, and/or Jacob specifically or to those whom the patriarchal writers of the biblical texts deemed the significant people of Israel's past generally, does occur. On the other hand, while one might not expect the term "matriarchs" to occur in the Old Testament, the term "mothers" almost never occurs either, and never in reference to Sarah, Rebecca, Rachel, and Leah.

The term "mothers" does occur in Gen. 32:12, but the reference there is clearly patriarchal, to the more-than-one mother of the children of Jacob. The few other references to "mothers" seem to refer to the vicissitudes of war. In Jer. 16:3, the prophet laments the futures of sons and daughters born from mothers and fathers; in Lam. 2:12, the exile's survivors cry to their mothers for food, and in 5:3, their mothers have become like widows. So much for the Old Testament.

The Greek of the New Testament uses two terms: *patres*, "fathers," and "patriarchs," *patriarchēs*.[42] While the term "fathers" is relatively common, the term "patriarchs" occurs only twice. Stephen's speech, which retells the history of salvation in synopsis form, includes the following:

> Then he (God) gave him the covenant of circumcision. And so Abraham became the father of Isaac and circumcised him on the eighth day; and Isaac became the father of Jacob, and Jacob of the twelve patriarchs. The patriarchs, jealous of Joseph, sold him into Egypt; but God was with him (Acts 7:8-9).

Clearly the Greek term is limited to denoting the sons of Jacob.

However, a cursory glance at various translations yields the following. The *New American Bible* translates with the term "patriarchs" six times. These include the two verses cited above, but also Rom. 9:5; 11:28; 15:8, and Jn. 7:22. While the Rom. 9:5 text could easily indicate the sons of Jacob, 11:28 seems broader:

> In respect to the gospel, they are enemies on your account; but in respect to election, they are beloved because of the patriarchs.

And, both Rom. 15:8 and Jn. 7:22 seem broader still, certainly intending to include Abraham, and also Isaac, and Jacob:

> For I say that Christ became a minister of the circumcised to show God's truthfulness, to confirm the promises to the patriarchs (Rom. 15:8).

> . . . Moses gave you circumcision — not that it came from Moses but rather from the patriarchs . . . (Jn. 7:22).

The *Revised Standard Version* uses the term "patriarch" in both Rom. 9:5 and 15:8, in addition to the two passages in Acts where the Greek term occurs; the *New Revised Standard Version* uses the term "patriarch" in addition to the two occurrences in Acts, in Rom. 9:5; 15:8, and Jn. 7:22. In other words, the translators were more patriarchal than the original authors.

You might ask, "Why, then, am I surprised and/or lamenting that Mary never received the designation 'matriarch'?" Or, "Am I suggesting that we begin to image Mary as Matriarch. Is my intention one of power and prestige? After all, several of the sons of Jacob — Zebulun and Dan, for example, do not seem to have been accorded corresponding power and prestige. What is my point?"

My point is this. Luke 1:46 might have been written, "And the prophet Mary said," introducing her prayer of thanksgiving and praise to God after Elizabeth's recognition of the new life with which Mary was pregnant, in the same way that Exod. 15:20 *does read,* "And the prophet Miriam, Aaron's sister, took a tambourine in her hand," introducing Miriam's prayer of thanksgiving and praise to God for Israel's victory at the Red Sea.

And, Lk. 1:38 might have read, "Then Queen Mary said," introducing Mary's acceptance of the angel's word, in the same way that 2 Sam. 7:18 *does read,* "Then King David went in and sat before the Lord and said," introducing his response to the Lord's word. Or, since the wise men clearly seek the "king of the Jews" (Matt. 2:2) whom Herod wishes to kill, Joseph might have been instructed to "take the child and the queen mother and flee to Egypt" (vs. 13). Whereas traces of New Testament tradition (in the form of Acts 7:8-9) and later translations of the New Testament designate Abraham, Isaac, Jacob, and the sons of Jacob as patriarchs, later tradition might have correspondingly designated Mary, not only as Mother, but also as Matriarch. At least several of the texts may indicate for her such an ecclesial role.

III. SOME CONCLUSIONS

What I have tried to suggest is that the images of Mary which can be derived from Scripture are multiple. The most obvious image of Mary is that of mother, the mother of Jesus.[43] Closely linked to the image of Mary as mother of Jesus, however, is the image of Mary as mother of the Church. These two images have together dominated the tradition. To complement these images, I have tried to suggest that some of the authors of the

New Testament, in spite of themselves, that is, in spite of the patriarchal culture in which they lived, depicted Mary as a character in her own right.

I have tried to suggest that the New Testament provides us with an image of Mary as prophet, a woman who stands in relationship to God as other prophets, both male and female. Rather than focus attention totally on the child whom she bore, I have tried to shift attention to the woman to whom God spoke, the woman who listened to that word, and the woman who consented to that word.

I have tried also to develop the image of Mary as queen, which I believe is also, though less obviously, derived from Scripture. Mary did not stand in history as a queen, but what happened to the king, to David, happened to her. The texts draw the analogy of David and Mary implicitly; I have teased out the comparison.

Further, I have tried to develop the image of Mary as queen mother. A king's mother is a queen mother. Jesus is the son of King David; Jesus is the king of Israel; Jesus is the king of the Jews. Jesus' mother is a mother who, by virtue of being a king's mother, is a queen mother. The New Testament texts lead us to such a conclusion, but refrain from making the assertion explicit. Granted, this image of queen mother is also the image of mother, focussing attention, consistent with the patriarchal culture of Jesus' day, on the son whom she bore. But, had her image of queen mother been developed more explicitly, then her proclamation of herself as servant (*doule,* in Lk. 1:38) of the Lord would have resonated even more clearly with her son's assertion that he came, not to be served, but to serve (Mk. 10:45; Matt. 20:28). Mary, although a queen mother, assumed a posture of servanthood, just as did Jesus, the king and her son.

Finally, I have tried to suggest the image of Mary as matriarch. My purpose in proposing this image is to suggest that what led the New Testament writers (and later translators!) to move from "fathers" to "patriarchs" is what might have moved later Christians to move from "mother" to "matriarch." But, such a linguistic shift never happened. A hermeneutics of suspicion must ask why.

Like Jane Schaberg, my intention has been to take a liberationist approach, though our findings are quite different. I, too, have been interested in what has been said about Mary, though it has not exactly been said "up front," as it were. My conclusion is not that she was raped; rather, I conclude that the patriarchal culture which pervades the New Testament texts prevented

Mary from receiving more explicit acknowledgment of the multiple images which must have emanated from her person.

By using imagination, I have tried to develop allusions and analogies and to read between the lines. The believing community has done the same for centuries. I have tried to develop images of a woman whose identity was not relational in a manner which derived her identity solely from motherhood; I have tried to develop images of a woman whose identity was, in fact, relational, but *a woman whose primary relationship was with God.* In addition, I have even tried to suggest images of a woman whose identity was relational in a manner whereby others' identity could be enriched from hers. I have dared to suggest that the Scriptures themselves contain images of Mary as a woman *in her own right* — before, and independent of the fact that, she became a mother.

NOTES

[1] *The Holy Bible. Revised Standard Version Containing the Old and New Testaments* (New York: Oxford University Press, 1973). *The New American Bible* translation (Nashville: Thomas Nelson Publishers, 1987) and the *New Revised Standard Version* (Nashville: Thomas Nelson Publishers, 1989) translate "born of a woman." The Greek *gunaikos* supports either rendering. Most biblical quotations which appear in this essay are from the *NRSV,* unless otherwise indicated, except that I have replaced "ancestor(s)" with "father(s)" in accordance with the original Hebrew and the culture which produced these texts. I have taken some liberty with the layout and spacing of certain biblical texts.

[2] On Gal. 4:4, see Alberto Vanhoye, "La mère du fils de Dieu selon Ga 4:4," *Marianum* 40 (1978): 237-47.

[3] John Charles Fenton, "The Mother of Jesus in Mark's Gospel and Its Revisions," *Theology* 86 (November 1983): 433-37. Most scholars believe that the Gospel of Mark preceded the Matthean account; I have chosen to pursue the Marian texts historically so as to be able to determine more easily the presence or absence of any theological development.

[4] Several biblical scholars note the reference to Mary as the last named in a genealogy which includes four other women — Tamar, Rahab, Ruth and Bathsheba — and seek commonalities among the women. See, for example, Francis J. Moloney, *Mary, Woman and Mother* (Collegeville: Liturgical Press, 1988), 11; and Raymond E. Brown, *The Birth of the Messiah. A Commentary on the Infancy Narratives in Matthew and Luke* (New York: Doubleday, 1977), 80.

[5] Mk. 15:40 refers to "Mary the mother of James the younger and of Joses," vs. 47 refers to "Mary the mother of Joses," and Mk. 16:1 refers to "Mary the mother of James." Since Mk. 6:3 identifies Jesus as "the son of Mary and brother of James and Joses. . . .," one must ask whether the mother of James and/or Joses is also the mother of Jesus.

Perhaps the references in Mk. 15:40, 47 and 16:1, in keeping with the thrust of Jesus' response in this passage, exclude Jesus in order to extend the familial intimacy. For additional comment on these verses, see Raymond Brown et al., eds., *Mary in the New Testament* (Philadelphia: Fortress Press, 1978), 68-72.

⁶The quotation from Isaiah 7:14 incorporated into this text has been used to support the virginity of Mary at the time of the conception of Jesus, though the Hebrew 'almāh may also indicate a young woman of marriageable age. When the Hebrew was translated into the Greek Septuagint, the term *parthenōs,* meaning "virgin," was used. On the subject of Mary's virginity, see Ignace de la Potterie, "La Mère de Jésus et la conception virginale du Fils de Dieu," *Marianum* 40 (1978): 41-90; and Joseph A. Fitzmyer, "The Virginal Conception of Jesus in the New Testament," *Theological Studies* 34 (1973): 541-75.

⁷Extraordinary circumstances regarding the birth of a child as an indication that the child will be extra-ordinary are common in the Old Testament. Recall the barrenness of each of the "matriarchs": Sarah (Gen. 11:30), Rebekah (Gen. 25:21) and Rachel (Gen. 29:31); of the mother of Samson (Jdgs. 13:2-3) and of Hannah (1 Sam. 1:5-6). Recall also the extraordinary circumstances surrounding the birth of Moses (Exod. 2).

⁸Mary Louise Gubler, "Luke's Portrait of Mary," *Theology Digest* 36 (Spring 1989): 19-24; and Deborah F. Middleton, "The Story of Mary: Luke's Vision," *New Blackfriars* 70 (December 1988): 555-64.

⁹John Brett, "Mary's Visit to Elizabeth," *Liguorian* 78 (December 1990): 18-21.

¹⁰As many as fifteen years ago, Elisabeth Schüssler Fiorenza pointed out, in an address delivered to members of the Catholic Biblical Association, that the Gospel of Luke, while it contains more episodes which include women than the other Gospels, actually is not less patriarchal than the other Gospels; it consistently relegates women to subservient roles. Despite Mary's response and initiative here, I concur with Fiorenza's reading of the way women are depicted in the Gospel as a whole. Cf. Jane Schaberg, "The Gospel of Luke," in *The Women's Bible Commentary,* ed. Carol A. Newsom and Sharon H. Ringe (Nashville: Westminster/John Knox Press, 1992), 275-92.

¹¹The ecumenical study by Brown and others includes a consideration of Lk. 3:23 and 4:16-30, though these texts focus, not on Mary, but on Joseph. See Brown et al., *Mary in the New Testament,* 162-65.

¹²Since the Gospel of Luke and the book of the Acts of the Apostles are believed to have been written before the Gospel of John, I consider Acts 1:13-14 here.

¹³Joseph A. Grassi, "The Role of Jesus' Mother in John's Gospel: A Reappraisal," *Catholic Biblical Quarterly* 48 (January 1986): 67-80.

¹⁴In Jn. 6:42, the Jews complain about Jesus' saying, "I am the bread that came down from heaven," because they know Jesus' "father and mother." Brown et al. consider this text as well as Jn. 1:13, 7:1-10, 41-43, and 8:41, though these latter contain no references to Mary, in *Mary in the New Testament,* 196-205.

[15]Exegetes studying this passage often point to the "hour" of Jesus inaugurated by this miracle. See, for example, Moloney, *Mary, Woman and Mother,* 31-50. Note that Jn. 19:25-27 (see below) also refers to the "hour" of Jesus.

[16]See Pheme Perkins' article, "Mary in Johannine Traditions," in *Mary, Woman of Nazareth,* ed. Doris Donnelly (New York: Paulist, 1989), 110, which notes Mary's function as symbol in the Gospel.

[17]Max A. Chevallier, "La fondation de 'l'Eglise' dans le quatrième Evangile: Jn. 19:25-30," *Études théologiques et religieuses* 58.3 (1983): 343-54.

[18]I have chosen not to include Revelation 12 which describes "a woman clothed with the sun, with the moon under her feet, and on her head a crown of twelve stars" (vs. 1), because I do not consider the verse to be an explicit reference to Mary. For related reasons, I have excluded from consideration Phil. 2:6-11, Rom. 1:3-4, Gal. 1:19; 4:28-29 which Brown et al. consider to have "potential Marian import." For their exposition, see *Mary in the New Testament,* 33-41 and 45-49.

[19]See, for example, Ignace de la Potterie, "La Mère de Jésus et la conception virginale du Fils de Dieu," *Marianum* 40 (1978): 41-90; André Feuillet, *Jésus et sa Mère d'après les récits lucaniens de l'enfance et d'après saint Jean* (Paris: Gabalda, 1974); "L'Heure de la femme (Jn 16:21) et l'heure de la Mère de Jésus," *Biblica* 47 (1966): 168-84; John McHugh, *The Mother of Jesus in the New Testament* (London: Darton, Longman & Todd, 1975); and John L. McKenzie, "The Mother of Jesus in the New Testament," *Concilium* 168 (1983): 3-11. That Mary is "mother of God" has allowed her to represent what would traditionally be considered feminine qualities of the divine. See, for example, Leonardo Boff, *The Maternal Face of God. The Feminine and Its Religious Expressions* (San Francisco: Harper & Row, 1987); and Elizabeth Johnson, "Mary and the Image of God," in *Mary, Woman of Nazareth,* ed. Donnelly, 25-68. It is this divine motherhood which has been the source of later theological/doctrinal developments regarding Mary, i.e., the Immaculate Conception and the Assumption.

[20]Matt. 12:46-50; Mk. 3:31-35; Lk. 8:19-21; 11:27-28; and Jn. 19:25-27.

[21]See, for example, Patrick Bearsley, "Mary the Perfect Disciple: A Paradigm for Mariology," *Theological Studies* 41 (1980): 461-504; Bertrand Buby, *Mary, the Faithful Disciple* (New York: Paulist, 1985); Anne Carr, "Mary: Model of Faith," in *Mary, Woman of Nazareth,* ed. Donnelly, 7-24; and Francis J. Moloney, *Woman: First Among the Faithful. A New Testament Study* (Melbourne: Collins Dove, 1984).

[22]In Judith Sanderson's commentary on the prophet Zephaniah in *The Women's Bible Commentary*, ed. Newsom and Ringe, 226, she warns of biblical texts which reinforce women's dependence. Whereas such texts were written by men who are themselves prone to arrogance in patriarchal cultures, they are inappropriate for women who are already too submissive.

[23]Donald Senior, "Gospel Portrait of Mary: Images and Symbols from the Synoptic Tradition," in *Mary, Woman of Nazareth,* ed. Donnelly, 92-108.

[24]Jane Schaberg, *The Illegitimacy of Jesus, a Feminist Theological Interpretation of the Infancy Narratives* (San Francisco: Harper & Row, Publishers, 1987). Her argument is based on four points: 1) the inclusion of Tamar, Rahab, Ruth, and the wife of Uriah in the Matthean genealogy, all of whom, she says, prepare for Mary's illegitimate conception; 2) the passive verb *egennēthē,* which she translates, "was begotten of Mary," in Matt. 1:16; 3) the omission of a fourteenth generation in the genealogy, which she understands as referring to the absent biological father; and 4) the translation of *parthenōs* as "young woman" and not "virgin." Her thesis is at least partially corroborated by others who point out that there is something "unusual" about some aspect of the sexuality and/or offspring of each of the women named in the genealogy. Moreover, I recently became aware of at least one rabbinic source which identifies Jesus as the son of Pan Tera, a name denoting a Roman soldier, though I have not as yet been able to track down the reference.

[25]According to John L. McKenzie, *Dictionary of the Bible* (Milwaukee: Bruce Publishing Co., 1965), 694-99, a prophet is "one who speaks for others." The Greek word *prophētēs* almost always denotes one who communicates divine revelation.

[26]This image of Mary is not entirely new. Though Mary's role as prophet was never really fully developed in mainstream theological circles, it did emerge periodically in more popular forms (sermons, etc.) where it received acknowledgment and attention.

[27]The most commonly available translation of the New Testament into Hebrew uses the phrases *'al yr'* and *māsā' hēn* for "fear not" and "find favor" in Lk. 1:30. These are the phases occurring in Gen. 15:1; 18:3, and Jdgs. 6:17,23.

[28]Elisabeth Schüssler Fiorenza has shown that the entire victory song was probably led by Miriam, but that patriarchal editing has resulted in the insertion of Moses' name in vs. 1. See her "Interpreting Patriarchal Traditions," in *The Liberating Word. A Guide to Nonsexist Interpretation of the Bible,* ed. Letty M. Russell (Philadelphia: Westminster, 1976), 39-61.

[29]*The Aramaic Bible,* vol. 10; trans., with an Introduction and Notes, Daniel J. Harrington, S.J., and Anthony J. Saldarini (Wilmington, Delaware: Michael Glazier, 1987), 105.

[30]See Gale A. Yee, "Hosea," in *The Women's Bible Commentary,* ed. Newsom and Ringe, 197, for Gomer rendered as promiscuous rather than as a harlot or prostitute.

[31]Richard J. Sklba suggests Mary's connection to prophetic call and ministry in his article, "Mary and the Anawim," in *Mary, Woman of Nazareth,* ed. Donnelly, 123-25, but he does not develop the insight.

[32]The close connection between the promise made by God to David through Nathan in 2 Samuel 7 and the promise made by God to Mary through Gabriel in Luke 1 has not been overlooked in Christian tradi-

tion. In fact, 2 Sam. 7:1-5, 8-11, 16 are read with Lk. 1:26-38 on the fourth Sunday of Advent, Year B. Ironically, however, the verses of 2 Sam. 7, which liken the message Mary received to the message David received, have been omitted from the liturgical reading. No doubt, this is to keep the focus on the child whom Mary will bear.

[33]The Greek *doulē* means "female servant" (Lk. 1:38). The Hebrew *bed* means "male servant." The Hebrew rendering of *doulē* is *siphā'*.

[34]On divine kingship, see, for example, George Cooke, "The Israelite King as Son of God," *Zeitschrift für die Älttestamentlichewissenschaft* 73 (1961): 202-25; Ivan Engnell, *Studies in Divine Kingship in the Ancient Near East* (Uppsala: 1943); and Aubrey R. Johnson, *Sacral Kingship in Ancient Israel* (Cardiff: 1967).

[35]Whether queens commonly lived longer than their husbands and, therefore, the queen mother ranked higher than the queen for which reason, if either were to be acknowledged, it would be the "queen mother," or whether Israel would have understood itself, if it had attributed to women the honorific title "queen" alongside the king, as according greater gender equality to women than the culture supported, we will never know. In this regard, see Jer. 13:18.

[36]The narrative also describes Jesus as preaching the kingdom of God (e.g., Matt. 4:23; Lk. 8:1).

[37]Joseph is the only other personage in the New Testament addressed as "son of David," and the only place that he is so addressed is Matt. 1:20. The Lord's messenger appears to him in a dream and assures him that the child whom Mary has conceived is from the Holy Spirit. In the patriarchal culture of ancient Israel, as elsewhere, while there is the designation, "queen mother," referring to a woman who is mother of a king (and presumably, but less significantly, wife of a former king), the designation, "king father," does not exist. For this reason, there is no reason to lament that Joseph (like Mary) is deprived of such a designation.

[38]Later tradition began to attribute to Mary the title of Queen; the "Litany of the Blessed Mother," for example, contains several appellations of Mary as queen of the apostles, queen of the saints, queen of martyrs, etc.

[39]Ezekiel describes finery "fit for a queen" in 16:13.

[40]One disservice performed by sex-inclusive language lectionaries is to disseminate the assumption that changing male-dominated to more inclusive language will eliminate the more subtle, but equally damaging, patriarchal biases which pervade the biblical texts. Donald Senior, for example, in response to a paper given by Sandra Schneiders at the Catholic Theological Society of America's meeting in June, 1992, challenged her assertion that the texts are permeated by the patriarchal culture which produced them!

[41]One such effort has recently been published. See Miriam Therese Winter, *The Gospel According to Mary* (New York: Crossroad, 1992).

[42]The Greek New Testament does not yield a corresponding term for "matriarch."

[43]Vatican II emphasized this derived identity as the basis for the other "honors" associated with her, i.e., the Immaculate Conception, the Virgin Birth, the Assumption.

Mary, Advocate of Justice

Mary T. Malone

When I speak about Mary in classrooms, parishes, and even in casual conversation, it often seems to me that no topic is excluded from the wide ranging nature of this powerful symbol. Today, Mary seems to be like a magnet, drawing all questions to herself. She is a catalyst for a whole host of discussions in the Christian community, and, in many ways, the issues surrounding Mary represent a kind of last frontier of critical questions, especially for the Roman Catholic community.

The topic presented for my reflection — Mary, Advocate of Justice — is an extremely rich one, and, in breaking it open, I find the same dilemma presenting itself to me. This topic seemed to attract every Marian issue to itself. The title seemed, in some sense, to be a microcosm of all the ecclesial dilemmas facing us today, and so, of necessity, some choices had to be made. The issues chosen for this reflection are personally relevant to me as a result of teaching and speaking at many levels of the Church and in many parts of the world. They do not, in any way, exhaust the topic.

The first necessary act in every form of Marian reflection is to be clear about the context of the discussion. So much Marian spirituality and theology has been, and continues to be, a kind of isolated product existing in its own world without connections to the rest of the Christian mystery. Since the writing of *Lumen Gentium,* it is no longer possible to speak of Mary outside the context of salvation history. The Second Vatican Council was a watershed in Marian reflection in this sense. Theoretically, a closure has been placed on the accumulation of titles for their own sake. Exploring the image of Mary as advocate of justice will not be another deductive exercise to extend the range of Mary's privileges.

73

The Apostolic Exhortation of Paul VI, *Marialis Cultus,* provides an especially creative set of guidelines for further Marian
discussion, and it is these guidelines that I intend to follow here.
In brief, he indicated that reflection on Mary should be rooted
in four principles. It should be scripturally based, liturgically
integrated, ecumenically sensitive, and anthropologically
sound.[1] Even though these guidelines are not being followed in
a systematic way throughout what follows, they govern the
whole approach to the topic.

In the same way, while a great deal of Mariology has accumulated in the tradition as a result of reflection on Marian privileges in a Christological context, the ecclesiological context has
been the basis of most post-Vatican II writing, and this correc-
tive seems profoundly important. To this must be added the tre-
mendous richness of exploring Mary within an eschatological
context, especially the notions of the fulfillment of promise, the
experience of "serene freedom" alluded to by Paul VI,[2] and the
avoidance of a certain unhealthy emphasis on Marian messages which point to present infidelities without a concomitant
emphasis on the outrageous hopefulness of the biblical tradition.

Every discussion of Mary and the realm of justice alludes to
her remarkable song of praise, the Magnificat: "My spirit rejoices in God, my Savior." It is this atmosphere of joy that seems
more and more to be a distinct need in Marian reflection in
recent times. Much talk of Mary has an edginess to it that
speaks of fear and latent, sometimes not so latent, hostilities to
Church authorities and those who do not share the speaker's
position or devotion. The miracle of the Magnificat has this
note of joy. The miracle of justice work today is the experience
of joy, the joy that raises and changes expectations and replaces
hostility, insecurity, staleness, and numbness with the soaring of
the spirit illumined by the graciousness of God.

An added experience of joy, especially for women, is the rediscovery of Mary's voice in Luke's great hymn. The restoration
of voice, the breaking of silence, is a central task for women
today. Every educator is faced with this, whether in exploring
the writings of the women of the Christian tradition — can we
really hear their authentic voices? — or in facing the next generation of students who struggle toward the expression of their
own voice in a system still bent on silencing them in so many
subtle ways. The many kinds of dogmatism surrounding the
person of Mary, both official and popular, often silence those
genuinely seeking to express new insights in order to create a
contemporary dialogue about Mary. This seems to have been

the goal of the Marian Year (June 7 to August 15, 1988), but the time was not then ripe, apparently, because no such discussion ensued.

Many Marian commentators speak of the apophatic period of Marian discourse after Vatican II. No doubt, this was partly occasioned by the necessary adjustments to Christian identity and experience stimulated by the great conciliar documents. But, it was also occasioned by the very inadequacies and "waffling" of these documents as they attempted to be faithful to the diversity of conciliar thought. At any rate, what was experienced by believers, despite a certain renewed clarity in biblical and theological thought on Mary, was a kind of lowering of the temperature of devotion. No single new image grasped the imagination as strongly as the old images did. Today, even such a biblically rooted and, by now, conventional image as Mary, the first disciple, has not unleashed the imaginations of believers. The disciple, Mary, has not been taken to heart, although, as we shall see, the prophet Mary has become a powerful new image in many parts of the Third World.

After exploring the separate images in our title — Advocate and Justice, this reflection will explore biblical images of Mary and Justice and then turn to specific instances of this advocacy of justice — the poor, laity, women, and, in particular, mothers. It will conclude with some pedagogical reflections rooted in the practice of Mariological reflection today.

The notion of Mary as advocate has never been far from the center of Marian devotion, although it has not been so popular in theology. Mary has appeared as intercessor for all before the throne of God ever since the proclamation of Mary as *theotokos* at the council of Ephesus. In the following centuries, Mary was an especial advocate of virgins and for virginity. In the Middle Ages, her advocacy extended to include all, even to the extent of being called upon as "Madonna of the Rogues." Folk tales, such as the ancient Legend of Theophilus,[3] added emotional power to this image, and everyone, from farmers to fishers, hunters to harlots, and women both seeking to find and escape husbands — all called on Mary to be an advocate for them before her son, Jesus Christ. Inevitably, the constant invocation of Mary as advocate, whether under the familiar titles of the Litany or the more heartfelt titles arising from the pain and suffering of the one in need, was both cause and effect of a certain elevation of the position of Mary to the detriment of the image of God. Even in Bernard's preaching[4] it was intimated that lay-folk should fear to approach the God of Judgment. Much better to approach the mother and allow her to act as advocate in their behalf.

This image still retains a strong hold on the hearts of many, but it continues often at the expense of a very inadequate experience of God. Despite its tenacity in many peoples' experience, this is not the notion of advocate pursued here. The recasting of the experience — as with most contemporary Marian difficulties at the pastoral level — awaits a strong evangelization so that the appeal to the advocacy of Mary in our behalf will grow from biblical testimony.

Throughout the Scriptures, advocates appear to be spokespersons for the people.[5] The advocate (*parakletos*) is the person called to stand beside us to testify in our behalf and to plead for us. The poor and those on the margins of society need advocates in a special way. In Luke's Gospel, Mary is such an advocate. She takes her stand as one of the *anawim,* one of God's poor. This is her status. The Magnificat, and indeed all the Lucan canticles, brilliantly express the piety appropriate to the *anawim.* Mary is the first spokesperson for the Reign of God, and she is given to speak with such biblical confidence that it seems that in her, the first disciple, the reign has found its home.

Mary speaks confidently for God, the just ruler, who acts without partiality and yet with the kind of partiality that demonstrates that care for the poor ones is the ruler's first charge. Throughout the Scriptures, advocates find the injustice of rulers particularly revolting — a vicious reversal of values. Justice belongs to the very nature of "the One who is mighty" and who has "done great things."

All those suffering injustice are given to understand that they have a claim on God, but God also demands justice. This is especially so with regard to worship. The justice of God cannot abide a mechanical cult that has abdicated its responsibility for the poor. Within the life of Jesus, the just reign of God is personified. Jesus brings justice, does justice, and is just. A new justice is proclaimed and experienced by believers, a justice that is the free gift of new life.

Justice is much on the ecclesial agenda in our time. In the context of the call to a "new evangelization,"[6] there is also inserted the call to a new justice: "Action on behalf of justice and participation in the transformation of the world fully appear to us as a constitutive dimension of the preaching of the Gospel, or, in other words, of the Church's mission for the redemption of the human race and its liberation from every oppressive situation."[7] More than twenty years ago, this was the call of the Sec-

MARY T. MALONE

ond General Assembly of the Synod of Bishops, and one senses
that these sentiments are repeated today with something approaching nostalgic awe. They represent a profound call to an
ecclesial change of heart which has significantly failed to mate-
rialize as general ecclesial consciousness.

In many contexts, the notion of justice has been hijacked by
the powerful, and it is with no small pain that Leonardo Boff
can ask, "justice for whom?" The reality of massive human suffering and misery faces us daily, with the need to transform our
calls for justice into a praxis of justice in behalf of the poor.
Ethical shock and indignation, instead of mobilizing believers
to action for justice, have often paralysed them. As we have so
often been reminded, the road to liberation lies through the
praxis of justice and not through the spiritualizing of justice in
search of our own peace of soul.

The Magnificat charts the journey for us. Justice is forever
intertwined with the coming Reign of God, and, together with
Mary, all disciples are called to be agents of this Reign. This is
not a call to a kind of sublime neutrality where all are theoretically treated equally, but a call to take sides with justice and
against injustice. This is such a difficult call for many disciples
today because the lure of a too easy reconciliation seduces them
into a false peace. Justice and injustice cannot be reconciled.
Advocates for justice do not call on those suffering misery to
reconcile themselves to injustice, but to recognize it, name it
and then act together to change injustice to justice. It is an area
where clarity above all is needed for privileged and affluent believers. Each choice aligns us either with justice or injustice,
and participation in the advocacy of Mary for justice for the
poor demands that "anyone who ventures to speak to people
about justice must first be just in their eyes."[8]

In the Gospel of Luke, Mary's call to justice is placed strategi-
cally on the margin between two worlds, and the margin is the
appropriate context for justice.[9] Mary's life appeared to have
been lived on the margin in a number of ways. Luke's infancy
stories place her in line with the prophets and spokespersons of
the Jewish people. She is surrounded by canticle-singing people
who are also on the edge — Zechariah, Simeon, and Anna. She
is the one who looks backwards and forwards, who sums up,
crystallizes and proclaims the future. Mary is also on the margin with regard to the very dimly seen history of the family of
Jesus. Her pregnancy raises questions; a certain tension is indicated with regard to her relationship to her son and his mission.
It is indicated that her role as mother must give way before her
discipleship. In so many scenes, one gets the feeling of Mary

looking in from the outside and apparently asking awkward questions. Indeed, one writer applies to her the words of the familiar children's rhyme, "Mary, Mary, quite contrary."[10]

As Luke's story continues, however, Mary is firmly ensconced as the first and model disciple. Mary is called to a journey of faith; she sets out with confidence and even "with haste," nourishes her journey with constant keeping and cherishing of the Word of God, and completes her journey by participating in the Pentecostal climax to the Paschal Mystery. And, as a prelude which is also a postscript, Luke portrays her as the woman of justice. She is the just one. Martin Luther is said to have remarked that the Magnificat is the swansong of all absolute rule. In this biblical charter of justice, Mary strongly denounces unjust use of power, wealth, and possessions that dispossess, oppress, and impoverish others.

The glorious context of this proclamation is the meeting of two relatives, two pregnant mothers, two of the *anawim,* those lowly, least likely people, who are chosen by God to further the history of salvation. One is almost tempted to trivialize the scene by placing it in a "Sound of Music"-like setting: babies are leaping in wombs, pregnant women are praising God with raised voices, and the "hills are alive . . ." But this, while a joy-filled proclamation, is no light-hearted, sentimental moment in salvation history. It is the proto-gospel, the charter of Christian living.

Much of the spiritualizing — or indeed ignoring — of this text has resulted from the mistranslation or misunderstanding of the word *tapeinosis.* It has almost universally been understood to mean lowliness in the sense of humility, and then the whole Magnificat was presented as an exemplar for women's humility. But, as Raymond Brown and others have pointed out, *tapeinosis* indicates that she is one of the *anawim,* one of the weak raised up to confound the strong. Mary was of low estate. She sings of her humiliation, her poverty. For Leonardo Boff, this means that she was one of the indigent, the poor, the despised ones. At the same time, exegetes ponder over what exactly Luke might have had in mind. All agree that the family of Jesus was not utterly poor and wonder whether or not there was some particular incident in Mary's life to which Luke might have been referring. Mary's virginity does not seem to be the occasion, although there is no doubt that virgins, along with widows and orphans, were among the *anawim,* i.e., those who had no one to depend on but God.[11]

More recently, Jane Schaberg has suggested an alternative explanation which can be rooted textually, to some extent, namely, that Mary may have been the victim of sexual violence at some time between her betrothal and marriage to Joseph. While this is not entirely new in the history of exegesis, it is certainly new in contemporary understanding of the text.[12] There is no necessity to explore this further here except to remark that Schaberg's suggestion always electrifies students when it is presented as part of a study of the Magnificat. Their response changes instantly from polite attention to a riveted fascination with the possibility of approaching the story of Mary from a context with which, unfortunately, they are more than familiar.

The concept of the *anawim* grew throughout Israelite history side by side with the understanding that God was not going to save the whole people, but only a remnant, and, throughout the centuries, this remnant was variously defined.[13] As the words of the Magnificat indicate, at the time of its composition this remnant included those who were the opposite of the proud, the wealthy, the mighty, and who lived a life of piety, fidelity, and reliance on God's promises. In the Lucan beatitudes, this is not an otherworldly concept, but is specifically directed against the rich. Brown and others also point to the antecedents of this attitude in the Scriptures — Hannah, Jael, and Judith.[14]

There is no doubt, then, that in the Magnificat we have a strong portrait of Mary as an advocate of justice. Mary plays a role of denunciation and proclamation. These are passages that, as Boff says, we should underline in red and insert "very important" in the margin of our texts. As we read these words today, Mary becomes instantaneously our contemporary. These are the struggles of the Christian community as we try to become reevangelized and to move beyond the numbness of over-spiritualization. Besides, these words force us to become conscious of our own situation and to discern where we stand — among the mighty and wealthy, almost certainly among those who are "proud in the imagination of their heart," or among the lowly. And, we are called to the same discipleship ministry of proclamation and denunciation. For most, this is a quite unexpected exemplary role for Mary.

There is no doubt whatever that on all fronts there is a renewed effort to integrate Mary today in ways that will be relevant to contemporary believers. As Paul VI pointed out almost two decades ago, Mary is not to be seen as out of contact with our reality.[15] The backdrop to Mary's hymn is a world that is disordered and in turmoil. As I write these lines, the disordered and tragic world of the Branch Davidians exemplifies the horror of misdirected fervor and the equally misdirected attempts of

society to channel these impulses. Mary's hymn of praise and
challenge reminds us that God has entered this conflict in our
behalf and that our songs of hope are not just whistling in the
dark, but profound expressions of faith. But, God's intervention
takes historical forms and is made concrete in historical, local,
and very specific actions. If the proud, the powerful, and the
wealthy are not to have the last word, there is a need for a new
anawim, a new kind of disciple, who will hear and do the word of
God with the integrity and commitment demonstrated in
Luke's portrait of Mary.

God's intervention once again calls us to a conversion of our
social and ecclesial relationships on very local, as well as global,
levels. The reversal of values and relationships proclaimed in
the Magnificat is not aimed at revenge, but at conversion, not
at antagonism, but at commitment to a new vision of social and
ecclesial reality. God, the song tells us, is unwilling to compromise with sinners, and this main theme of Mary's words shows
up the hollowness of much of our conventional language of
"fairness" and "justice," especially when these are interpreted as
giving to all according to their merit or place in society, rather
than according to their need.

This challenge to the spiritualization of Mary is timely at a
moment of renewed attention to apparitions and their attendant
apocalyptic spiritualities. At the same time, it is interesting to
note that the "messages" reported from these events are often
directed to those who today might be included among the *anawim.*[16] The restoration of Mary's place among the believing disciples — the first and greatest of these — demands her removal
from otherworldly realms and her situation among those who
seek inclusion among the humanly saved. Leonardo Boff invites us to make our own the prayer of Dom Helder Camara to
Our Lady of Liberation:

> O Mary, Mother of Christ and of the Church,
> we prepare for our evangelizing mission.
> We must continue it, enlarge it, and perfect it.
> And so our thoughts are on you . . .
> You took no complacency in your blessedness,
> but concentrated your thoughts on the whole human race.
> Yes, you thought of everyone,
> but you made your forthright option for the poor,
> the same option as your Son would make one day.
> What is it in you — in your words, in your voice,
> when you announce in your Magnificat
> the humiliation of the mighty
> and the exaltation of the humble,
> the satisfaction of the starving

and the dismay of the rich —
what is it in you that no one dares call *you* a revolutionary,
or regard you with suspicion?
Lend us your voice!
Sing with us!
Beg your Son to accomplish in us, in all their fullness,
his Father's plans.[17]

Another bishop-poet adds his reflection on *Mary of Liberation* and awakens those in the "first world" to new understandings of the import of Mary's call to justice. This is Pedro Casaldaliga, the courageous bishop of Sao Felix do Araguaia in Brazil. Casaldaliga celebrates Mary as the "songstress of the Magnificat, the prophetess of the poor made free, the mother of the people, the outcast mother in Bethlehem, in Egypt, in Nazareth, and among the great ones of Jerusalem." Perhaps it is only the poets who can enter into the biblical vision of human salvation with the eyes of faith. Casaldaliga writes:

Singer of the grace offered to little ones,
for only the little ones know how to receive it;
prophetess of the liberation that only the poor can achieve,
for only the poor can be free . . .
Teach us to read the Bible — reading God —
as your heart knew how to read it . . .
Teach us to read history — reading God
reading human beings —
as your faith intuited it . . .
Teach us to read life — reading God,
reading ourselves —
as your eyes, your hands, your sorrows, your hope
went along unveiling it.[18]

What, then, does it mean today for Mary to be an advocate of justice for the poor? When he visited Santo Domingo recently for the Fourth General Conference of the Latin American Episcopate, Pope John Paul II reflected on the ever-widening gap between the rich and the poor and the new forms of Christian commitment which this phenomenon demanded of believers. He quoted the Puebla document as follows:

When we draw near to the poor in order to accompany them and serve them, we are doing what Christ taught us to do when he became our brother, poor like us. Hence service to the poor is the privileged, though not the exclusive, gauge of our following of Christ. The best service to our fellows *(sic)* is evangelization, which disposes them to fulfil themselves as children of God, liberates them from injustices and fosters their integral development.[19]

John Paul had already placed himself in continuity with Medel-
lin and Puebla in reaffirming the preferential option for the
poor. He went on to root this preferential option in a renewed
Christian anthropology, a new pilgrimage of justice for the
whole Church and renewed attention to inculturated Mariolo-
gies. It seems that today the links between Mary and justice are
never far from believers' minds and hearts.

In an earlier work, *Salvation and Liberation,* Leonardo and Clodovis Boff had asked the very pertinent question: Justice for
whom?, where?, and why?, and proceeded to answer from their
immersion in the reality of the misery of the poor. For them, the
only possible point of departure is the reality of misery and massive human suffering. From here, they ask the question: which
praxis will be of help? How can we be Christians in a world of
misery? Rooting themselves in a biblical understanding of the
poor, they respond that we can act with a faith that is salvific
only if it passes by way of the praxis of love.[20] In a way that
forecasts the Pope's words at Santo Domingo, they point out
that we live in a world which is permanently violating the dignity of the human person so that all of us live in a situation of
"social sinfulness."[21]

It is always necessary to remind ourselves of the dimensions
of a justice spirituality and praxis, rooted in the exemplary vision of the Magnificat, and the Boff brothers, with their inimitable clarity, outline for us the dimensions of such a vision. The
starting point is the acquisition of a liberating spirituality,
rooted in the knowledge and experience that, with the poor, one
experiences God. This was Mary's experience as one of the *anawim*. This conversion experience — which is passed over, or almost assumed, by the writers, but which we know is the task of
a lifetime, leads us to a liberative reading of Scripture. We read
with new eyes, with a cleansed vision, and with newly opened
ears and hearts. Feminists have also discovered this vivifying
experience and have come to realize that, once the reader's/
believer's eyes are opened in one area, they are newly alert to
blindness in other areas.

The next stage is a rereading of theology for its liberating
content. A huge task of reprocessing awaits the pilgrims of justice as they traverse anew the familiar, but profoundly challenging, mysteries of God, Christ, grace, the sacraments, and
Mary, with a new experience at heart and a new praxis in mind.
This inevitably leads to a theological reflection on the analysis
of the reality of poverty, misery, and injustice so that the mechanisms of oppression will be clearly seen and understood. At the
heart of this process is a turn to the subject, to the poor themsel-

ves and especially to their potential for resistance so as to become agents of their own liberation. One of the most impressive aspects of the Magnificat, viewed in this light, is the strong, womanly moral agency of Mary as she speaks in her own voice and from her own experience as a disciple, her profound convictions about the working out of salvation history.

This leads to a "popular pedagogy of liberation" which combines the enormously fruitful insights of Paulo Freire and the long and rich history of Christian catechesis. This latter aspect is not spelled out, but the resources of traditional catechesis, in its emphasis on the gradual nature of conversion, the centrality of the subject, the dialogical nature of the interaction, and the essential rootedness in Scripture and in ecclesial community, parallel in remarkable ways the findings of Freire.[22] It is no less remarkable the way the journey of discipleship for Mary, outlined in the Lucan and Johannine texts, follows the same path.[23]

Essential to this journey is the recovery of memory because, as Leonardo Boff points out, the winners have destroyed the memory of the losers. This is another stage in the journey of discipleship familiar to feminists and to anyone engaged in the task of the "new evangelization." Our capacity for blindness and deafness is paralleled only by the skill of the dominant tradition in excising from memory the contributions and very lives of those at the bottom. The final stage of the process of developing a biblically-rooted praxis of justice is the development of a theory of liberation theology.

Those who journey along this way will experience three different kinds of conversion or three levels of awareness. Each of the first two levels usually engages us in work for justice which is perhaps highly motivated, but inadequate. The first level is that of empiricism which focuses on the accumulation of facts, a first naïve awareness of the realities of human misery in a particular situation, and the urge to help. This perhaps may be the situation of most believers: inundated with facts and constantly called upon to respond to crisis after crisis. With no further analysis, numbness results, as so many food banks and various kinds of national appeals are discovering. At the risk of a certain naïveté, this stage can be said to parallel the position of Mary at the Cana wedding, a most extraordinary story evocative for people at many different levels. All of us are familiar with the rush of sympathy, the urge to help, and also with the frustration of knowing that it is never enough, often misguided, and often productive of results quite the contrary of those we intended. This was not, of course, the situation at the wedding feast of

Cana, but the confusion and tension around the request for
help and the response parallel many a donor's reality.

The second level of conversion moves us to a more critical
perspective. We are led to seek the origins of misery — it is not
an accident, but a direct consequence of planning in one sector
of reality for the benefit of that sector. This leads to a search for
more efficacious ways of entering the process, which require as
their necessary prerequisite the interpretation of the reality in
the light of faith. The solutions which offer themselves to us at
this stage are ones which aim at the reestablishing of a certain
equilibrium in society. It is clearly perceived at this stage that
society is like a body, that there are interconnections at all levels. The massive gaps between the rich and the poor, to which
the Pope referred in Santo Domingo, are one example of dis-
harmony in the body that must be put right. The response at
this level of analysis and conversion is usually towards reform.
The horrible truth that eventually wrecks this analysis is the
realization that, despite our reforming efforts, the body gets
sicker and the rich get richer and the poor poorer. The fre-
quency of this last statement in every kind of analysis over the
past several decades serves only to indicate that there must
needs be another level of analysis and praxis which may perhaps be more efficacious.

This last analysis can be done only on a global level because
the intricacies of every local dynamic of wealth and poverty are
rooted in the international structural network of late twentieth
century capitalism. It is only by a truly radical critique that we
can unearth the patterns and connections whereby each one of
us individually, collectively, nationally, and globally is hooked
into this system. It is only through the enormous effort involved
in this critique that we become aware of the *ongoing* mechanisms
of poverty and marginalization.[24] The contribution of liberation
theology is the bringing to bear of a strong faith-filled theological analysis to these global realities. The Reign of God is
enfleshed in the justice proclaimed by Mary, advocated by
Mary, and, just as the *Theotokos* gave flesh to the Logos of God,
so, too, in the words of Boff, history is *gravida Christi*. Mary,
Theotokos, is the prototype of salvation history.

To be an advocate of justice means that, of necessity, Mary
and all disciples must also be agents of justice. We do this by
giving alms to the needy, by living generously, by seeking to live
simply, by "downward mobility," by preaching the Good News
to the poor, by standing with the poor in order to share the
beatitudinal privilege of poverty, and especially by working for
justice for the poor. But, we cannot idealize poverty. It is an

affront to the justice of God.[25] Neither can we be neutral and
pretend a certain detachment from the issues in the interests of
clarity of judgment or cool-headed decision-making. Being an
advocate of justice is not done from a stance of objectivity, but
from one of passionate commitment to the bringing about of the
community of topsy-turvy values envisioned by the voice of
Mary in the Magnificat. Mary's life is the concrete sign of the
sub-version and re-versal of the established order, wrought by
the Incarnation of the Word, and, contrariwise, the raising up
of the weak, the poor, and the hungry. Those of us who have
become rich, in whatever way, must deal seriously with the dis-
pleasure of God articulated by Mary against the "mighty." As
Ivone Gebara says so well, when God looks at the *anawim* and at
the arrogant, God's heart inclines towards the former.[26]

The sorting out process does not wait until the end of time.
Starting from the moment of our evangelization, we are called
on, like Mary, to issue and to live some resounding "noes" as
well as some resounding "yeses." The "God will cast down"
words of Mary must become as familiar a part of our life of faith
as the "let it be done" words with which we are much more familiar.

Throughout history, each period of "new evangelization" has
had Mary close to its center. The creation of a Christian consciousness in medieval Europe, in fact the creation of Christen-
dom, was accomplished by the Rosary, the *biblia pauperum,* as
much as by anything else. The first evangelization of the peoples of Latin America relies on devotion to the Lady of Guadalupe for one of its saving graces.[27] As Leonardo Boff points out
in his book, *New Evangelization,* evangelization is always and
everywhere a mutual project. It is the poor who will evangelize
the Church today, they who themselves have been evangelized
through their devotion to the Lady of Liberation. It is the kind
of evangelization, he says, that will not produce a new ecclesiastical structure, but the gathering of communities around the
message of the Gospel.[28] Virgil Elizondo points out that an
evangelizing process was introduced at Guadalupe that is ecumenical at its core because it engages us at the level of our image
of God. It is indeed at this level that the core Christian theological dialogue is taking place today. The central religious symbol
of Christianity is being radically challenged, probably for the
first time since the great Trinitarian debates of the fourth and
fifth centuries. The proclamation of Mary as *Theotokos* at Ephesus in 431 saved an essential element of the mystery of the
humanity/divinity of Christ then. It is not at all unlikely that
the question of God and God language will proceed hand in

hand with a new exploration of the evangelizing role of Mary for today. Such a process has been well entitled the "dogmatics of the poor."[29]

Despite the glowing phrases of the Vatican documents and the more recent encyclical, *Christifideles laici,* it is not untrue to call the laity the poor of the Church. They are still variously described as the gullible, simple, easily confused section of the *ecclesia.* The laity are still often seen as passive, uncooperative, and unreliable. They are consigned officially, over and over again, to some mythical "temporal sphere" of reality where certain ecclesial privileges do not apply to them. Roman Catholic laity have no official voice in the *ecclesia.* They are the silent and silenced majority.

Another picture has emerged, however, and has been growing in clarity and strength over the past decades. The *Christifideles laici* have been uncovering the meaning of fidelity, discipleship, and the joy of being pilgrims in the faith. Over the past twenty odd years, lay people have become evangelized, catechized, and have experienced the profound joy of exploring and entering into the Good News. The great biblical themes of creation, election, covenant, prophecy, incarnation, salvation, reconciliation, and resurrection are entering into the very bones of the Christian people and are being lived as part of the fabric of their lives. A new evangelization has begun to be conducted both by and for lay people. Some discover the journey of discipleship in the process of following the Rite of Christian Initiation of Adults, whether as participants, sponsors, or members of evangelizing communities. Others begin the journey through study and the need to make sense of a strong faith inherited through a believing family or a strong Catholic culture. Others, again, begin the journey with a sense of outrage against many forms of injustice and mine the tradition for its rich resources of prophetic challenge and saintly commitment. There are as many other routes as there are people — retreats, spiritual direction, modelling of family and friends, healing and recovery from the multiple injustices of racism, sexism, and so many other forms of exploitation — but, whatever the contributing factors, a new lively, committed world community of lay disciples has been emerging.

The relationship of Mary to these groups is hard to gauge. Many have rejected her as incompatible with their new biblically based faith. Many live uneasily with remembered and loved childhood devotions that have not taken on the maturity of adult commitment. Many feel guilty at the absence of Mary in their lives and make spasmodic attempts to restore recitation of the Rosary or other devotions. And, many continue with an unreflected devotion to Mary that continues to enhance their lives just because they once fell in love with Mary, and the love affair has never ended. For all of these people, a kind of Marian justice is due. They need to be able to complete their journey of faith, as Mary did, by being welcomed at the heart of the Church. They need to engage in the act of mystagogy, as Mary did, by being enabled to give voice publicly to their ecclesial stance and to name what they have come to know as believers.

Several Mariologists, already mentioned, have commented on the apophatic period of Mariology immediately following the Second Vatican Council.[30] This was the period that there was little or no evidence of any integration of Mariological reflection into the standard postconciliar writings on ecclesiology, soteriology, Christology, and liturgy. While this situation has begun to change in theology, it remains within the academy and has hardly penetrated the pastoral scene. Very little has been written on Mary that is accessible to the generally educated laity. The Church's mystagogical task on Mary, as indicated by Chapter Eight of *Lumen Gentium,* has not been accomplished. This chapter, while articulating the wisdom of the tradition on Mary without adding any new doctrine, nevertheless did point out directions for such an act of mystagogy. It seems that these directions were not followed anywhere. What the laity heard was a hortatory suggestion about ecumenical sensitivity — something that was, of course, necessary — and also about tendencies to credulity. But, the implications of this teaching were never taken up pastorally.

The Magnificat proclamation about the scattering of the proud and the raising up of the lowly can apply quite readily to the relative abandonment of the people by official teaching on the postconciliar view of Mary. It is not that the sources are not there. First of all, there is the enormously rich resource located precisely in the life of the people. The laity as theological resource offers abundant richness to the ecclesial community, but this resource has not been tapped. On the contrary, this resource is constantly being ruled out of order and deemed unessential to the life of the Church. The recent struggles over the United States Catholic Conference statement on Women and the Church is a case in point.

At all levels of the Christian community, there can be heard a cry from the heart for intelligible teaching on Mary. It is more than likely that the now familiar reporting of Marian apparitions and the intense interest they arouse point to a significant lacuna in the spiritual and ecclesial life of the laity. Just as the image of Mary is actualized anew in each age, so, too, in each age, Mary acts again as an advocate of justice for the laity. She is no longer seen as the Madonna of the Rogues, but the same sense of abandonment by officialdom is often perceived. In this age, too, the laity are finding a new actualizing of their identity. They are seeking full participation in the ecclesial community, not in the sense of a creeping clericalism, but beyond the false dualism of the secular and the sacred.

The dignity of the laity, affirmed so often in papal teaching,[31] has not been made perceptible in practice. Many of the laity do not feel dignified. They feel second-rate. What is undoubtedly the teaching of the Church on their dignity has not become received teaching by them in a way that integrates this experience with their full participation in the Church. Starting from the incipient insights of *Munificentissimus Deus* in 1950, the Church in the intervening years has been adding to its store of wisdom about the life of the lay faithful. It is not an accident that this encyclical, one of the first contemporary articulations of human dignity, was made in the context of the proclamation of the dogma of the Assumption. Pius XII voiced his hopes that this action would help people to "realize more and more the value of a human life entirely dedicated to the will of God."[32] The image of saved humanity is mirrored in Mary. What is affirmed of her can also be affirmed potentially of every human being.

This opening to the subject is seen with special clarity in the encyclical of Pope Paul VI, *Marialis Cultus*. The National Liturgical Bulletin of the Canadian Bishops names this document as one of the most explosive since the Council. This did not necessarily make it a better known document. From a pastoral perspective, it was hardly ever read, taught, integrated, nor reflected on in the Christian community. It is worth while, then, to quote a few of its noteworthy anthropological sections. The Pope indicates that a rereading of the Scriptures "will help us to see how Mary can be considered a mirror of the expectations of the men and women of our time."[33] He continues:

> Thus the modern woman, anxious to participate with decision-making power in the affairs of the community, will contemplate with intimate joy Mary who, taken into dialogue with God, gives her active and responsible consent, not to the solution of a contingent problem, but to that "event of world importance," as the Incarnation of the Word has been rightly called. . . . The modern woman will note with pleasant surprise that Mary of Nazareth, while completely devoted to the will of God, was far from being a timidly submissive woman or one whose piety was repellent to others; on the contrary, she was a woman who did

not hesitate to proclaim that God vindicates the humble and the oppressed, and removes the powerful people of this world from their privileged position.[34]

In the light of these statements and of the faith experience of the community, the preaching of an exemplary and typological Mariology is no longer adequate. It is no longer sufficient to exhort people to be humble and submissive like Mary, or even to be strong and believing like Mary, unless the true circumstances of both her life and their lives are taken into account. A true evangelization proclaims the whole Gospel, not just parts chosen on stereotypical grounds. The dialogical and mutual nature of evangelization needs to be taken into account here, also. Mary stands beside the people as advocate for true and just discipleship, just as she stands beside the poor as advocate for true and just living conditions.

Another "path of cultural encounter" which has been largely ignored in official teaching is the encounter with those who are wholly taken up with what has been called "popular devotion" to Mary. We have referred briefly to the phenomenon of popular Marian piety in Latin and Central America; here, we wish to turn to the same phenomenon in North America. It is time to question the "wait-and-see" attitude of the official teaching Church in this area. Such an attitude too easily leaves the field open to enthusiasts, if not outright charlatans. This is not a questioning of the sincerity of the participants, but some questioning of the astonishing lack of episcopal and theological leadership must be undertaken. In courses on Mary at both undergraduate and graduate levels, students express shock and dismay that not a single reference is made to the phenomenon of apparitions in any of the three major contemporary documents: *Lumen Gentium,* Chapter Eight, *Marialis Cultus,* or *Redemptoris Mater.* The general approach is fairly clear — one waits to discern the fruits of such devotions. But, that general wisdom has significantly failed a particular segment of the Christian community in our day, and a situation of real injustice prevails.

The results are obvious. Many people rush from one apparition to the next in the hope that some message of guidance from heaven will be received to fill the lacuna of spiritual guidance on earth. Whole industries have come into being peddling these messages, thereby trivializing both the phenomenon and the participants. An apocalyptic atmosphere reigns where there is feverish attention to present infidelities and promised doom which is wholly alien to the spirit of the Gospel. Anti-clericalism flourishes when the official teachers are seen to shy away from the whole Marian scene and resort sometimes to ridicule, some-

times to unfounded criticism. Mary is seen again as an opposi-
tional symbol — the one standing over against the mainline tradition and accusing it of infidelity. An atmosphere that can only
be called "gnostic" arises as some claim secret knowledge and
secret access to information not generally available.

So much energy is being poured into what is essentially a
detour from the Gospel. The phenomenon of apparitions is being isolated, and a truly faithful popular Marian piety is rendered almost impossible. A huge pedagogical task awaits the
emergence of a new Marian prophet who can, at one and the
same time, adhere to the biblical dynamics of a vital evangelization and also enter, in a spirit of mutuality, into a true dialogue
with those who participate in popular Marian devotion. History shows that often the end result of such a division in the
Church is the imposition of legislation to prevent the worst excesses. How much better to tackle the more challenging task of
evangelizing and catechesis in a spirit of profound respect and
along the lines of the criteria laid down by Pope Paul VI. The
concept of the *consensus fidelium* surely plays a part here.

In what direction is this consensus pointing? It points to a
deeply felt spiritual vacuum that is apparently not being as-
suaged by the normal life of the Catholic communities. People
speak of feeling betrayed and abandoned by their spiritual leaders. There is a thirst for access to God, for a sense of closeness,
of reassurance. There is a distinct absence of a pedagogy of love
in the Christian community, a love that was for so long directed
towards Mary, but seems to have no true focus today. Though it
is probably true that the Marian devotees would not acknowledge this dimension, it, nevertheless, seems clear that there is a
thirst for what might be called the "feminine face" of God. In no
way is this meant to indicate that Mary should take on divine
characteristics — on the contrary, it is precisely in her humanity
that she serves as such a powerful symbol — but, that the un-
yielding maleness of the Church no longer satisfies all the profound religious aspirations of believers.

Mary can be — and is — truly an advocate of justice for the
lay believer. Over and over again in the pages of *Redemptoris
Mater,* John Paul II refers to the journey of faith undergone by
Mary. In fact, in sheer numbers of references, this image of
Mary the journeyer and pilgrim far surpasses the image of
Mary the virgin. The Pope seems to be implying that this is the
key Marian symbol today.[35] If anything is true of the Christian
community today, it is this journeying in faith. It is so easy to
lose sight of the goal and allow the vision to pale. In this context, apocalyptic visions of doom and destruction, though ini-

tially satisfying as reassurance that we are not mistaken about the state of the Church, nevertheless, serve only to focus attention on the self, on present infidelity, and away from the Good News. The strong proclamatory words of the Magnificat presume a believer's grasp on the meaning of the coming Reign of God. Apparitional messages, however timely, without this context, are distractions.

In Luke's Marian theology, the parable of the sower seems never to be far from his mind. The word of God arouses many different responses in the hearts of believers. The true disciples are those who take it to heart, chew on it, live it fully, and bring forth fruit one hundred-fold. But, the word must be grappled with. It is not an accident that so many Marian scenes in the Scriptures show Mary either asking questions or being apparently rebuffed for presuming that she knew the next step. This image of Mary, the theologian, grappling with the meaning of the message of salvation can awaken in believers a renewed confidence in their ability to struggle, likewise, with the saving truth of the Gospel. The eschatological "Yes" that was asked of Mary did not mean that her life followed a blueprint thereafter. No, she is being asked to risk everything for the one thing necessary. The peace of her life is shattered and continues to be shattered as she follows the pathway of her son toward its inevitable end. Mary, the just one, struggles with the call to discipleship. Perhaps the real injustice to the lay faithful is the sense that there are too easy reassurances along the journey, that the appeal to authority can resolve the dilemmas of the heart in the matter of faith. The safety-net of commandment and dogma can easily become minimalist patterns of believing and do not open the human heart to the great drama of discipleship. With Mary, this drama can be rediscovered.

As he opened Marian reflection to the anthropological question, so, too, did Pope Paul VI open it definitively to the question of the significance of the symbol of Mary for women. Mary, the advocate of justice and the model of discipleship, is advocate and model for all — women and men. But, it is especially to women that Mary has been presented as the principal model for their lives. In fact, in homiletics and in many an official document, the implication persists that Mary is the model for women and that Jesus is the model for men. Apart from the distinctly skewed theology in this suggestion, not to mention its heretical potential, this suggestion is restricted to a very small section of biblical testimony to Mary, and even this became distorted as the centuries proceeded. It is necessary, then, to explore the theme of Mary as an advocate of justice for women in order to bring centuries of Christian piety in line with biblical witness.

When Marian reflection broke upon the scene in what has been called the "golden age" of patristic literature and faith, it was in the context of the extraordinary enthusiasm for virginity awakened by desert asceticism. In an ecclesial atmosphere of fear of, and contempt for, the body, and in particular for the carnality of women, daughters of Eve, the great teachers of the day were yet haunted by the Good News of creation, salvation, reconciliation, and, in particular, the belief in the resurrection of the body. The truth of the Gospel and the facts of life as they experienced them in their varied personal faith journeys were in constant warfare. The image of Mary, the Virgin, even more the *aeiparthenos,* the perpetual virgin, seemed a wonderful solution to this dilemma. The redemption of the woman, which, in some writings, was understood to be two-fold — the first, from female carnality through which women were understood to "become male," the second, from the common sin of humanity — was seen to be accomplished and perfectly mirrored in Mary, the Queen of Virgins.

This led to an outpouring of creative patristic writing on the role of women and on the doctrine of virginity. The image of Mary was recast as the model fourth century Roman nun. It was in the context of this debate that the doctrine of Mary's virginity was hammered out — incidentally against some very strong opposition in the persons of Helvidius and Jovinian. All the resources of the Church went into the promotion of virginity for women, and few or none of the resources of the Church went into reflection on the Christian dimensions of motherhood or any other dimension of women's lives. Of course, official teaching was usually more spare in its language than was the fervent rhetoric of a Jerome; nevertheless, an atmosphere of distrust was created, and the "truth" was often articulated that the life of virginity was always and everywhere far superior to marriage and motherhood. So little has been recorded about the married lives of ordinary women Christians that it is virtually impossible to form any opinion on the way they might have experienced this life. A great deal has been recorded about the lives of virgins and nuns, however, and is just recently being translated and made accessible.

Two aspects are immediately apparent. First of all, the life of virginity for women, as it was organized in the various forms of monasticism and later religious communities, presented women with an avenue to education, the company of women, a guiding spirituality, and the opportunity to know the wonder of dedicating one's life irrevocably to God, that would otherwise never have been available. These women experienced an extraordinarily effective ministry of leadership which included, in particular moments, even quasi-episcopal status. The atmosphere of convent life provided an ideal setting for prayer, study, and the practice of mystical encounter with God, which has left such an abundance of literature to succeeding generations. But, in order to stake a claim on such a life, many women had to encounter formidable obstacles — the most formidable being the cultural and parental requirement that they marry. The stories of such women are rife with incidents of horrific family violence, and in incident after incident the struggling young woman turns to Mary as her one source of help.

Mary, the compassionate mother, is the most frequent form of Marian intervention in these stories, used often to counteract the violence and hostility of an earthly mother toward her daughter's vocation. The justice which Mary seeks for these women is portrayed as the freedom to follow their journey toward the God of their hearts.[36] Throughout the Middle Ages, especially, this scene is played out over and over again, whether in the soaring hymns of Hildegard of Bingen, the pathos-filled visions of Christina of Markyate, or the astonishingly beautiful poetry of Hadewijch of Brabant. In their struggles to defy the conventions of society, including the convention of obedience to parents and fulfilment of marriage arrangements, in order to follow their particular journey of discipleship, hundreds of women had only Mary the Advocate of Justice to rely on. On the other hand, the relating of a Marian vision of support was often all that was needed to draw the attention of ecclesiastical leadership to their plight.

There are, however, no such stories of mothers calling on Mary for help. In the spirituality that was popular throughout most of Christian history, pregnancy and motherhood were a stain on virginity and left married women in a state always suspiciously sinful. There is fierce hostility to sex in most Christian writings through the ages, as well as strictures that advocated, for both women and men, the need to refrain from Eucharist after even legitimate sexual encounter. Indeed it was this restriction which paved the way for the imposition of clerical celibacy in 1139.[37]

There have been severe criticisms of the effects of certain strains of Mariology on the psyches of most women throughout Christian history, and one cannot but agree with the gist of these criticisms. Mariology, it is said, has sapped and deflected the energy and legitimate aspirations of women. It has been

cruelly alienating and oppressive to women, and the presentation of Mary as a "cosmic Lady Bountiful" and "sentimental
pleader to those higher up" has been a calculated misuse of the
spirit. While this is certainly true, there are, at the same time,
millions of the very poor for whom Mary is the central religious
focus of their lives and the source of all their spiritual energy.
We know this to be true today. It was likely also true at the time
of the composition of the *Salve Regina,* when the voices of the
"poor, banished children of Eve" cried to the one they experienced as sweet and loving. This is not an attempt to justify the
distorted theology which had deprived these women of the good
news of their salvation to the extent that Eve was their focus of
identity, but to point to the fact that Mary was the one image of
justice in lives blighted by centuries of misogyny and neglect.[38]

There is no doubt that Mary and women are linked by historical, cultural, and gender bonds. Mary is the most outstanding
figure in the Western world, the one most frequently portrayed
in art and extolled in poetry. It is also true that, through the
image of Mary, attitudes toward women were communicated
and deeply internalized by all. Christian feminists have rightly
insisted that such images both of Mary and of women be revised
today. Images of Mary as sexless and all pure, humble and submissive, virgin and mother, present for women an impossible
and inimitable model. Centuries of Christian spirituality offered women the dualistic choice of being imitators of Mary or
Eve, the one impossible, the other at least familiar.

The heart of most ecclesiastical writing about Mary as model
for women has little to do with the real women who have struggled to live their lives of faith, but with an ecclesiastically constructed image of womanhood. Few real women break through
the pages of history to relieve this stereotype, because an essential part of the stereotype was the silencing and privatizing of
women's experience. In an attempt of justice to restore womanhood to Mary and Mary to womanhood, several avenues have
been explored. One of the key generative symbols in writing
about women today is the symbol of women's voice, the recovery of their own voices, the recognition and critique of "voices of
authority," and the ability to distinguish among the many forces
that serve to silence women's voices, and, when they do speak,
to prescribe and control the content of women's speech.

This is a task familiar to teachers, both as a personal quest
and as an educational task. One avenue to the rediscovery of
women's voices is the recognition of the strong voice of Mary of
the Magnificat. Mary speaks as one who has both received and
proclaimed the truth of revelation. She speaks from the core of

her experience as disciple, in Luke's portrait, and, as a woman, calls for the liberation of the oppressed. The loud voice of the proclaiming woman cuts through the false ontological categories created for women's lives and restores the voice of women to history. It is no surprise that Mary speaks from the margin, not only in the Magnificat, but in so many biblical scenes. The Markan scene which portrays Mary as outside the circle of disciples is a familiar location for many women trying to articulate their experience of Christian discipleship.[39]

Mary appears in the Magnificat as the voice of authority, almost the sole representative of womanly theological authority in the whole tradition. The "elevation" of Teresa of Avila and Catherine of Siena as Doctors of the Church has added two more female names to the roster, but there the story ends, from the official perspective. Mary can be called upon as an advocate of justice for women, especially in this regard. What an abundance of theological insight has been lost to cumulative Christian teaching at every level, by the silencing of the voices of women. And, what an enormous loss to today's Roman Catholic experience when the voice of women believers is deemed unnecessary to the Church's self-reflection and self-critique. Claiming an authoritative Christian voice will be a particular struggle for Roman Catholic women for years to come. It seems abundantly clear that any renewal in Marian devotion will await the sounding of this voice.

The dealings of Jesus with women in the Gospels are rooted in the quality of their faith and not in the roles they play. The quality of Mary's faith has been raised to the level of exemplar in the ongoing tradition, but, for all other women, the faith that they exemplify has been subordinated to the roles they play. From the perspective of using a voice of authority or a voice of proclamation, the main role is framed in negative terms — women are not among the ordained. The links among celibacy, power, ordination, and voice become clear here. It is the renunciation of marriage, of contact with women, which has been made, especially in recent times, the core symbol of the right to raise one's voice in the Church, whether in proclamation, praise, forgiveness, or healing. Any linking together of the symbol of Mary with the advocacy of justice cannot avoid the issue of the sexual identity of women and the way that sexual identity restricts them from playing the normative role of discipleship indicated by Mary, the model disciple. As I suggested at the beginning of this essay, the exploration of the image of Mary in the Church today seems to draw to itself all the most pertinent issues of the day. Mary has always been, and continues to be,

one of the icons of humanity. When we reflect on Mary and
women, we have to acknowledge the fact that, for most of Christian history, the full humanity of women was denied. Women's
nature is still described as "special," and "woman" is still allotted
the rights appropriate to her "special nature."[40] When we speak
of Mary as advocate of justice for women, the question of humanity returns. Will Mary be the one who will move us beyond
stereotypical fumbling with notions of masculinity and femininity to an exploration of the full meaning of humanity, using all
the resources of all women and men of all races and creeds? It
would indeed be a traditional role for Mary.

Perhaps one of the most ambivalent images of Mary is the
image of Mary the mother — mother of Jesus, mother of the
Church, our mother, the mother of priests, mother of God (finally used in official documents only at Vatican II) — so often
Mary is invoked as mother. Seldom, though, is any consideration given to what exactly this motherhood means. The language used is either nauseatingly sentimental, symbolically
confusing, theologically in a kind of neutral zone, or ethically
lost in the realm of the impossible. The experience of real mothers is hard to find in this welter of imagery, and so one turns to
the image of Mary as advocate of justice, to explore the possibilities of theological and actual justice for real mothers.

The recent novel of P. D. James, *The Children of Men,* illustrates in an extraordinarily moving way the vision of a world of
universal infertility. No babies have been born for decades. The
sale of dolls and a raging pornography industry attempt both to
keep maternal instinct alive and to titillate the sex drive of a
country that now has no need for sex. There are no education,
no future. And women, without the opportunity to be mothers,
are shown as pathetic creatures who shrivel to total insignificance. There is no use for them. It is a horrific vision.

More recently, in another horrific inferno, another element
of the motherhood myth was held up before the world and
found wanting. In Waco, Texas, the representatives of law and
order justified their attack on the Branch Davidian compound,
in part, by saying that they were relying on the maternal instinct of the mothers to save their children in the face of invasive
and punishing tear gas. Such maternal instincts were not found
to be present. In the midst of such a show of force, it seemed like
an astonishingly narrow thread by which to justify the extinc-
tion of lives.

The symbol and mystery of the mother is one of humanity's
oldest objects of reverence. The giving of life from one's own
body remains one of the greatest mysteries, despite our scien-

tific, medical, and psychological sophistication. There has never been such emphasis on motherhood as we see today and, likewise, never such a concerted attack on real mothers. From certain segments of the men's movement to some pro- and anti-abortion activists, from accusations of welfare fraud to the appalling prevalence of wife battering, the place of mothers in our communities has never seemed to be under such stress.

Several recent works have begun to explore the role of mothers, especially as a result of the very useful distinction between motherhood as cultural and, we might add, theological construct and motherhood as the experience of mothers.[41] Several themes begin to emerge. First of all, there is a very strong critique of the theological use of the symbol of mother in more and more damaging ways. It is obvious that real mothers have never been invited to contribute to the formulation of this image. Likewise, it is clear, historically, that the constant invocation of a kind of spiritual and ecclesial motherhood, linked to the image of Mary, has served to alienate women from the profoundly creative and religious dimensions of mothering — from giving birth to the ongoing mothering skills of nurturing, enabling, enduring, suffering, and loving. The theme of the "bringing forth of spiritual children" has been frequent. In his Holy Thursday letter to priests, *Behold Your Mother,* Pope John Paul II pursues such a theme with quite extraordinary language:

> It is worth recalling these scriptural references (i.e. to Gal. 4:19 and Eph. 5:29), so that the truth about the Church's motherhood, founded on the example of the Mother of God, may become more and more a part of our priestly consciousness. If each of us lives the equivalent of this **spiritual motherhood** in a manly way, namely, as a **"spiritual fatherhood,"** then Mary, as a figure of the church, has a part to play in this experience of ours.[42]

It is hard to see what this kind of language has to do with motherhood as mothers know it. The tragedy of such language is that the experience of motherhood by women has never been seen as a theological locus. As Marie-Thérèse Van Lunen Chenu remarks, the Church, "rather than drawing conclusions from its statement on the equality of the sexes, for the benefit of its own ecclesiology and in order to produce a more acceptable ethical code of sexuality, . . . is more concerned with developing the **vision which it has of itself as bride and mother,** according to anthropological models which are currently under challenge."[43]

Another theme is that of the insidious link between poverty and motherhood today. Women are penalized today by state, religion, and culture for becoming mothers, especially if there are no men in the picture, for whatever reason. Society and Church take refuge in demeaning terms, such as "single mother," in order to ignore the fact, and its implications, that women are indeed the heads of households. Almost daily, the service and welfare arms of governments comment on the drain on the national finances represented by female heads of households. The services provided for mothers living alone with their children are directly focused on the needs of the children. The mother is supported only in her capacity as child-bearer and child-carer. Beyond that, her health and welfare are not provided for.[44] In such a context, the theme of maternity as a semi-sacred ontological reality, divorced from all human coloring, seems simply scandalous.

Women who are mothers, believers, and theologians, either by profession or self-designation, are beginning to write about being mother from a Christian perspective, with a distinct lack of sentimentality. They speak of the everyday slog of rearing children, of the fact that a mother cannot escape when the situation becomes intolerable.[45] They speak of discovering the mistake of "sacrificing" the self for the sake of children and of the frustration which results. This daily experience of mothers directly contradicts the reflections on a woman's true femininity by Pope John Paul II where, in a passage describing the mission of women, he says, **"Woman can only find herself by giving love to others."**[46] This is not the experience of mothers today — if it ever were, and one wonders about the continued theological relevance of an image which has no basis at all in reality. What women discuss, by way of experiential contrast, is the loss of the self when one engages in this eternally self-giving behavior.

Throughout the history of Christianity, the experience of motherhood was seen as the antithesis of holiness and accessibility to God. One of the most astonishing examples of this is the life of Margery Kempe who, though the mother of fourteen children, spent a good part of her life trying to prove that she had attained the dignity of virginity and manages almost never to mention her children. Margery, with genuine Christian insight, wanted to experience herself as a "new creatur," and one might almost say that she wept herself into this experience, as her gift of tears continued copiously for ten years. It is interesting that many contemporary and medieval writers turn to the motherhood of God and Jesus rather than to the motherhood of Mary for validation and inspiration of the religious experience of motherhood. The best known medieval mystic to use this metaphor is Julian of Norwich: "This fair lovely word 'mother' is so sweet and so kind in itself that it cannot truly be said of any-

one or to anyone except of him and to him who is the true
Mother of life and of all things. To the property of motherhood
belong nature, love, wisdom and knowledge, and this is God."[47]

Similarly, Margaret Hebblethwaite speaks of the discovery of
God as mother. She says that the experience of motherhood
made this means of address seem natural and meaningful. She
likens prayer to the experience of breast-feeding and delights in
finding confirmation of her own experience in the writings of
Catherine of Siena, among others.[48] As I searched this literature, which is still relatively scarce, I could find little reference
to the motherhood of Mary, and, as I read, I came to understand the distance that has been created between the actual experience of motherhood by Mary and the Church's unceasing
use of it for its own purposes.

Mary is the mother of Jesus. As a young Jewish woman, she
experienced what every human mother experiences — the pain
and anxiety, the joy and exhilaration of giving birth. Our claim
on the humanity of Jesus demands this realization. If the word
"mother," used of Mary, does not connect with the experience of
all mothers, then the word, theologically, has become devoid of
meaning. It is not from further theological speculation, then,
but from an exploraton of the experience of motherhood by
mothers that liberating and healing release will return to Marian reflection on motherhood. For too long, motherhood has
been clothed with notions of either sinfulness or disease. For too
long, the experience has been taken out of mothers' hands and
placed in the hands of physicians. A grandmother commented
recently on the ridiculous banning of the word "pregnant" from
the airwaves lest it offend the ears of sensitive women: "Where
did they think women were during the birthing process?" The
human dynamics of motherhood were lost in such a process.
What we need, and are just barely beginning to find, is a mystagogy of motherhood — the naming, claiming, and celebrating
of the extraordinary richness of this experience. Says Margaret
Hebblethwaite: "God gave and gave beyond our hopes because
it was her good pleasure."[49]

The home needs to be reclaimed as a sacred place; ". . . we
have not learnt to relate to the sacred in the family home, so that
just by walking around the house of a Christian family we can
feel we are drinking in draughts of God. We have not dared to
think in these terms."[50]

A moratorium must be called on male clerical reflection on
motherhood with regard to Mary — Leonardo Boff is no more
successful than the Pope in his attempt to create a Marian ma-
ternalism — until women have had a chance to tell their story of

motherhood, to reflect on it from the depths of their knowledge and Christian experience, and to celebrate it publicly and liturgically in rituals designed by themselves. Perhaps the image of Mary's Immaculate Conception can be reactivated in the interests of highlighting the immaculate beauties of the gift of bringing forth new life. Sally Cuneen describes a spontaneous discussion of the spiritual significance of pregnancy, birth, and nursing, and remarks on the novelty of this experience in middle-class culture. There is a new insistence on being conscious during birth, of participating actively in the process with one's partner, and even of directing the process. This is not intended to negate the benefit of medical help in case of emergency, but an entirely natural process has been medically orchestrated, often for the benefit of the medical establishment and not of the mother.

It is difficult to explore any spiritual experience other than as victim when one is neither a conscious participant nor the lead actor. Cuneen quotes Carol Ochs as follows:

> The decentering of self achieved through asceticism can be accomplished as well by true devotion which is first and foremost physical caring. In caring for their infants, mothers don't seek to mortify their sensitivities — they simply know that babies must be diapered and that infants who spit up must be cleaned. They count the action as no great spiritual accomplishment. By merely doing what must be done, their spiritual development proceeds without pride and without strain — it gracefully unfolds.[51]

The Song of Mary is a song of liberating nurturance. In the Reign of God, bodies will be attended to. This song is not about souls or a distant future, but a call to act in the present as embodied persons who need to be fed and nurtured and who are responsible for the feeding and nurturing of all peoples on earth, especially our own children. It is also a song about the neglect of the bodies of the poor and the hungry, and the source of this neglect is the misuse of wealth and power. Mary's song of praise and proclamation invites us to attend to the realities of human living — acts of finding and preparing food, acts of feeding and providing food for the hungry. These acts are as holy as acts of fasting. The art of creating the sacred space we call home is as holy as the art of creating the sacred space we call convent, church, or monastery. Mary and Joseph did not create a monastery for Jesus, but a home.

Sometimes humor illustrates the point effectively. A young Irish priest visited the mother of ten children and watched her struggles to feed and care for them during an evening meal. He felt an encouraging comment was necessary, so he suggested that the mother remember the Holy Family and its immaculate mother. The Irish human mother responded: "I do remember her and the fact that *she* had only one to look after." This natural common sense has always been a part of the wisdom of motherhood — now it needs to inform the theological reflection on motherhood, including the motherhood of Mary.

Speaking of Mary as advocate of justice is always open to the temptation of isolating Mary from mainstream theology, something that has frequently happened to Marian reflection in the past. It is also open to the temptation of isolating parts of Mary's life for attention and of ignoring other parts as not patent to theological reflection. Ever since the explosion of Marian devotion in the fourth and fifth centuries, she has acquired enormous and far-reaching symbolic value. The real Mary, the young Jewish woman, receded from view, and in her place arrived the powerful elasticity of the mother-virgin-queen-intercessor imagery of Christian imagination. In the overall development of Marian reflection, it is precisely the scriptural testimony which has had least influence on the tradition; so, also, we can say that the real humanity of Mary has had remarkably little influence on the person presented for veneration to the Christian community. The whole apparition tradition arises from statuary and its imaginative reconstructions and not often from any biblical sense of Mary's personality. The presence of certain anti-Jewish strains in this tradition is not difficult to find — it was even used by Hitler as proof that Mary was not a Jew. At any rate, the humanity of Mary has been lost in the sheer volume of imagery that has inundated the Christian tradition.

Not so today. Many women continue to regard Mary with some suspicion. They have abandoned their childhood devotion and have not found an adequate adult expression with which to replace it. It is interesting how few and spartan are the references to Mary in current Christian reflection on motherhood. There was little in Marian tradition to throw light on their experience of motherhood. Women's identification with Mary was interpreted through the experience of motherhood, but it was a motherhood unknown to any female of the human species. For men, Mary can be an object of fantasy, longing, admiration, or veneration, but, for women who share womanhood with Mary, she is an identification figure and one whose example they are invited to follow. It is not surprising that one of the great outbreaks of Marian devotion followed close upon the imposition of clerical celibacy. At the institutional level, the emphasis on virgin-motherhood made this identification impossible in the area where it was most encouraged.

It is time, then, for the advocacy of some justice for Mary, and it seems that this can be done only by listening to women as they speak of Mary. From the imposed institutional starting point of male celibacy, such reflection and such justice would seem to be impossible. Mary is not an object; she is a person. Women are not objects; they are persons with full humanity and full moral agency. Listening to women speak of Mary brings radically new insights to the discussion. They are insights about pain and blood and the horrors of holding one's dead child in one's arms, and insights about the unimaginable joy and ecstasy of giving birth and bringing life to life. Without such stories, the significance of Mary will not be recovered. We must cease looking for appearances of Mary only in the heavens and discover her in the midst of the routine of life — the life of hungry, poor, and marginalized women, as well as the life of more affluent women who try to live a Christian commitment of resistance to false values. Here, Mary will be found as companion and justice advocate.

Thousands seek Mary today. Pilgrims return from Medjugorje and dedicate their farms and homes as places of prayer and pilgrimage. Often there is not much evidence of the spectacular and the apparitional. Many people acknowledge having met visionaries, but not being themselves among their number. But, there is a great deal of emphasis on living a new and quietly joy-filled life of companionship with Mary. There are, of course, excesses and thrill-seekers and those who try to manipulate events for their own purposes, but, on the whole, a low-key renewal is occurring.

Little is taking place at the official level. Mary seems to strike universal fear into clerical hearts. But, a quiet murmuring of renewed Marian reflection can be heard. It is spoken in whispers around kitchen tables and enroute to pilgrimage sites. It is a delicate thing, which, if raised too soon to the light, might be prematurely destroyed. Ecumenically, believers from many traditions are marvelling at the believers' skill in selectivity when it comes to Marian texts. Even the most avid devotees of the Word manage to ignore the sections that do not seem to be immediately relevant. The phenomenon of the resistant reader is not new. Fidelity to the word of God takes many forms, most highly selective.

A longing for justice at many levels informs the life of the contemporary Roman Catholic Church. For some decades, segments of the North American Church basked in international attention because of its creative leadership and especially its courageous stands on women's issues. That period seems to have concluded. Perhaps the image of Mary as advocate of justice can reactivate our imaginations beyond the sterile attention to orthodoxy and orthopraxis which seems to preoccupy Church leadership today. Just care is at the heart of just action. It is time for the loud and rushing images of the Visitation to provide a newly creative and generative symbol for lovers of Mary and lovers of justice.

NOTES

[1]The Apostolic Exhortation, *Marialis Cultus,* issued 2/2/74; E.T., *True Devotion to the Blessed Virgin Mary* (Washington, D.C.: USCC, 1974), #29-37. (Henceforth designated *MC*)

[2]*MC,* 55.

[3]Hilda Graef, *Mary: A History of Doctrine and Devotion* (Westminster, MD: Christian Classics, 1985).

[4]*Sermon for the Nativity,* 288.

[5]John L. McKenzie, *Dictionary of the Bible* (Milwaukee: Bruce, 1965).

[6]Pope John Paul II, "Opening Address at CELAM," *Origins* 22/19 (1992).

[7]"Justice in the World," Introduction, in *Proclaiming Justice and Peace,* ed. Michael Walsh and Brian Davies (Mystic, CT: Twenty-Third Publications, 1991), 270.

[8]Ibid., Part III, 277.

[9]Phyllis H. Kaminsky, "Teaching Women and Sexuality in the Christian Tradition: Mutual Learning and Pedagogical Issues of Voice, Authority, and Power," *CSSR Bulletin* 21/1 (February 1992), 2.

[10]Ben Kimmerling, "Mary, Mary Quite Contrary," *The Furrow* (May 1988): 279-88.

[11]Raymond E. Brown, *The Birth of the Messiah* (New York: Doubleday 1977), 330ff.; Leonardo Boff, *The Maternal Face of God* (San Francisco: Harper and Row, 1987), Part III, 107-21.

[12]Jane Schaberg, *The Illegitimacy of Jesus: A Feminist Theological Interpretation of the Infancy Narratives* (NY: Crossroad, 1990), especially 97-101.

[13]Brown, *op. cit.*

[14]Ibid.

[15]*MC,* 37.

[16]See, for example, Mary Craig, *Spark from Heaven: The Mystery of the Madonna of Medjugorje* (Toronto: Hodder and Stoughton, 1988).

[17]Boff, *op. cit.,* 202-203.

[18]Pedro Casaldaliga, *In Pursuit of the Kingdom* (Maryknoll, New York: Orbis Books, 1990). Quoted in *Catholic New Times* (Toronto), 25 October 1992, 3.

[19]*Origins* 22/19 (1992), 16.

[20]Leonardo and Clodovis Boff, *Salvation and Liberation* (Maryknoll, NY: Orbis Brooks, 1985), 16ff.

[21]Ibid., 37.

[22]Ibid., 25ff. See also, Paulo Freire, *Pedagogy of the Oppressed,* trans. Myra Bergman Ramos (New York: Seabury Press, 1970).

[23]John Paul II, *Redemptoris Mater;* E.T., *Mother of the Redeemer, Origins* 16/43 (April 9, 1987), *passim.*

[24]*Salvation and Liberation,* 9ff.

[25]Jacques Dupont, O.S.B., "The Poor and Poverty in the Gospels and Acts," in *Gospel Poverty: Essays in Biblical Poverty,* ed. Augustin George, S.M., et al. (Chicago: Franciscan Herald Press, 1977), 25-52.

[26]I. Gebara and M. Bingemer, *Mary Mother of God, Mother of the Poor* (NY: Orbis Books, 1987), 16ff.

[27]Virgil Elizondo, "Mary and the Poor: A Model for Evangelizing," in *Mary in the Churches (Concilium* 168) (NY: The Seabury Press, 1983), 59-65.

[28]Leonardo Boff, *New Evangelization: Good News for the Poor* (NY: Orbis Books, 1991).

[29]Gebara and Bingemer, *op. cit.,* 121ff.

[30]See the comprehensive article, "Mary in Postconciliar Theology," by Stefano de Fiores, S.M.M., in *Vatican II: Assessment and Perspectives, Twenty-Five Years after (1962-1987),* ed. René Latourelle, S.J. (NY: Paulist Press, 1988), I: Part III, Chapter 17.

[31]See especially, *Christifideles laici,* 1988.

[32]Mary T. Malone, *Who Is My Mother? Rediscovering the Mother of Jesus* (Dubuque, Iowa: Wm. C. Brown Company, 1984), 129.

[33]*MC,* 37. See *National Bulletin on the Liturgy* 11 (January-February, 1978): 47-51.

[34]*MC,* Ibid.

[35]See especially Part III, "The Mother of God at the Center of the Pilgrim Church."

[36]One of the most accessible anthologies is Elizabeth A. Petroff, ed., *Medieval Women's Visionary Literature* (New York: Oxford University Press, 1986). For Christina of Markyate, 144ff.

[37]Anne Llewellyn Barstow, *Married Priests and Reforming the Papacy: The Eleventh-Century Debates* (New York: Edwin Mellen Press, 1982).

[38]H. Cox, *Seduction of the Spirit, The Use and Misuse of People's Religion* (NY: Simon and Schuster, 1973, 1975).

[39]Mark 3, 31ff.

[40]*Mulieris Dignitatem* (Washington, D.C.: USCC, 1988), 30 and *passim.*

[41]The point seems to have been made first by Adrienne Rich in *Of Woman Born: Motherhood as Experience and Institution,* Tenth Anniversary Edition (NY: W.W. Morton & Co., 1986). See also, Anne Carr, Elisabeth Schüssler Fiorenza, *Motherhood: Experience, Institution, Theology (Concilium* 206) (Edinburgh: T & T Clark, 1987).

[42]John Paul II, *"Behold Your Mother": Mary in the Life of the Priest* (1988), No. 4.

[43]"Between Sexes and Generations: Maternity Empowered" (*Concilium* 206), 37.

[44]Mercy Amba Oduyoye, "Poverty and Motherhood" (*Concilium* 206), 23-30.

[45]Margaret Hebblethwaite, *Motherhood and God* (London: Geoffrey Chapman, 1984).

[46]*Mulieris dignitatem,* 30.

[47]*The Book of Margery Kempe,* trans. and ed. R. A. Windeatt (NY: Penguin Books, 1985), and Julian of Norwich, *Revelations of Divine Love,* trans. and ed. Clifton Walters (NY: Penguin Books, 1966).

[48]Hebblethwaite, *op. cit.,* 134.

[49]Ibid., especially chapter 16.

[50]Ibid., especially Chapter 13.

[51]Sally Cuneen, *Mother Church: What the Experience of Women Is Teaching Her* (NY: Paulist Press, 1991), 134.

Mary: A Sign of Contradiction to Women?

Doris K. Donnelly

The source for the familiar question posed in the title of this essay is the Gospel of Luke 2:34. The setting is the presentation of Jesus in the temple; the speaker is Simeon who tells Mary that her son will be "a sign of contradiction" or "a sign spoken against," as the *Revised Standard Version* has it.

The intriguing challenge before us is to uncover the ways Mary, too, may be understood as a sign of contradiction. How is she "a sign spoken against"? How well does Mary measure up against women's agenda? And, what do women do when they identify contradictions associated with Mary?

For Mary, the problems surrounding contradictions are exacerbated because, unlike her son for whom exist biblical sources accounting for his actions and enabling the reconstruction of some elements of an historical Jesus, we do not have parallel advantages for his mother. There are very few historical data from which to construct any analogous "quest for the historical Mary."[1]

In the absence of these sources, however, the contradictions converge straightaway around two poles — the pole of women's experience and the pole of the Christian tradition surrounding Mary. Women have experienced contradictions bouncing against these poles, sometimes cancelling out both reference points. Or, women have felt compelled to choose between the contradictions — for example, between Mary's virginity *or* motherhood as her point of identification with them or else to throw up their hands in frustration and walk away from a virgin-mother model that seems to make no sense to human beings of the female gender.

First, let it be noted that there *are* contradictions. Yet, for all the exasperation connected with the contradictions facing them, many women have been unwilling to surrender Mary, but instead have contributed three important insights to the cause of reconciling opposites: (1) the certainty that their own experience as women is valuable in dialogue with the Mary of the tradition; (2) the identification of the contradictions as institutionally based and of theologizing done by men without benefit of consultation with women's experience; and (3) the sense that the contradictions could be accommodated in a both-and dialectic rather than an either-or negation. Anne Carr phrases well this last option:

> Mary as virgin and mother need not be understood as an impossible double bind, an inimitable ideal, but as a central Christian symbol that signifies autonomy *and* relationship, strength *and* tenderness, struggle *and* victory, God's power *and* human agency — not in competition but cooperation.[2]

The starting point for dealing with the contradictions lies with the experience of women, recognizing that a collaborative effort on the part of all women is needed so that the Marian tradition speaks credibly to all Christians. Thus, voices of biblical scholars, theologians, professional and grass-roots women, white women and women of color, both in the United States and elsewhere, are represented in these pages. Voices of men who share the same interests have also been included.

Because the issues raised by women could touch all aspects of women's experience as well as all areas of Marian doctrine and devotion, expediency prompts narrower parameters for this study. To that end, it will concentrate on women's experience of motherhood and the way that event is understood for Mary.

The points of view of both women of color and their white sisters regarding the experience of motherhood are acknowledged in Part I. Part II considers some theological formulations about the motherhood of Mary, contradictions associated with them, and women's responses to these concerns. A brief conclusion points to directions for the future in women's dialogue and experience of Mary.

PART I: FEMINISTS, WOMANISTS, MUJERISTAS AND THE EXPERIENCE OF MOTHERHOOD

Since women's experience has been the focal point of feminist scholarship in recent decades, it seems appropriate to turn there, predominantly, but not exclusively, for data for this study.

In the large body of literature that has accumulated in recent decades, feminists recognize that it is important to "be the definers rather than the defined,"[3] as Toni Morrison exhorts. Feminism reclaims the lost history, memory, wisdom, and experience of women, acknowledging in the recovery of their "subjugated knowledge"[4] a powerful critique of a society where dominant forms of power and knowledge reign supreme. "The critical principle of feminist theology," simply stated by Rosemary Radford Ruether, "is the promotion of the full humanity of women."[5] Feminism recognizes that human rights and talents and weaknesses are not divided by sex and that, in basic terms, all forms of sexism, racism, and classism are distortions of the plan of the Creator and the message of the New Covenant in Jesus Christ. The feminist critique applies especially to institutions, including Christian churches and theologies, that perpetuate stereotypes and other forms of inequality.

Although common denominators exist, women of color have identified feminism in recent years as a white middle-class movement, often with racist roots, and they have become articulate spokespersons, in their own right, of experiences not addressed in mainstream Western feminist circles. This essay proposes that different insights about motherhood emerge from white feminists and feminists of color which in turn influence their appropriation of symbols around Mary. In the final analysis, women of color and white women collaboratively must construct a theology of Mary true to the tradition and to their own experience.

In spite of common ground and the sensitivity of many prominent white feminists, women of color have felt excluded from feminist circles. "What Chou Mean We, White Girl?,"[6] they ask, with voices inflected to underline the "we." African American women claim that "Black women's existence, experience, and culture and the brutally complex systems of oppression which shape these are in the real world of white . . . consciousness beneath consideration invisible, unknown."[7] Many women of color prefer Alice Walker's term "womanist" as descriptive of who they are and what they are about. Walker's definition includes four elements: first, a connection with the word "womanish" in contrast to "girlish"; it refers to black females or females of color. Second, it includes woman's interest in the survival of all — a theme that recurs explicitly in the experience and writings of women of color. Third, womanist celebrates who and what it is that woman loves — food, roundness, struggle, dance, music, etc. Fourth, Walker offers a comparison: womanist is to feminist as purple is to lavender, thus emphasizing the strength and passion of womanists compared with those of feminists.[8]

It is not only black women who feel excluded from feminism as defined by white women. Cherrie Moraga and Gloria Anzaldua address the "blank spots" in white feminism that either stereotype women of color, marginalize, or patronize them.[9] Ada Maria Isasi-Diaz writes of the Hispanic woman's "invisible invisibility" and identifies "engagement" as the missing element in her contact with feminists.[10] Latina feminist Jo Carillo speaks of the hypocrisy of feminists towards mujeristas in her poem, "And When You Leave, Take Your Pictures With You":

> And when our white sisters
> radical friends see us
> in the flesh
> not as a picture they own,
> they are not quite as sure
> if
> they like us as much.
> We're not as happy as we look
> on
> their
> wall.[11]

Kwok Pui'lan offers still another indictment of Western female scholarship as not compassionate enough to allow the harsh reality of Third World women to challenge the feminist paradigm shift they hope to develop. Feminist scholarship, she believes, will remain disembodied until it pays heed "to the daily rice of Asian women."[12] From Nelle Morton, Pui'lan has learned that oppressed women must learn four languages to ensure their survival — the languages of the white male, the white female, men-of-color, and their own language. She also recognizes the wisdom of Audre Lorde who advised that "the master's tools will never dismantle the master's house."[13] It may be important, however, to become familiar with the master's tools in order to beat the master at his own game, but women of color are aware of the need to learn their own language if they ever intend to build a house of their own, to say nothing of housebuilding in the context of a pluralistic feminism.

Chela Sandoval neatly sums up a messy situation. Her voice resonates with the writings of many other women of color when she speaks of a hierarchy that places the white man on top, white women after that, black men following them, and women of color at the bottom in the fourth and final category "against which all the other categories are provided their particular meanings and privileges."[14] What is clear for our purposes is that women of color identify white women as part of the problem, not part of the solution.

The struggle between white women and women of color highlights the difficulty in forming a generic description of women's experience of motherhood. Recognizing that it is impossible to speak for *all* feminists, womanists, or mujeristas, we realize that enough general impressions have emerged from these divergent constituencies to allow speaking for the experience of *some*. Still, the essay remains fully aware that a homogenized experience of motherhood does not exist.

Two other difficulties deserve comment.

First, taking the critique of feminism by women of color at face value, one observes it often happens that a class issue emerges where white women represent the middle-class and women of color, the poor. This frame of reference reflects the literature at hand, where women of color, even when they are not poor, often speak in solidarity with the marginalized and poor, and white women, like me, often speak from perches of privilege.

Second, the essay rejects, but is aware of, a prevalent, sometimes subtle, romanticized version of motherhood as well as the uneven, unjust and manipulative ways that it has been used by men to keep women subservient, forever catering to the needs of their children. To speak of women's experience of motherhood, therefore, in no way condones the oppressive ways it has been used in patriarchal societies, nor does it support any theory that equates motherhood with women's nature, or motherhood as the only routing for fulfillment open to women, nor does it approve of institutions, the Church among them, that render women subordinate as members, yet extol, almost exclusively, their role as mothers. On the other hand, once the oppression is clearly denounced, this essay supports the very positive experience of motherhood expressed by women themselves, concerning both their own experience as mothers as well as in relation to the symbol of Mary as mother.

A. FEMINISM AND MOTHERHOOD

If it is true that a gap exists between white women and women of color, it should be possible to uncover different perspectives in their experiences of motherhood. Even though the spectrum is a broad one, and even though we recognize that we speak for only *some* white women, it is possible to identify four recurrent, though not exhaustive, emphases when white women reflect on their experiences of motherhood.

1. Motherhood threatens self-identity. The guiding thesis of Betty Friedan's book, *The Feminine Mystique*,[15] challenged the "mystique" that women were to be defined principally through their roles as daughters, wives, and mothers. It urged women not to accept derivative status, but, rather, to seek fulfillment (if they chose) outside the home/family context. Friedan's words resonated with women. Locked into a system where their whole identity depended on their husbands and children, they sought ways, *not always selfishly*, to find themselves, to be something different from someone's wife or someone's mom, even when the "someone" was a person they loved dearly.[16]

Feminism still challenges the view that women's place is in the home, at the kitchen sink, preparing meals and serving others in other supportive ways without any attention to their self-development. Jean Baker Miller has noted that, when women "are encouraged to transform their drives into the service of another's drives; and the mediation is not directly with reality, but with and through the other person's purpose in that reality,"[17] the emotional and physical health of the woman is often jeopardized. Living through others has lost its appeal for many women when it contributes to an inferior social stereotype and a psychological theory in which women seemed neither to have opinions, tastes, nor identities of their own.

More important, however, as a white middle-class woman contemplates child-rearing, is the narrow social structure connected with motherhood. The mother is cook, chauffeur, tutor, nurse, comforter, guide, and chief bottlewasher. The social framework operative in middle-class families presumes that she alone is responsible for the total care of her child. She may be the fortunate wife of a sensitive, modern, caring husband receptive to shared parenthood, but the middle-class white woman is also aware that there will be significant changes in her life and her identity, more so than for her husband, once the baby arrives. She is told that she is "giving up everything" to have her baby, that rearing the child is easily a full-time job, and that children demand total attention. If she fails, of course, a child therapist could be hired to repair the damage, but that is certainly a small consolation. Apart from her husband (not always a very reliable back-up), the white middle-class woman does not have many places to turn. The nuclear family design leaves her with few options. Her family does not live close by; her friends have jobs; but, even if family and friends were nearby and free, the white middle-class woman hesitates to impose upon them. It is just not her way.

Closely conjoined with this issue are the child care agenda. But, child care as a political and domestic priority has been long in coming and only recently has come to the forefront of national debate.[18] Without adequate child care, the identity issue of white middle-class women remains threatened.

2. Motherhood limits career advancement and/or creativity. In a helpful article, Joyce Little distinguishes between conspicuous and inconspicuous achievements.[19] Conspicuous achievements are public, recognized and honored by society, and almost always happen outside the home and away from the family.[20] Women may choose (and some do) to pursue conspicuous avenues of accomplishment. If they are childless when they make their choice, they soon become aware of the tick of the biological clock; it is possible that they may forgo forever the possibility of giving birth to children of their own. When women with children enter the marketplace, they frequently compromise their advancement by moving on the slower paced "mommy track" rather than on the more aggressive fast track. Because mommy trackers in executive suites (and occasionally on factory floors) assume responsibility for children, obligating them to leave work promptly at the end of the day or shift, they are not so free to travel, take overtime assignments, socialize with their coworkers at the close of the day, or accept reassignments and the promotions that accompany these things as are their fast-track-counterparts. In addition, they routinely deal with the conflict of responding to the needs of a sick child at home and an urgent assignment at the office, often in the same day.

In an enlightening article not to be confused with the way the "mommy track" has been hybridized above, the consultant and business executive Felice Schwartz proposes that there are, in general, two groups of women in the marketplace — the career-primary woman and the career-and-family woman.[21] The career-primary woman is ready to make the same trade-offs traditionally made by men who put their careers first. In point of fact, however, career-primary women may make greater sacrifices, for, as Schwartz points out, "the decision [to put career first] requires that [women] remain single or at least childless or, if they do have children, that they be satisfied to have others raise them."[22] She points out that 90% of executive men, but only 35% of executive women, have children by the age of 40.[23] But, Schwartz encourages the corporation to notice, encourage, and reward women who want to be both mothers and productive workers outside the home. Given the extent of the professional training that companies have invested in these bright, capable women, it is to the company's advantage, Schwartz argues, to find ways to accommodate them. Career-and-family women offer something unique to the business world. Because the talented and creative ones among them are willing to trade some career growth and compensation for the freedom to spend more time, temporarily, with their children, both the women and the company benefit. Companies are able to keep their best people who continue to perform well until the time their children are in school and the women are less fragmented. Meanwhile, these mothers are able to combine home and career on their terms and with lessened stress in both areas of their lives.

A second point connected with Little's distinction between conspicuous and inconspicuous achievements has to do with motherhood's inhibiting women's contributions to art, music, and literature. The totally consuming commitment connected with motherhood has deterred women from actively nurturing their own creative gifts which, similarly, require total undivided commitment. When Shulamith Firestone asks the "tired question," "What were women doing while men created masterpieces?,"[24] the possible response is twofold: they were mothering, or they had no need of masterpieces because they were busy "creating" children. But, neither answer seems entirely satisfactory.

What white middle-class mothers have identified is that, at a time in their lives when they would like to have it both ways — to be mothers and creative workers/artists, they are forced to make choices. And, the choices are difficult, painful, and they entail sacrifices that women often wish were not part of the picture.

3. Motherhood must challenge patriarchal systems.
Adrienne Rich succinctly describes patriarchy as

> the power of the fathers: a familial-social, ideological, political system in which men — by force, direct pressure, or through ritual, tradition, law and language, customs, etiquette, education, and division of labor, determine what part women shall or shall not play, and in which the female is everywhere subsumed under the male.[25]

The situation in which most mothers find themselves is saturated with patriarchal history and overtones. Rich facilitates the conversation when she distinguishes between motherhood as

experience and institution. From the "experience" flows "the potential relation of any woman to her powers of reproduction and
to children."[26] This is different from motherhood as an institution "which aims at ensuring that potential — and all women —
shall remain under male control."[27] When motherhood is detached from the bondage of patriarchy, it has the possibility of
being a transforming experience. What is needed, according to
Rich, is not to abolish motherhood, but "to release the creation
and sustenance of life into the same realm of decision, struggle,
surprise, imagination and conscious intelligence, as any other
difficult, but freely chosen work."[28] Given the pervasiveness of
patriarchy, Rich registers astonishment at ". . . all we have
managed to salvage, of ourselves, for our children, even within
the destructiveness of the institution: the tenderness, the passion, the trust in our instincts, the evocation of a courage we did
not know we owned."[29]

This approach differs significantly from the one offered by
Shulamith Firestone. She imagines a future when technology
will offer the option of artificial reproduction through artificial
fetuses to free women from their bodily ties to reproduction.[30]
Rich is closer in thinking to Rosemary Ruether who argues that
to surrender the traditional link of women with nature would be
to "buy into that very polarization of which we have been the
primary victims."[31]

The point, therefore, is that there is a need to revision the
motherhood experience, detaching it from restrictive anthropological and sociological strictures, so that it may be appreciated
by more women as a life-giving and creative experience. But,
the danger to be avoided in reacting to a history of patriarchal
oppression is surrendering the motherhood experience —
throwing away the baby with the bathwater, as it were.

4. Motherhood is a spiritual awakening. While there are
women who see motherhood as confining and some who resent
its intrusion in their careers, others are surprised to find sheer
joy in the experience of pregnancy, birthing, and mothering.

Jean Bolen, a California physician who had delivered more
than 50 babies before she gave birth to a son and who valued the
scholarly and intellectual parts of her career enormously, reports that she was stunned by the transforming effect of her
pregnancy when she realized "that what was in my uterus was
more important and more wonderful than anything in my
head."[32] Bolen and others do not deny that mothering, as practiced in patriarchal societies, has been oppressive; they seek
only to point to an alternative. They have managed to spiral

through the mine field others claim as negative and to identify motherhood as a very positive experience.

An important voice in this area, echoing Bolen's experience, but framing it critically and pushing its limits, belongs to Sara Ruddick. Ruddick believes that all thinking is rooted in, and shaped by, the activities in which people are engaged.[33] She explores in detail the way the day-to-day effort involved in rearing children — including peacemaking, patience, and flexibility — offers a blueprint for the kind of work that needs to be done to promote world peace. Ruddick grants that men can develop the practice of mothering if they are willing to engage in such work as a primary commitment, but she contends that this is comparatively rare.

Ruddick knows that not all women are intrinsically peaceful, but she contends that the demands placed on the mother for preservation, growth, and social acceptability of her child put her in a privileged position to experience the contradictions among giving birth, preserving and sustaining life, and military thinking that hurts and destroys. In light of those contradictions, Ruddick develops a model of maternal thinking that involves a simple rationale for protection and growth of the child. Particularly for those intrigued by Carol Gilligan's model of care as "another voice,"[34] Ruddick integrates Gilligan's care model and Gandhi's model of peace and links feminist politics with the nonviolent peace tradition. She gathers testimony from women's experiences, not only to challenge the politics of war, but also to show the value of nonviolence as life-giving and creative. Ruddick's reflective awareness of the link between maternal practice and maternal thinking is a theoretical complement to the praxis-based contribution of Third World women and a helpful connection to new ways women have for understanding Mary.

B. WOMANISTS/MUJERISTAS/ASIAN WOMEN AND MOTHERHOOD

The question is whether the motherhood experience among women of color offers perspectives different from those of white women. Does the Black or Latina or Asian woman's experience of motherhood, either in the context of the United States or elsewhere, evoke different moods? Does it derive from different roots? The answer to both is yes. Three points in particular deserve notice.

1. Motherhood is experienced as a communal activity.
The lifeline that supports women of color is a communal theology rooted in a praxis of caring. Delores Williams writes that "womanist reality begins with mothers relating to their children and is characterized by black women (not necessarily bearers of children) nurturing great numbers of black people in the liberation struggle."[35] Elsa Tamez identifies the point of departure for theology as a praxis of caring. Such praxis is "a non-hierarchial, non-imperialistic, non-patriarchal structure finding women who advocate . . . collegial relations between men and women, older and younger people and children, between all people."[36]

The same may be said of the experience of motherhood. The Latina, the Black, and the Asian woman are united in their understanding of the need for a social reality that claims a woman is not only mother of her child, but of all children. What this means in the practical order is that there exists for women of color a community sense stronger than that known to Anglo middle-class women. Contrary to the theories of anthropologist Bronislaw Malinowski who established the individual family as the center of societal interaction, Marianne Katoppo, an Asian woman theologian, asserts that, in virtually all tribal societies with which she is familiar, any woman in the household will respond to a child's cry for "mommy," and, conversely, all children will call their mother's sisters "mother."[37] She cites the Batak society where the mother's older sister is Inang Tua (elder mother) and the younger sister is Inang Muda (younger mother). Katoppo further comments that "the extreme individualization and alienation of the person, as may be the case in western society, is quite uncommon"[38] in that culture.

The mothering role, undertaken by women in Asia, Latin America, Africa, and in ethnic communities in the United States, is not merely a spiritual motherhood of well wishing and support from the sidelines. It assumes real hands-on involvement in the life of a child, with women aware that the cards are stacked against their children and that only if they join together in support of them do these boys and girls have a chance to succeed against staggering odds. Even in United States innercities, where violence is epidemic and boys and girls must stay indoors to avoid bullets, drugs and gangs, the fragile network of grandmothers, aunts, and neighbors attempts to stay in place to guarantee support and some measure of sanity and safety.[39] Would that these mothers could afford to stay home and assume full-time mothering for their "at risk" children! But, as Jacqueline Jones points out in her own historical research on black women, work, and the family, any valid sociological study of black motherhood she did had to take account of the family context *and* the work context.[40] Mothers had no choice; they had to work. What Jones writes of black women could also be said of Chicana and Asian working class mothers.

Meridian, the protagonist of one of Alice Walker's novels, lives out the truth of the communal core to the motherhood experience.[41] A teen-age mother, beleaguered with the pressures and demands of full-time motherhood, Meridian contemplates suicide and/or killing her own baby. Instead, she commits what she deems to be the ultimate sin against black motherhood — giving her child away. At the end of the novel, however, Meridian has reinterpreted the meaning of the word "mother" to include those who nurture the possibility of a decent life, not only physically, but spiritually, and not only for her child, but for all children. Meridian's maternal vocation lies in becoming the mother of a movement of liberation for her people. Motherhood redefined in that context is salvific for her and for her community.[42]

Valerie Saiving did the women's movement a favor years ago when she pointed out that the most pernicious sin for men may be prideful self-assertion, but that for women the root sin is not pride, but "triviality, distractibility, and diffuseness; lack of an organizing center or focus, dependence on others for one's own self-definition, tolerance at the expense of standards of excellence; inability to respect the boundaries of privacy; sentimentality . . . and mistrust of reason — in short, underdevelopment or negation of the self."[43]

To that valuable contribution, Susan Thistlethwaite offers another. From the writings of Zora Neale Hurston and Katie Cannon, she identifies the sin of the black woman (and by extension, I submit, this is the sin recognized by all women of color), to set oneself outside the community: "The besetting sin of black women, consists in turning away from their community and their ancestors, in denying their heritage of social responsibility to their people and to oppressed women everywhere."[44]

2. The experience of slavery influences the experience of motherhood. American slavocracy, that bound black men and women in an oppressive system of economic, social, physical, and sexual exploitation, wreaked its havoc with particular brutality on the black woman. Black women were not only dishonored by white men, but they were brutalized by white women as well. Often enough, they were mistreated by black men, too.

Slavery forced black women to surrender their own children to be sold and to submit to the breeding instincts of their Christian masters who were eager to satisfy their lust or produce more slaves. In the novel, *Uncle Tom's Cabin*, the slave woman Eliza responds to her master's threat to sell her child by assuming perilous risks and escaping the system that imprisoned her.[45] For most women, however, there were no escape routes. Instead, they bore the excruciating pain of separation from their own flesh and blood. Perhaps Sojourner Truth's plea is the most eloquent: "I have borne thirteen children, and seen 'em mos' all sold off to slavery, and when I cried out with my mother's grief, none but Jesus heard me! And ain't I a woman?"[46] As the backdrop to her novel *Beloved*, Toni Morrison uses the historical incident of Margaret Garner, a runaway slave in Kentucky, who, in 1855, killed her daughter rather than have her returned to slavery. Bluntly, boldly, poignantly, Morrison dedicates the novel to "sixty million and more" slaves sacrificed and virtually forgotten.

In addition to the savagery of separating mothers from their children, black women were routinely raped by their masters. Margaret Walker reminds us, in her historical novel *Jubilee*,[47] that Sis Hetta, a self-possessed, graceful, high-spirited young woman when she came to the Dutton plantation as a "gift" to Master Dutton from his father, gave birth to 15 of his children. She died in childbirth at the age of 29, with thighs and legs almost completely covered with varicose veins, mourned by friends and a husband who knew about, but were powerless to counter, the forced breeder relationship.

Delores Williams reminds us that, while "the male dominated economic sector exploited the black women's reproductive capacities" for more slaves and more money, "the female-dominated domestic sector exploited black women's nurturing capacities in order to provide greater comfort for families of the white ruling class."[48] Certainly, this is vividly brought to consciousness in Alice Walker's novel *The Color Purple* when Sophia tends to the mayor's household and children and is denied a promised visit with her own family at Christmas.[49] Bell Hooks tells of the punishment meted out to a slave girl when her white mistress discovered her husband raping her. The girl was locked in a smokehouse and beaten daily for several weeks. When slaves on the plantation confronted the white mistress and claimed that the girl submitted to an act of force by the white husband, the mistress responded: "After I've done with her, she'll never do the like again thru ignorance."[50]

These experiences are reflected in the working conditions even now for immigrant and migrant women in the United States. Even the upwardly mobile among them can relate to Bernice Zamora's lament. Oppressed by her Chicano lover and also by the gringo who robs her of $20,000-30,000 a year of pay she calculates is due her, she composes a prose poem:

> And so I write about how I
> worked in beet fields as a child.
> About how I worked as a waitress
> eight hours at night to get through
> high school, about working as a
> seamstress, typist, and field
> clerk to get through college,
> and about how in graduate school
> I held two jobs, seven days a week,
> still alone, still asking, "Can
> I feed my children today?"[51]

Slavery has many faces; women of color have worn most of them. Their gripping, poignant, and angry stories rehearse a passionate commitment to their children's welfare, but they remind us, too, that, for women of color, the ladder from the cellar into the light has been, and still is, a difficult climb.

3. Motherhood involves suffering. On the subject of suffering, some statistics are relevant:

- In Argentina, children ages eight to ten are trained in prostitution centers and then sold to the U.S. and Arab countries.[52]
- In the brothels of Manila and Bangkok, the port district of Rio de Janeiro, and the backrooms of Frankfurt, pimps hawk the services of children as young as 8 to 13 years old by emphasizing that they are "clean" (i.e., free from the AIDS virus), though this judgment is probably "naive," according to experts reporting in Brussels at a conference organized by Unesco on "the sex trade and human rights."[53]
- In Brazil, 400,000 children younger than five die each year from curable illnesses. Last year, 740 minors were assasinated.[54]
- The conflict in Guatemala has orphaned or displaced 210,000 children.[55]
- The January-February, 1993 issue of the *Harvard Business Review* used as a case-study the conscience dilemma of a U.S. manufacturing company confronting child labor (some children possibly as young as 8) working for no wages in its Lahore, Pakistan, plant.[56]

It is not the intention of this essay to suggest that working class women of color suffer more than white middle-class women. Rather, it is to call to the reader's attention the history of inequality and injustice that is, and has been, theirs *in excelsis*.

Through the linkages of motherhood with community and the experience of slavery and oppression, the outlines of suffering have already been clearly established. But, there is a particular suffering we vicariously experience when we watch mothers in inner-city Detroit walk the gauntlet with their young children from the projects to school and vice versa so they are not harassed by older children in acts of gratuitous violence. The suffering endured by these women is part of the package of motherhood in Soweto, Buenos Aires, Nicaragua, the south side of Chicago, the Bushwick section of Brooklyn, and many places in between. It is a suffering of women who try not to endure it passively, but who enter into it and actively experience and encounter it. It takes super human courage to do what these women do, and they do it, not incidentally, on behalf of children who are not their own as well as those who are.

What these mothers learn in the process of their sacrifices is that they are capable of turning destructive anger into a powerful force demanding change. Through their collective Bible study groups, women in Latin America begin to become aware of new roles beyond taking care of their houses and going to Church. In their community action groups on the south side of Chicago, women know themselves as voters who can alter school districting lines, budgets, teachers' salaries, and after school programs. Women realize that, if they want a different future for themselves and their children, they must suffer to make it happen. Denise Carmody writes:

> From the underside of history the poor women of Africa, Asia and Latin America fight to do what is right. Even in the most trying circumstances most of them struggle to protect their children, hold their families together, and endure sufferings without cursing God.[57]

This is not suffering for suffering's sake, of course, but rather suffering to effect change and even transformation. For these mothers, it is worth the price.

PART II. MARY AND MOTHERHOOD

Like many women, when the American novelist Mary Gordon became a mother, she looked to Mary for a woman with whom she could relate, woman-to-woman: "I have wanted to create for myself a devotion to Mary that honors her as a woman, as a mother, that rejects the wickedness of hatred and sexual fear."[58] Gordon was aware, at least implicitly, of Elizabeth Johnson's assessment that

> Concentration on Mary's motherhood in the tradition has served to reinforce the perception that motherhood is the raison d'etre of a woman's life, the one divinely approved accomplishment. . . It has thereby legitimated domesticity as the primary vocation for women.[59]

For a new relationship to emerge, it was necessary for Gordon to forget the blue veil on the holy card pictures, the slouching posture, the downcast eyes, the halo, the insecure demeanor, the vacant look on the statues in parish churches, and words like "handmaiden," "submissive," and "obedient." She needed a vigorous and courageous woman who could help her sort through sorrows and joys, who could help her exchange pain for enlightenment. Liturgist Shawn Madigan offers as a blueprint for those who share the same search a return to the only four Marian liturgical festivals that have a scriptural foundation: the annunciation, the visitation, the motherhood of God, and the sorrowful mother of the passion.[60]

Madigan's suggestion frames this section of the essay. An earlier preference to elicit a theological base of reflection and exegesis from as wide a cross-section of women, and occasionally men, is not only still operative, but is critical to allow for divergent points of view to challenge and enlighten conversation.

A. THE ANNUNCIATION

The trouble with contradictions starts here. An all too common reading of this story pictures Mary in the passive role of a girl unable to figure out the plot, let alone the subtext, of the drama unfolding before her. Without ego or self-possession, Mary seems to shrug her shoulders and go along with a plan too deep for her comprehension. She agrees to be a passive team player, content with a background supportive role. As a woman, she "never tries to steal the show, but is always in her proper place cooperating with her son in the salvation of the world."[61] In addition to her docility, the Scriptures affirm her virginity; tradition will subsequently uphold Mary's virginity before, during, and after the birth of Jesus. The miraculous conception of Jesus does not involve sex, and, in due course, sex becomes associated with humankind's baser instincts, clearly less preferable than virginity as a way of life and only somewhat mitigated as an appalling negative when a child results from the act.

An often overlooked part of Luke's narrative, however, discloses Mary, contrary to stereotype, as a young woman who is comfortable discussing sex with the heavenly messenger. Poised and articulate, she is aware of, and unembarrassed by, the facts of life as she questions the impossibility of the proposed pregnancy. In a conversation that would befuddle many contemporary teenagers weaned on MTV and PG-17 movies, Mary raises an objection ("How shall this be, since I have no husband?" Luke 1:14), and she expects an answer.[62]

Mary's fiat is all the more impressive, given her active participation in the dialog. Hardly the passive acquiescence of a dolt or the uncomfortable consent of a reticent prude, Mary freely assents to be a partner in the plan of salvation: "She is a self directed person, consulted in advance [and] gives her consent; thus she becomes an active, personal agent in the drama of God's Incarnation."[63] One theologian comments that "Mary emerges from the 'infancy narratives' as an actor in command of her own choices, including the disposition of her own body."[64]

Given Luke's text, it is something of a surprise that a fear of female sexuality develops in the Marian tradition.[65] Consistent with its fear of female sexuality, the Christian tradition placed Mary on a pedestal where she was safe, virginal, and unthreatening to celibate males; at the same time, the tradition looked to Mary's diametrically opposite symbol, Eve, for its temptress imagery. Mary is the pure one; Eve, defiled. Mary is innocent; Eve, cunning. Mary is holy; Eve, sinful. Mary is of the spirit; Eve, of the flesh. The Eve-Mary dichotomy, to no one's surprise, elevated Mary as the woman to behold, but not copy, because she was inimitable. Women were given Eve as their model and for countless generations considered themselves among "her poor banished children," as they prayed the popular prayer, the *Salve Regina*. To its credit, in *Behold Your Mother*, the United States National Conference of Catholic Bishops avoided reference to Mary as the "new Eve" and focussed, instead, on her role as liberator.[66] Indeed, this pastoral letter is even sensitive to the misuse by Church fathers of Mary as "new Eve" and the categorical identification of all other women as "old Eves."

Reflecting the grass roots experiences of Latina women and their experience of the extended family and inclusive community, theologians Ivone Gebara and Maria Clara Bingemer attempt to ignore the Eve-Mary dichotomy by claiming both women as their sisters — as part of the family. Eve is the mother of the living; Mary "is Eve in the totality of her being — mother of the living, mother of life."[67] Mary does not replace Eve, but is an extension of her — Eve is the older sister, Mary, the younger one. Not only are Mary and Eve perceived as sisters to each other, but they are sisters to all women by virtue of their creative capacities. Latina women seem more interested in the ties that bind these two women and less interested in the features that separate them.

From the white First World sector, biblical scholar Phyllis Trible urges women who approach Genesis 2-3 not "to read to reject," but to "reread to understand and to appropriate."[68] In the rereading, and with Trible's guidance, Eve emerges as more intelligent, sensitive, and ingenious, in contrast to the man, Adam, who is passive, brutish, and inept. Thus, the rereading leads to fresh perspectives, uncluttered by patriarchal biases, and allows women to take pride in being daughters of Eve.

Trible, Bingemer, and Gebara point to new ways to read the Eve-Mary symbolism that has served to divide women in the past. In their hands, the Eve-Mary dichotomy seems less threatening and more collaborative. Revisioning Mary at the annunciation scene renders Mary as a model contemporary women would regard favorably: she evidences a high comfort level with her own sexuality, grace under pressure, confidence in new settings, an unusual degree of self-awareness, and uncommon generosity in responding to an exceptional challenge.

B. THE VISITATION

Luke's account of the visitation (1:39-56) centers on two women: Mary, newly pregnant and carrying Jesus, and Elizabeth, six months along in her pregnancy with John. Their link is not only pregnancy, but the roles their sons will play in the drama of redemption. John will herald the birth of Jesus who will redeem Israel. This story reveals the way the virgin-mother symbol has been a sign of contradiction associated with Mary, with each element in the equation, at different moments in history, functioning as a "sign spoken against."

As women are aware, Mary as virgin-mother has served to separate Mary from women who can relate to her either as virgin or mother, but not as both. Unfortunately, her uniqueness sets her apart from the experience of all women as "the great exception rather than the type."[69]

What Marian theology often overlooks, however, is that both women in the story conceive their sons in remarkable ways. Elizabeth is past her prime. She and her husband Zachary have adjusted to her barrenness and life without children. But, the barrenness of Elizabeth's womb is miraculously reversed through the unexpected power of God who is able to do the impossible. Elizabeth conceives; the curse of barrenness is lifted, and the child inside her leaps excitedly when Mary comes onto the scene.

Parallel to Elizabeth's story is Mary's extraordinary conception of Jesus. In Mary's case, it is not old age that stands in her way, but rather her virginity. We have been so often programmed to appreciate virginity as a pearl of great price and the gift above all others that it is possible to miss a curious twist in this story. Instead of understanding virginity as a "treasured virtue," the biblical theologian Donald Senior proposes of Mary's virginity that "there is reason to suggest that Luke considers it an impoverishment, a promise unfulfilled."[70] She of low estate, she the handmaid, she the poor one has been filled with good things. Once again, however, Donald Senior points out, contrary to interpretations and extrapolations exalting Mary's virginity, that "'the low estate' of Mary in Luke's narrative is her virginity . . . Into the poverty of her virginity, God brings new and unexpected life."[71]

Thus, in addition to their mutual pregnancies and the overlapping destinies of their sons, Mary and Elizabeth are connected by virtue of their conception stories — for Elizabeth, the impossibility of pregnancy because of old age (a tragic situation within the context of the culture), and for Mary, the impossibility of pregnancy because of the impoverishment of her virginity. The parallel is reinforced even further when God breaks through the limitations of barrenness in one case and virginity in the other, and new life pulsates in the bodies of these two women. Elizabeth and Mary may exemplify two different experiences of promises unfulfilled, but God's intervention is clearly the cause of the joy these mothers-to-be share with each other. Elizabeth recognizes in Mary a kinswoman who trusted in the promise of God to redeem "the emptiness of her virginity,"[72] and she refers to Mary's trust "that there would be a fulfillment of what was spoken to her from the Lord" (1:45). Elizabeth's words hardly reflect a passive obedience on Mary's part, but rather an active, alert, expectant hope that God would not renege on his promises and that Mary, too, would be faithful to hers.

In all of the symbols and themes that surround Mary in the Gospel, it is also crucial to remember that she is a woman who carries her baby to term. Trimester after trimester, month after month, Mary remains actively engaged with the new life within her, nourishing the child in her womb, pondering the plan, involved with her husband in preparation for the birth of their child. God's promise to Israel is linked to the total care with which Mary agrees to give birth to new life.

This approach to Mary's virginity points to the fundamental understanding of virginity, for Mary and for other women, as a signal of the person independent and complete unto herself. As so, it is a statement of freedom, not lack. It expresses a wholeness that need not always be understood in physical terms. To be a virgin also carries with it psychological, emotional, and spiritual components.

One is reminded in this context of Virgilio Elizondo's remarks about girls and young women sold into prostitution in Latin American countries, whom he calls virgins.[73] Measured in scientific terms exclusively, these women were violated; in a very real medical, but restricted sense, they are not virgins. But, Elizondo's pastoral sense encourages him to take the longer view. At a more profound level, and in a more complete way, his judgment seems accurate.

Perhaps Alice Walker's novel, *The Color Purple*, provides a similar insight regarding virginity. In a moment of self-awareness, after Shug and Celie share intimacies about their sexual histories, Shug reaches a similar conclusion about Celie. Raped by the man who claims to be her father, Celie is also the mother of two children and the wife of an abusive husband, but she confides to Shug that she has never, ever enjoyed sex. Shug assesses the situation simply: "Why Miss Celie, she say, you still a virgin."[74]

Shug is aware of the physical side to Celie's experience, but she is aware of the spiritual side, too. She knows that there is more to measuring virginity than a clinical examination. So, her assessment stands, for Celie is a woman complete unto herself. It is the better part, not to be taken from her.

Perhaps in the context of this discussion concerning virginity, it is possible to rethink the inherent contradiction in the virgin-mother symbol accorded to Mary. Rather than an either-or separation through which women have routinely been forced to choose between one or the other of these dual roles, perhaps what is at stake after all is a both-and.

At a profound, but real, level, Mary *is* virgin *and* mother, for she was at the same time fully actualized, integrated, and a whole person complete in herself who offered herself completely to another. She was not dependent on her child for fulfillment because she mothered and let go when the time came to do that. She was not dependent on a man for her fulfillment, but on God. The nineteenth century black abolitionist and feminist, Sojourner Truth, once responded to a white preacher's claim that women could not have equal rights with men because Christ was not a woman. Truth asked: "Whar did your Christ come from? . . . From God and a woman! Man had nothin' to do wid' Him!"[75]

The contradiction between virgin and mother rests on a revisioning of these symbols. Contemporary women welcome ways of joining the two with an "emphasis . . . placed neither on bodily generativity alone nor on the value of the purely independent woman,"[76] but rather in ways that support balance in women's lives. So far we have hints at responses, no solutions, but a conviction that pondering Mary is the place to begin.

C. THE MOTHERHOOD OF GOD

Although Mary of the tradition is the source of mixed signals for women, when the contradictions swirl about her core identity, the split falls between those who claim her motherhood and those who claim her response to the word as defining who she is.

There has been a clear preference in recent years among both male and female Marian scholars to move away from Mary's motherhood and towards Mary as hearer and doer of the word as her defining moment. There are at least two reasons for this. One is Jesus' response to the woman who blesses Mary's blood ties to Jesus: "Blessed rather are those who hear the word of God and keep it" (Luke 11:28). But, the excessive maternal emphasis of the past is also responsible for the current accent, primarily because of the way the symbol was used as the rationale to limit women's identity to childbearing and mothering.

Claiming Mary as a hearer and doer of the word is a fitting category for Mary because she is an exceptional listener. She listens to the word of God and lets the Word/word incubate in her being. Listening to the word, however, is a dangerous activity because it encourages disciples, Mary primary among them, to take risks. When Mary hears the deliberate, daring promises of God at the annunciation, she says "yes" and risks the security of her reputation. Trusting God's promises, she risks safety and lives under Herod's rule. Later, she risks both safety and family life in her homeland when she travels to Egypt with her husband and son and lives there until Herod's death. Mary risks letting her son go into the hands of those who will betray him.[77] And, her final risk involves hanging on to her son's promises and their joint venture when all seems lost with his death, and all that remains is a fragile hope.

Women in Third World countries take similar risks daily and look to Mary, not as a princess in dainty white linen robes, but as a sister and companion in native dress, struggling as they do to make a go of things. Perhaps the Jungian author, Clarissa Pinkola Estés, pushes the model of Mary's mentoring role a bit too far when she refers to her as "a gang leader in heaven,"[78] but this kind of insight is closer to the bone than one might at first think.

Mary as hearer and doer of the word is a very appealing point of identification for all women, but, for Latin American women involved in bible study in their base communities, meeting Mary in the Scriptures is often a transforming experience. Women whose culture encouraged them to keep quiet and take a back seat in all activities except those going on in the kitchen find in Mary an active agent who challenges the status quo and makes possible a revolutionary transformation of the social order. Hearing the word of God has been the starting point for women "in demanding their own rights and their own opportunities," according to Luz Beatriz Arellano.[79] They recognize that "their role was to be history-making subjects of their own liberation, and hence to take part in the struggles to transform their country."[80]

Rosemary Ruether points out that Mary is not merely the advocate on behalf of the lowly ones, but that "(she) herself embodies that oppressed people. . . . She is herself the liberated Israel, the humiliated ones who have been lifted up, the hungry ones who have been filled with good things."[81]

This woman-to-woman link with Mary testifies that "liberation Mariology" is "far more at home with Third World women than with many North American Christians, many who regard themselves as near, if not exactly *on*, the thrones of the mighty."[82] For the Latina, African, or Asian Third World woman, however, Mary's appropriation of the word is a source of power these women never knew they had. It is a power that propels women from their previous horizon of home and family to the broader reality of paid labor and other forms of public life. There, they speak the words of Mary's Magnificat so boldly that the prayer is grounds for arrest in some sections of the world.[83] The power of the prayer rests simply in its ability to identify injustice and to proclaim a readiness to suffer for the sake of the new homeland, confident that change can and will happen.

Not only do some women listen to what the word says, but there are some women, especially First World white middle-class women, who have listened to what the word is *not* saying. For example, some find no convincing evidence for a clear rejection of women from ordination to holy orders in the Roman Catholic Church. Other women have revolutionized biblical

study by uncovering stories of our foremothers and their importance as apostolic witnesses of Jesus' ministry, death, and resurrection, *as well as* the inclination of writers of the New
Testament "to play down the women's role as witnesses and
apostles of the Easter event."[84] In addition, Elisabeth Schüssler
Fiorenza questions the accuracy of androcentric traditions:

> . . . the New Testament does not transmit a single androcentric
> statement or sexist story of Jesus, although he lived and
> preached in a patriarchal culture. . . . These women believe
> they have a responsibility to act on what they have *not* heard the
> word say, and there exists a sense of responsibility among these
> women to develop the appropriate strategies to make known
> their findings.[85]

Still other women are writing to ensure that feminine images of
God that they hear spoken in the Scriptures are not lost.[86]

Whatever attention needs to be paid to Mary as hearer and
doer of the word, there are also voices of women asking that her
role as physical mother not be forgotten. Women of color, in
particular, have found in her motherhood the connection they
have sought to honor their roots, their culture, and themselves
as the center of roots and culture. The Guadalupe Mary, for
example, is honored precisely in light of her affirmation of the
indigenous Indian women (and all people) of Mexico, politically suppressed, sexually violated, and economically exploited
by the Spanish conquistadors, beginning in 1521.

When Mary appeared to the Amerindian Juan Diego at
Tepeyac, the color of her skin was brown. She was clearly a *mes-
tiza*, part of the people subjugated by the colonizers. And, the
fact that Mary appeared on the site where the pagan goddess
Tonantzin appeared just a short time before was also not lost on
the indigenous people. However, according to Mary De Cock,
the most important liberation the Guadalupe Mary offers the
Indians by her dark-skinned image

> . . . was her prophetic critique of the racism in the church. The
> image of Santa Maria de Guadalupe — mediator, evangelist,
> prophet, disciple, and theologian — was also that of a young
> pregnant woman, clearly identified by her garments with the
> dignity and power of a conquered nation. She is a symbol
> women can identify with today in their slave status within the
> family, society and church.[87]

But, Guadalupe is one place in a long list of apparitions to the
poor. In addition, there is ". . . the black Aparecida who allowed herself to be found in the waters of the river Paraiba in

Brazil, Nicaragua's Purisima, Cuba's Virgin of Charity . . ."[88]
and more.

What all of these apparitions have in common is the potential
for Mary's solidarity with the oppressed. That potential is activated when women in countries where these apparitions have
taken place take time and are encouraged to wonder about
them. The meaning of the apparitions cannot be imposed from
the outside. For example, in a fascinating study of the Guadalupe Mary, Andres Guererro uncovers a connection between
Mary's appearances and the macho culture of Mexico.[89] But,
Guererro was sensitive during the preparation of his study to
allow indigenous women to discover their own experiences and
make their own connections. Furthermore, as Mary De Cock
points out:

> For centuries the common folk of the pre-patriarchal church, the
> peasant women of the middle ages, the pueblas of Mexico and
> the fishing villages of Nicaragua have found in Mary some sort
> of personal symbol that the theologians have missed.[90]

In cultures populated by women of color where motherhood
is a collaborative vocation, Mary's motherhood gives new
weight and meaning to her title, Mother of all Christians. She
reflects the mothers in south central Los Angeles and Flatbush,
New York, who understand their roles as corporate ones. A similar self and vocational understanding links the Madres de
Plaza de Mayo in Argentina, the mothers in Bolivia, Nicaragua, and El Salvador.

Women in Latin America, like women the world over, understand that the motherhood idealized image offered to them is
the precise reverse side of the exploitation they suffered as victims. Motherhood "gave (woman) back, or tried to give her
back, as a mother, what had been taken from her as human
person and as woman: her dignity, her participation, and the
chance to be not just one who reproduces human life but also
one who creates life and transforms her own society and her
own culture."[91] White women in North America recognize the
same sleight of hand that enables the patriarchal system to take
away with the left hand what it gave with the right. The
strength for women to unmask such hypocrisy comes from pondering Mary. At least, this is explicitly so among Latinas.

But, women who have revisioned the motherhood of Mary in
positive liberating fashion balance that identity with a self-
understanding as hearers and doers of the word. Posed with the
contradictions, it is possible to distinguish Mary as mother
from Mary as hearer and doer of the word without separating

them from each other. The experience of women connects with Mary's concern for our *temporal* and *eternal* happiness brought into being when justice rolls down and all forms of domination are levelled. Such a hope, however, is predicated on antennae sensitive to inequity wherever it is found, but especially when it threatens the powerless in the family network. When they are threatened, the response of women, mothers among them, is to resist, to exert their collective power to say "no." The "no" is also said to anyone who attempts to maintain irreconcilable opposites between hearing/doing the word and motherhood because, in their own experience, one includes the other.

D. SORROWFUL MOTHER

Mary as Mother of Sorrows presents us with two images perceived to be contradictory: her spiritual maternity and her physical motherhood. Yet, women — those professionally trained in exegetical and theological method as well as *campesinas* and descendants of slaves who "do theology from daily life" — say that both parts of the Marian mystery deserve attention.

Emphasis on Mary's spiritual motherhood often marginalizes the importance of the body. The body becomes dispensable. The spirit matters. One unfortunate consequence of this way of thinking is that it enables us to regard poverty, deprivation, and even death as tragic situations, but not as things that need to be contested: things of the earth, including the body, will pass, but a heavenly reward awaits those who endure. There is the possibility that even the death of Jesus would elicit tears and a shrug of the shoulders, but not necessarily action on behalf of justice opposing the status quo. In addition, a spiritual motherhood allows Mary to be otherworldly and untouched by life's harsher side. It derives from a maximalist Mariology, according her privileges that properly belong only to God, permitting Mary a supernatural connection with the plan of salvation, shielding her from the sting of deep, perduring sorrow. Accordingly, Mary would comprehend beyond the ordinary, and her sorrow at the death of her son, though real, would be mitigated by some extraordinary knowledge that lessened her pain. The net effect of this kind of theologizing would separate women from Mary, because no woman is so protected and privileged.

Ivone Gebara points to still another distancing effect. She writes of the way "spiritual motherhood" was extended to the life of women religious. The term implied renouncing the body as an ever present temptation and overcoming "the limitations of the 'material' body" as the canonical religious woman "approached the angelic ideal."[92] Gebara sees this as a consequence of vows and related issues, such as style and place of living, types of relationships and a language which reflected submission to a Church governed by men.[93]

In a strange turn of events, Mary's spiritual motherhood is being revisioned by women through the lens of their experiences. Rather than seeing this function of Mary's role as limiting and as a denial of the body, they perceive it as a way of strengthening their physical links with each other. Your child *is* my child; I am co-responsible with you (and you with me) for our children's future. They find that they have a way of maternal thinking in common that is based on preservative and attentive love. Women see themselves as united in the cause of creating a better world for their children in ways that transcend blood ties. Powerful coalitions of women in brutal and oppressive situations testify to this profound solidarity. For example, from one Chilean woman come these words:

> Because of all this suffering we are united. I do not ask for justice for my child alone, or the other women just for their children. We are asking for justice for all. All of us are equal. If we find one disappeared one I will rejoice as much as if they had found mine.[94]

Even without Puebla's documentation declaring that Mary belongs to the identity of Latin Americans, especially in situations of peril and oppression, women of color know this spiritual connection instinctively.[95] On one hand, women deflect the macho lauding and male deception concerning motherhood (theirs and Mary's), but, on the other hand, they know that Mary surrendered a womb like theirs to announce and embody the kingdom of justice and peace. A popular Nicaraguan hymn expresses these simple sentiments:

> Mary virgin bird,
> Joyful virgin bird.
> You with the aching feathers,
> You with the thorns and roses.
> Little bird in the cotton fields,
> bird in the coffee fields,
> brown-skinned virgin bird,
> black bird in the canefield.
>
> We pray to you through your son,
> the beloved one from your womb,
> the worker, the peasant,
> the humble one, the exploited one.
> We pray to you through your people.

> Virgin bird, when you fly,
> don't let your flight be stained,
> little bird of peace.[96]

While there exist ways to rethink Mary's spiritual mother-hood, there is no doubt that women have reestablished the womb-to-womb connection with Mary: "For Asians, the concentration of human hope is in the womb, where past, present and future converge."[97]

A theology that ratifies the importance of the physical part of Mary's mothering experience leads women to ponder their involvement in nine month pregnancies that lead to the possibility of maiming or death in war. When Mary suffers the ultimate injustice — the death of her innocent son, women understand the tragedy of losing what it took so long to knit together in the human body. Rather than telling her story from the vantage point of Easter, women pause and ponder the devastation Mary experienced as mother on Good Friday.

There are various representations of this tragic suffering. The lithographs of Kathe Kollwitz have special appeal because Kollwitz herself initially supported her younger son's service in the German military during the First World War and even accepted her dead son as a hero.[98] Gradually, she came to think differently, as do so many other women coopted into the ethos of war. Kollwitz' diaries trace her progressive move from war and towards nonviolence. In 1938, when she was in her seventies, Kollwitz sculpted a bronze Tower of Mothers that "depicts a circle of defiant mothers, arms outstretched, joined to protect the children behind them."[99]

Still another image is Michelangelo's Pieta which perhaps most eloquently captures the pathos of the scene where Jesus' limp body lies on Mary's lap, and, in a gesture that defies the spontaneous clutching of a child to her bosom, Mary offers him to the world, much like the way that the mothers of Hiroshima did and the mothers of Johannesburg and Nicaragua still do. Mary's gesture proposes to us that the death of an innocent person should never have happened. The symbol of the Pieta challenges a civilized world to see to it that it never happens again.

Mary personalizes grief. In a world inured to the ravages of war where death to children, men, and women is counted as "collateral damage," Mary shows what the pain of death looks like.

A television reporter once approached another mother, in a different culture and a separate time, as she visited the Vietnam War Memorial in Washington, D.C. The mother told of her trip from Houston and her need to touch her son's name, en-

graved among the 56,000 dead, "because war is names and not
numbers."[100] This mother from Houston knew the same thing
that the mothers from Latin America, Palestine, Beirut, and El
Salvador know. She knew that the only way humans can allow
and support war is by intellectualizing, computerizing, and
producing it in an elliptically harmless and antiseptic fashion
for television and the press. She also knew what the Pieta expresses: that war is flesh and that death has a face — the face of
a brother, mother, father, sisters, daughter, husband, wife, or
son.

This may well be the Pieta's strongest and most enduring insight for us. Mary's most important struggle on behalf of peace
may be her refusal to allow death to have the final word. In her
grief, Mary as the sorrowful mother invites us, as we see her
hold the limp and dangling body of her son, to take seriously the
flesh: "No woman who is a woman says of a human body, 'it is
nothing' . . ."[101] Clearly, the events surrounding the mother of
sorrows attests that matter is real, flesh is good, and the physical
is holy.

Sara Ruddick writes about the peacemaker's hope as a milita-
rist's fear. She is convinced that "the rhetoric and passion of maternity can turn against the military cause that depends on it."[102]
Ruddick believes that a feminist maternal politics of peace can
create "a suspicion of violence, a climate in which peace is desired, a way of living in which it is possible to learn and to practice nonviolent resistance and strategies of reconciliation."[103]
Together, mothers, feminists, and women in resistance to war
are members of an "imaginative collective." These are women in
the barrios, at the Plaza in Argentina, in the streets of South
Africa, in cities like New York, Houston, and Los Angeles, who
value the bodies of the children they helped bring into this
world. Collectively, they speak of their hope that these bodies
(and minds and spirits) will grow and flourish. The hope of
these mothers is tangible, real, and passionate. And, it does not
seem too far fetched to count Mary among these women.

CONCLUSION

The key to resolving the contradictions surrounding Mary
lies with women themselves. Together, they are capable of healing the wounds suffered by the Mary of the tradition. Women
have the power to reconcile opposites, not as part of an aca-
demic exercise twisting patriarchal categories for their own benefit, but because the symbols surrounding Mary have

emancipatory elements of their own. The following observations and suggestions are offered toward the healing process.

For the resolution of contradictions surrounding Mary, these steps seem critical.

1. A theology of Mary must begin with women of color in dialogue with white women. "Interdependency between women is necessary if we are to make ourselves into active, creative selves,"[104] writes Toinette Eugene. This is already being done in some quarters. In other places where Mary is not the direct beneficiary of a pluralist-feminist theology, women are recognizing the need for dialogue across race, class, and religion lines.[105] Women's wisdom is the key to a Mariology that will speak to men and women alike, but no one group — neither Latina, African, Asian, nor Anglo women — alone possesses the truth. The effort needed is collaborative, supportive, and freeing.

2. The agenda of women of color must be at the forefront. Feminist theologian Mary Grey phrases this point well:

> If *all* women are included in the agenda of liberation theology, the living conditions of women from ethnic minorities must be at the center, not at the periphery: this means that an *authentic* feminist liberation theology grasps the nettle of the *two-fold* ethic of liberation language and becomes sensitive to whether it is speaking to oppressor or oppressed. It must be sensitive, too, to the fact that women are *both*.

3. For reconciliation to happen, white women must acknowledge their responsibility regarding the oppression of their sisters of color. The reconciliation needed with regard to Marian contradictions and between Mary and women begins when women are at peace with each other. As long as there are anger, resentment, mistrust, or exclusionary language and/or behavior, the strength of women will be diluted in accomplishing the task at hand.

4. A revisioning of God as mother must not be displaced in the process of formulating a contemporary theology of Mary. The temptation is great and the seduction subtle to substitute Mary as the feminine face of God and leave a theology of creation and redemption fraught with male imagery. Feminists are paying close attention to this danger and are redirecting maternal images to the Creator God at the same time that they are reconstituting a theology of Mary. Both tasks must be done, and one must not imperil the other.

5. Particular attention needs to be paid to folk religion, to the stories of unlettered women, to a praxis-oriented theology. Mary De Cock writes poignantly of this need and of the hazard of intellectualizing Mary's message: she holds that the symbol of Guadalupe, for example, still holds some power of liberating hope for women "because it has largely escaped sophisticated theological analysis."[107]

6. Forgiveness needs to be practiced towards the patriarchy. Mary Gordon called this, appropriately, a "forgiving vigilance,"[108] but, in any form it is a gesture of reconciliation. Sooner or later, women will have to place this step in their long or short range plans. Because what is at stake is true forgiveness, not one of its many counterfeits, Margaret Wold's counsel is practical and wise. She writes:

> While forgiveness must be permitted to bring its *shalom* into our lives, the *shalom* woman cannot do those whom she forgives the disservice of allowing them to remain in anti-shalom positions. While she loves and forgives the ones who sin against her, she can no longer permit the sins of sexism (and racism) to continue wherever they become identified.[109]

Wold speaks eloquently of the confrontative work associated with forgiveness. It is not an exercise of putting band aids over wounds, but rather of cleansing them and allowing them to heal.

If Mary is to speak a liberating word to the community of Christians of which she is the most exemplary member, it is fitting that her sisters help bring this word into being. Women of color and white women, young and old, strong and weak — women together are the source of the theology of Mary the Church needs. The future of the Marian tradition and the faith community rests with women who are approaching tasks like this with imagination, vigor, hope, and creativity. Both the Marian tradition and the Church have a hopeful future in their hands.

NOTES

[1]See the general survey of data in R. Brown, K. Donfried, J. Fitzmyer, and J. Reumann, eds., *Mary in the New Testament* (New York: Paulist/Philadelphia: Fortress, 1978).

[2]Anne E. Carr, *Transforming Grace* (San Francisco, CA: Harper & Row, 1988), 193. See also Elizabeth A. Johnson, "The Marian Tradition and the Reality of Women," *Horizons* 12:1 (Spring, 1985): 116-35, for another approach to revisioning the Marian tradition in light of women's experience.

[3]Toni Morrison, *Beloved* (New York: Alfred A. Knopf, 1987), 190.

[4]This theme of "subjugated knowledge," defined by Michael Foucault, receives attention from numerous feminist writers. See Fou-

cault, *Power/Knowledge: Selected Interviews and Other Writings 1972-1977*, ed. Colin Gordon (New York: Pantheon Books, 1981).

[5]Rosemary Radford Ruether, *Sexism and God-Talk* (London: SCM Press, 1983), 18-19.

[6]See Lorraine Bethel, "What Chou Mean We, White Girl?," *Conditions: Five* (Autumn, 1979), 86-92.

[7]Barbara Smith, "Toward a Black Feminist Criticism," in *But Some of Us Are Brave: Black Women's Studies* (Old Westbury, NY: Feminist Press, 1982), 157.

[8]See Alice Walker, *In Search of Our Mother's Gardens* (San Diego, CA and New York: Harcourt, Brace, Jovanovich, 1983), xi-xii: "From the black folk expression of mothers to female children, 'You acting womanish,' i.e., like a woman. Usually referring to outrageous, audacious, courageous or *willful* behavior. Wanting to know more and in greater depth than is considered 'good' for one. . . . 2). *Also*: A woman who loves other women, sexually and/or nonsexually. . . . Committed to survival and wholeness of entire people, male and female . . . Traditionally capable, as in: 'Mama, I'm walking to Canada and I'm taking you and a bunch of other slaves with me.' Reply: 'It wouldn't be the first time.' 3). Loves music. Loves dance. Loves the moon. *Loves* the Spirit. Loves love and food and roundness. Loves struggle. *Loves* the folk. Loves herself. *Regardless*. 4) Womanist is to feminist as purple to lavender."

[9]*This Bridge Called My Back: Writings by Radical Women of Color,* ed. Cherríe Moraga and Gloria Anzaldua (Watertown, MA: Persephone Press, 1981); *Making Face, Making Soul, Haciendo Caras: Creative and Critical Perspectives by Women of Color*, ed. Gloria Anzaldua (San Francisco, CA: Aunt Lute, 1990). Also see "Special Section on Appropriation and Reciprocity in Womanist/Mujerista/Feminist Work," *Journal of Feminist Studies in Religion* 8(2) (Fall, 1992): 91-122.

[10]For the citation concerning "invisible invisibility," see Ada Maria Isasi-Diaz, "Toward an Understanding of *Feminismo Hispano*," in *Women's Consciousness, Women's Conscience*, ed. Barbara Hilbert Andolsen, Christine Gudorf, and Mary D. Pellauer (Minneapolis: Winston-Seabury Press, 1985), 51-61. For her comment on "engagement," see *"Viva la Diferencia!,"* a subtitled commentary from "Special Section on Appropriation and Reciprocity in Womanist/Mujerista/Feminist Work," *Journal of Feminist Studies in Religion*, 100.

[11]From *This Bridge Called My Back: Writings by Radical Women of Color*, 63-64.

[12]"A Vision of Feminist Religious Scholarship," (Pui'lan as respondent), *Journal of Feminist Studies in Religion* 3(1) (Spring, 1987): 102.

[13]Audre Lorde, "The Master's Tools Will Never Dismantle the Master's House," in *This Bridge Called My Back: Writings by Radical Women of Color*, 99.

[14]Chela Sandoval, "Feminism and Racism: A Report on the 1981 National Women's Studies Association Conference," in *Making Face, Making Soul*, ed. Gloria Anzaldua, 64.

[15]Betty Friedan, *The Feminine Mystique* (New York: Dell Publishing, 1963).

[16]Rita Crowley Turner is one feminist who pointed out the fallacy of Friedan's premise "was linking the notion that being a wife and mother actually rules out the possibility of being a person." Cf. *The Mary Dimension* (London: Sheed and Ward, 1985), 10-11.

[17]Jean Baker Miller, *Towards a New Psychology of Women* (Boston: Beacon Press, 1976), 76-77. In this connection, cf. Patricia A. Harrington, "Mary and Feminity: a Psychological Critique," *Journal of Religion and Health* 23(3) (Fall, 1984): 205-17. Harrington uses Freud to critique the symbolism and theology of Mary in contemporary Roman Catholicism.

[18]Cf. Anna Quindlen's comments from her column in *The New York Times*, National Edition, 28 February 1993, 15: "At a professional meeting last week, one woman after another talked about the sick sitter, the late sitter, the illegal sitter paid off the books, while the others nodded with sisterly solidarity. What you could clearly see *were the beginnings of a middle-class all-female movement. .*" (Italics mine)

[19]Joyce A. Little, "Mary and Feminist Theology," *Thought: A Review of Culture and Ideas* 52 (December, 1987): 343-57.

[20]Little points out, however, that sometimes the inconspicuous activity of having a baby may, in fact, be a conspicuous achievement.

[21]Felice N. Schwartz, "Management Women and the New Facts of Life," *Harvard Business Review* 71(1) (January-February, 1993): 65-76.

[22]Ibid., 69.

[23]Ibid.

[24]Shulamith Firestone, *The Dialectic of Sex: The Case for Feminist Revolution* (New York: William Morrow, 1970), 121.

[25]Adrienne Rich, *Of Woman Born: Motherhood as Experience and Institution* (New York: W. W. Norton, 1976), 57.

[26]Ibid., 13.

[27]Ibid.

[28]Ibid., 280.

[29]Ibid.

[30]Firestone, *op. cit.* See especially Chapter 10: "The Ultimate Revolution: Demands and Speculations," 183-201.

[31]Rosemary Radford Ruether, "Motherearth and the Megamachine: A Theology of Liberation in a Feminine, Somatic and Ecological Perspective," in *Womanspirit Rising*, ed. Carol P. Christ and Judith Plaskow (San Francisco, CA: Harper San Francisco, 1992), 51.

[32]Sherry Ruth Anderson and Patricia Hopkins, *The Feminine Face of God* (New York: Bantam Books, 1991), 76.

[33]Sara Ruddick, *Maternal Thinking* (New York: Ballantine Books, 1990).

[34]Carol Gilligan, *In a Different Voice* (Cambridge, MA: Harvard University Press, 1982).

[35]Delores Williams, "Womanist Theology: Black Women's Voices," *Christianity and Crisis* 47(3), 2 March 1987, 68.

[36] *Through Her Eyes: Women's Theology from Latin America*, ed. Elsa Tamez (Maryknoll, NY: Orbis, 1989), v.

[37] Marianne Katoppo, *Compassionate and Free: An Asian Woman's Theology* (Maryknoll, NY: Orbis, 1979), 14.

[38] Ibid.

[39] In a 1993 series of profiles of at-risk children in *The New York Times*, National Edition, one article after another reinforced this maternal concern, but see especially Sara Rimer, "Shawn, 17: Running Past Many Obstacles," Sunday, 25 April 1993, 1ff.

[40] Jacqueline Jones, *Labor of Love, Labor of Sorrow: Black Women, Work and Family from Slavery to the Present* (New York: Basic Books, 1985).

[41] Alice Walker, *Meridian* (New York: Washington Square Press, 1976).

[42] Professor Sue Houchins of Pomona College was generous with insights concerning *Meridian*; these are gratefully acknowledged. See also Susan Thistlethwaite, *Sex, Race and God: Christian Feminism in Black and White* (New York: Crossroad, 1989), 54, 83, for her fine analysis of *Meridian* and her contribution to a feminism that bridges feminists and womanists. Thistlethwaite's insights and leads were invaluable sources for this essay. In particular, it is her work that led me to Stowe, Sojourner Truth, Hooks and Jones.

[43] Valerie Saiving, "The Human Situation: A Feminine View," in *Womanspirit Rising*, 37.

[44] Susan Thistlethwaite, *op. cit.*, 85.

[45] Harriet Beecher Stowe, *Uncle Tom's Cabin* (New York: W. W. Norton, 1993).

[46] Sojourner Truth, quoted in Thistlethwaite, 35.

[47] Margaret Walker, *Jubilee* (New York: Bantam Books, 1966). I was led to this book by Delores Williams, "Women's Oppression and Life-Line Politics in Black Women's Religious Narratives," *Journal of Feminist Studies in Religion* 1(2) (Fall, 1985): 59-71.

[48] Delores Williams, "Women's Oppression," 69.

[49] Alice Walker, *The Color Purple* (New York: Harcourt, Brace, Jovanovich, 1982), 90-92.

[50] Bell Hooks, *Ain't I a Woman. Black Women and Feminism* (Boston: South End Press, 1981), 37.

[51] Bernice Zamora, "Notes from a Chicana Coed," in *Making Face, Making Soul*, 131.

[52] See "Children Beyond the Margins," *Christian Century*, 20 January 1993, 50.

[53] Marlise Simons, "The Sex Market: Scourge on the World's Children," *The New York Times*, National Edition, 9 April 1993, 4.

[54] From "Children Beyond the Margins," *Christian Century*, 50.

[55] Ibid.

[56] Martha Nichols, "Third-World Families at Work: Child Labor or Child Care?," *Harvard Business Review* 71(1) (January-February, 1993): 12-23.

[57] Denise Carmody, *Virtuous Woman: Reflections on Christian Feminist Ethics* (Maryknoll, NY: Orbis, 1992), 74.

[58]Mary Gordon, "Coming to Terms with Mary," *Commonweal* 109, 15 January 1982, 12.

[59]Elizabeth A. Johnson, "The Marian Tradition and the Reality of Women," *Horizons* 12:1 (Spring, 1983): 116-28.

[60]Shawn Madigan, "Do Marian Festivals Image 'That Which the Church Hopes to Be'?," *Worship* 65(3) (May, 1991): 194-207. See especially 196.

[61]Virgilio Elizondo, *Mary Prophetess and Model of Freedom for Responsibility* (San Antonio, TX: Mexican American Cultural Center, n.d.), 1.

[62]Cf. Raymond E. Brown, "Mary in the New Testament and in Catholic Life," *America* 146(19), 15 May 1982, 374-79. According to Brown, Mary brings up a major obstacle to the messenger's plan: "The angel is thus given the opportunity to explain how this child will be conceived" (376).

[63]Rosemary Radford Ruether, *The Feminine Face of the Church* (Philadelphia: Westminster Press, 1972), 32.

[64]Mary De Cock, "Our Lady of Guadalupe," in *Mary Among Women* (Kansas City, MO: Sheed and Ward, 1985), 130.

[65]Walter Ong offers one of the most provocative explanations for male anti-feminism and for the war between the sexes initiated and sustained by men. Marshalling a vast range of sociobiological evidence, Ong proposes that the male fetus must secrete androgens to offset the mother's hormones, and, after only a brief identification with the mother's body in infancy, the male impulse is "to fight" the feminine, to separate from its safety, and to prove its masculinity over and against it. Male insecurity, risk-taking, and the will to dominate are all functions of each other and are all traceable to the womb. See *Fighting for Life: Contest, Sexuality and Consciousness* (Ithaca, NY: Cornell University Press, 1981).

[66]See *Behold Your Mother* (Washington, DC: USCC/NCCB, 1973), #42.

[67]Ivone Gebara and Maria Clara Bingemer, *Mary Mother of God Mother of the Poor* (Maryknoll, NY: Orbis, 1989), 99.

[68]Phyllis Trible, "Eve and Adam: Genesis 2-3 Reread," in *Womanspirit Rising: A Feminist Reader in Religion*, 74.

[69]Elizabeth A. Johnson, "The Marian Tradition," 123.

[70]Donald Senior, "Gospel Portrait of Mary: Images and Symbols from the Synoptic Tradition," in *Mary: Woman of Nazareth*, ed. Doris Donnelly (Mahwah, NJ: Paulist Press, 1989), 104. Note Senior's reference to Mary Callaway, *Sing, O Barren One. (A Study in Comparative Midrash)*, Dissertation Series 91 (Atlanta: Scholars Press, 1986), esp. 100-107.

[71]Ibid., 106.

[72]Ibid., 105.

[73]Virgilio Elizondo, *Virgen y Madre: Reflexiones biblicas sobre Maria de Nazareth* (San Antonio, TX: Mexican American Cultural Center, 1983); "Mary and the Poor: A Model of Evangelizing," in *Mary in the Churches, Concilium* 168 (New York: Seabury, 1983): 59-75; "Mary in the Struggles of the Poor," *New Catholic World* 229 (1986): 245-46.

[74]Alice Walker, *The Color Purple*, 69.
[75]Sojourner Truth's quote comes from Delores S. Williams, "Womanist Theology: Black Women's Voices," *Christianity and Crisis* 47(3), 2 March 1987, 70.
[76]Elizabeth A. Johnson, "The Marian Tradition," 134.
[77]Only "the psychologically sound woman knows how to relinquish," says Ong, *op. cit.*, 100.
[78]See the interview with reporter Dirk Johnson on Jungian author Clarissa Pinkola Estés: "A Message for all Women: Run Free and Wild Like the Wolf," *New York Times*, National Edition, Sunday, 28 February 1993, Section E:7.
[79]Luz Beatriz Arellano, "Women's Experience of God in Emerging Spirituality," in *With Passion and Compassion: Third World Women Doing Theology*, ed. Virginia Fabella and Mercy Amba Oduyoye (Maryknoll, NY: Orbis, 1988), 139.
[80]Ibid.
[81]Rosemary Radford Ruether, "She's a Sign of God's Liberating Power," *The Other Side* (May, 1980): 18.
[82]Ibid., 19.
[83]Anne Carr, *Transforming Grace*, 173.
[84]Elisabeth Schüssler Fiorenza, "Interpreting Patriarchal Traditions," in *The Liberating Word*, ed. Letty M. Russell (Philadelphia: Westminster Press, 1976), 49. Deserving special mention is the contribution by Elisabeth Schüssler Fiorenza to which so much of feminist theology is indebted. See her *In Memory of Her: A Feminist Theological Reconstruction of Christian Origins* (New York: Crossroad, 1983); and *Bread Not Stone: The Challenge of Feminist Biblical Interpretation* (Boston: Beacon Press, 1984).
[85]Ibid., 52.
[86]See especially Sallie McFague, *Models of God: Theology for an Ecological, Nuclear Age* (Philadelphia: Fortress Press, 1982); Elizabeth A. Johnson, "The Symbolic Character of Theological Statements about Mary," *Journal of Ecumenical Studies* 22:2 (Spring, 1985): 312-36; Elizabeth A. Johnson, *She Who Is: The Mystery of God in Feminist Theological Discourse* (New York: Crossroad, 1992).
[87]Mary De Cock, 126-27.
[88]Maria Clara Bingemer, "Women in the Future of the Theology of Liberation," *SEDOS Bulletin* 22 (15 February 1990), 26.
[89]See De Cock for further information about Guererro's study, 127ff.
[90]De Cock, 136.
[91]Arellano, 143.
[92]Ivone Gebara, "The Mother Superior and Spiritual Motherhood: From Intuition to Institution," in *Motherhood: Experience, Institution, Theology*, Concilium 206 (Edinburgh: T&T Clark, 1989), 44.
[93]Gebara, "The Mother Superior," 42. In fact, although Gebara revisions spiritual motherhood, she writes that the basic nucleus around which it exists in religious communities is deeply patriarchal.
[94]Marjorie Agosin, "Emerging from the Shadows: Women of Chile," *Barnard Occasional Papers on Women's Issues* 2(3) (Fall, 1987): 21.

[95]Third Conference of Latin American Bishops, *Puebla*, official English translation (Washington, DC: USCC/NCCB, 1979), #283.

[96]Arellano, 149.

[97]Marianne Katoppo, *Compassionate and Free*, 83, quotes this line from Asian theologian C. S. Song without a full citation.

[98]Sara Ruddick, *Maternal Thinking: Toward a Politics of Peace* (New York: Balantine Books, 1989), 157-159. See also Mary Condren, "To Bear Children for the Fatherland: Mothers and Militarism," in *Motherhood: Experience, Institution and Theology, Concilium* 206, 82-90.

[99]Ibid., 159.

[100]Doris Donnelly, "Maternity's Raw Faith," *Sojourners* (November, 1983): 24.

[101]Olive Schreiner, *Women and Labour* (London: Virago Press, 1978), 172.

[102]Ruddick, 157.

[103]Ibid., 244.

[104]Toinette Eugene, "On Difference and the Dream of Pluralist Feminism," as part of the "Special Section on Appropriation and Reciprocity in Womanist/Mujerista/Feminist Work," *Journal of Feminist Studies in Religion* 8(2) (Fall, 1992): 92.

[105]In this regard, see *God's Fierce Whimsy: Feminism and Theological Education* (New York: Pilgrim Press, 1985), 36, especially for the exchange of letters between Katie Cannon and Carter Heyward on whether we can be different, but not alienated. Susan Brooks Thistlethwaite devotes her book, *Sex, Race and God: Christian Feminism in Black and White*, to this issue. See also Maria C. Lugones, "On the Logic of Pluralist Feminism," in *Feminist Ethics*, ed. Claudia Card (Lawrence, KS: University of Kansas Press, 1991), 35-44; Elizabeth V. Spelman, *Inessential Woman: Problems of Exclusion in Feminist Thought* (Boston: Beacon Press, 1988); Barbara Smith, "Racism and Women's Studies," in *Making Face Making Soul — Haciendo Caras: Creative and Critical Perspectives by Women of Color*, 25-28.

[106]Mary Grey, *Feminism, Redemption and the Christian Tradition* (Mystic, CT: Twenty-Third Publications, 1990), 9-10.

[107]De Cock, 137.

[108]Mary Gordon, *op. cit.*, 12.

[109]Margaret Wold, *The Shalom Woman* (Minneapolis, MN: Augsburg Publishing House, 1975), 120.

Images of Mary in Popular Devotion: Universalizing the Mother in the Late Twentieth Century

Sandra L. Zimdars-Swartz

Introduction

The Virgin Mary has been known through the centuries by various titles, to name but a few: Mother of God, Mother of Sorrows, Mother of Mercy, Queen of Heaven, Second Eve, Ever-Virgin, and Blessed Virgin. Many of these titles and the images associated with them have waxed or waned in popularity, reflecting the devotional needs of particular times. Elizabeth Johnson has demonstrated, for example, that, during the medieval period, depictions of Mary responded to the environmental, social, and political insecurities of the times, and that Mary, the great *Theotokos* of the patristic period, became the tender human mother suckling her baby. Mary became less a symbol of the Church and more of an individual with her own joys, sorrows, and glory. Surrounded by images portraying her as God's Treasure, the Mother of Mercy, and the Madonna of the protective mantle, medieval Christians no doubt found it easier than Christians of earlier centuries to relate to Mary in immediate and personal ways, finding in her and through her a more personally focused salvation.[1]

In this last decade of the twentieth century, Roman Catholics
in the United States are experiencing a Marian revival of significant proportions. Responding perhaps in part to the lull in
Marian devotion following the Second Vatican Council, many
Catholics today are embracing anew images of the Mother of
God as a vehicle for their spiritual lives. Contributing to this
late-twentieth century resurgence of Marian devotion are the
words and activities of a pope, John Paul II, who is personally
very much devoted to Mary and who actively encourages devotion to her among the Catholic faithful; new images of Mary
which have emerged from recent biblical and historical scholarship, which depict her as an autonomous individual who, of her
own volition, actively participates in the events of salvation history; and, finally, the international popularity of the alleged apparition of Medjugorje.

I suggest that, of these three things, it is the apparition at
Medjugorje that is most directly responsible for the recent revival of Marian devotion in the United States. This essay will
examine some of the issues and ideas that were emerging in
popular American culture and in the mass media with respect
to Mary in the years following the Second Vatican Council; the
impact here, especially in the past five or six years, of the apparition at Medjugorje; and the way proponents of this apparition
have responded to these issues and ideas. And, it will call attention, finally, to the image of Mary as a Universal Mother that is
emerging now in the wake of Medjugorje in some popular
American Marian devotion and especially in the messages associated with some of the recent Marian apparitions reported in
the United States.

I am not proposing in this essay that popular devotion to
Mary is reducible to those beliefs and practices which surround
the reports of appearances of Mary. But, I do suggest that Marian apparitions are one important place in which the images of
Mary most relevant and appealing to a particular cultural context are manifested — and where there is creative testing of the
boundaries, by persons who claim to be devoted to Mary, of
what beliefs and practices may be accepted by the institutional
Church. As William Christian, Jr., has suggested, Mary's directives in apparitions are for many people a way of learning
what God wants at a particular place and time, without the kind
of detailed study of, and extrapolation from, Scripture and tradition that tends to be the province of professional theologians.[2]
Contemporary apparitions, then, provide important clues to
the issues that are most troubling contemporary Roman Catholics and to the images of Mary that they find most relevant. It

should also be noted that I am not making any judgments about whether Mary is actually appearing in any of these apparitions. My goal is simply to elucidate the meanings that Marian devotees in recent years have found in the image of Mary as Universal Mother.

Controversy and Change in U.S. Marian Devotion after Vatican II

The controversy that has developed around the image of Mary in the United States in the wake of the Second Vatican Council and some of the changes that have been taking place which have fueled this controversy may be illustrated by examining two articles that appeared in the popular press, one in 1972 and the other almost twenty years later, in 1991. While these articles were not based on rigorous research, they were typical of their times, and they offered to their respective audiences some very interesting analyses of Mary's status and some interesting prognostications about her future.

The first article, "The Liberation of the Virgin Mary," by John O'Connor, appeared in the December, 1972, issue of *Ladies Home Journal*.[3] O'Connor argued that, prior to the Second Vatican Council, Mary was in something of an ontological limbo, having a status beyond that attainable by real women by virtue of her virgin motherhood, but not quite achieving the rank of divinity. This was undoubtedly due, he thought, to the fact that her image had been defined by men who may have had unrealistic views of women, some of whom may have regarded sex as something "low, bestial, and nasty." In recent years, perhaps as a result of this ambiguous male-defined status, it seemed as if Mary had "disappeared, as if whisked off to wither away in some geriatric nursing home."

But, O'Connor found that, in those waning months of 1972, things were changing, and he attributed this, at least implicitly, to the women's movement. For, he said, "as women gain a new consciousness of their human dignity, rights, and mission, Mary must be counted among them."[4]

As evidence of a new interest in Mary, O'Connor cited a renewed examination of Mary on the part of Protestants. He noted, for example, the work of theologians Hans Asmussen (Lutheran), Max Thurian (Reformed), and E.L. Mascall (Anglican). This new Protestant interest was concerned to maintain a balance between the traditional reverence for Mary as the mother of Jesus and her humanness, while avoiding an enthusiasm that would equate her with, or place her above, her Son.

O'Connor found this concern echoed in Catholic circles, where popes and theologians alike had warned against excesses in Marian devotion. Father Eugene Walsh is quoted as saying, "There is very little evidence of Mary in Scripture, but there has been a lot of theological speculation. Now she must be rescued from the debunkers who would throw out everything, and from those advocates of an unbalanced piety, the plastic statue crowd."[5] O'Connor also noted the debate that was taking place among theologians over the meaning of Mary's virginity, contrasting those who insisted on a literal, physical understanding of Mary's virginity before, during, and after the birth of Jesus, to those who understood it as a symbol of the integrity of Mary's faith, her faithfulness to the will of God, and her steadfastness to the call of God.

O'Connor noted also that Mary's status had changed as a result of the documents of the Second Vatican Council. By placing Mary in the Constitution on the Church, the Roman Catholic Church had emphasized that Mary was a part of, and not separate from, the people of God. Moreover, new biblical scholarship was finding that Mary was "where the action is" and was depicting her as an activist, perhaps even a subversive, a "liberated woman" of her time. A new image of Mary was emerging, he argued, "not the medieval virgin queen, but the personification and prototype of the Christian mission — a woman who humanizes the world by being present where needed."[6]

It is interesting that, while O'Connor included among the factors contributing to this new image of Mary the "new dignity of women" that was associated with the modern women's movement, all of the experts whose views of Mary he cited were male. If past images of Mary, as O'Connor noted, had been defined by men, so, it would seem, were the new images of Mary suggested in his article. In addition to Asmussen, Thurian, Mascall, and Walsh, already noted, O'Connor cited as authorities Fathers René Laurentin, Eamon Carroll, Patrick Peyton, Gregory Baum, and Professors L. Gordon Tait, Howard P. Kainz, and Kristen Skysgaard.

The recent article, by Richard Ostling, entitled "Handmaiden or Feminist," which was the cover story of the December 20, 1991, issue of *Time Magazine*,[7] reflects many of the changes that have taken place in the last twenty years, both in popular American images of Mary and in the structures of authority which have been affecting and shaping these images. Ostling begins his article by noting that the past decade has seen a "grass-roots revival" of faith in the Virgin around the world, and he cites as evidence for this a significant increase in pilgrimages at major Marian shrines. He notes that at Lourdes (France), for example, the number of visitors had increased ten percent in the previous two years and had now reached an annual total of five and a half million pilgrims. The shrines at Knock (Ireland) and Czestochowa (Poland), both of which received visits from Pope John Paul II in 1979, had also seen dramatic increases in attendance, the number of visitors at Knock increasing two-fold to an annual total of one and a half million, and the annual total at Czestochowa climbing to five million. At the National Shrine Grotto of Our Lady of Lourdes, in Emmitsburg, Maryland, attendance had doubled the previous year to five hundred thousand. And, prior to the recent outbreak of war in the former Yugoslavia, the apparition site at Medjugorje had, since June of 1981, been visited by an estimated ten million pilgrims.

Ostling attributes some of this increase in Marian devotion to Pope John Paul II, whose personal devotion to the Mother of God is well known. As a bishop, Ostling recalls, he put a golden "M" into his coat of arms, and he adopted as his motto "Totus Tuus," both referring explicitly to Mary. And as Pope, he has encouraged devotion to Mary by including visits to Marian shrines on almost all of his foreign trips and by invoking Mary's aid in virtually every discourse. He is said to firmly believe that it was her personal intercession that preserved his life in the assassination attempt on May 13, 1981, which is symbolically important as the anniversary of Mary's first appearance to the three children at Fatima. And, just as Mary, as the Black Madonna of Czestochowa, patroness and protectress of Poland, was hailed by many Polish Roman Catholics for turning back the enemies of Poland in past centuries, so John Paul II is said to be convinced that it is Mary who has brought about the collapse of Communism in Poland and indeed in all of Eastern Europe.

Ostling notes that Pope John Paul II continues to give voice to conservative interpretations of Mary's life in papal documents, for example, his 1988 decree, *Mulieris Dignitatem* (On the Dignity and Vocation of Women), in which Mary was held up as the preeminent model of the two states in which women would achieve a sense of dignity, that is, virginity and motherhood. But, Ostling also credits John Paul II with a relatively enlightened view of Mary in some respects, noting, for example, that he does not use her domesticity to argue against women pursuing careers, and that his praise of her submissiveness has reference to her relation to God and not to men.

The most striking example, however, of the changes that have taken place in thinking about Mary in the nineteen years separating O'Connor's article from Ostling's comes, not in the latter's discussion of the views of John Paul II, but in his discussion of what he calls the "much more aggressive view of Mary emerging from feminist circles within the church, emphasizing her autonomy, independence, and earthiness."[8] As authorities for this new "revisionist" view of Mary, Ostling turns, not to traditional, male theologians associated with institutions of higher learning, but to women, some of whom are indeed theologians associated with universities or seminaries, but some of whom are known chiefly for their religious activism or for their involvement in some kind of social service. He cites, for example, Sister Lavinia Byrne, who works with non-Catholic groups in Britain, as a spokesperson for the view that Mary was the one who remained faithful during the crucifixion, while all but one of the male disciples fled. And, French writer Nicole Echivard is quoted as saying, "The Mother of God is the one from whom women are created in their preference for love and for people, rather than for power or machinery. Mary is the most liberated, the most determined, the most responsible of all mothers."[9]

But still, after nineteen years, something of the uneasy ontological status of Mary as quasi-human, quasi-divine, which was noted by O'Connor, apparently remains. The recent increase in devotion to Mary is understood by some, Ostling says, as "a delayed backlash" to the relegation of Mary in the Constitution on the Church of Vatican II to the humble status of one person among many in the community of believers. But among others, he notes, there is an uneasiness over the perception that, in the new Marian devotion, Mary could become "a competitive divinity" who is quite independent of her son. Ostling seems to see both of these views as diverting attention from a more fundamental point — which is that, in the increased attention to Mary through a variety of images, including "devoted mother," "militant, independent female," and "suffering parent," one can see the continuation, and some new manifestations, of the power that has always been associated with Marian imagery. And, he concludes by saying of those who are being drawn to Mary today, "whatever aspect of Mary they choose to embrace, those who seek her out surely find something only a holy mother can provide."[10]

It is interesting to note that, while these articles arose in rather different times and manifest some rather different concerns, both are in fact interested in Mary's universality. In the 1972 article, this takes the form of an interest in her appeal to non-Catholics, and the non-Catholic men cited here as "authorities" are an indication of a willingness to grant that, if Mary is indeed universal, one may have to look somewhere other than to traditional Catholic authorities in order to see the full range of her importance. In the 1991 article, this is more or less taken for granted; traditional authorities, such as the Pope, are brought together here and seen as basically consonant with the experiences of the laity, including lay women; and the theme of Mary's universality is brought to focus here especially in the interest in her importance for women and in the question of just how one ought to understand Mary's motherhood.

The existential dimension and meaning of Mary's universal motherhood, which I believe is the focal point of contemporary Marian devotion today, may best be explored through the religious experiences that have been generated in and around contemporary Marian apparitions.

Medjugorje and Its Impact in the United States

A particularly important factor in the upsurge of Marian devotion in the United States in the past five or six years has been the alleged apparition of Mary to six young people in Medjugorje, which began in late June, 1981. Mary's reported daily appearances to these young people (four women, two men) in this small town in Bosnia-Herzogovina, near the border with Croatia, attracted some attention and drew some pilgrims from the United States as early as 1983 and 1984. Publicity about Medjugorje in the United States became widespread, however, only in the mid 1980s, and a glance through the *Catholic Periodical Index* suggests that it was not until 1987 and 1988 that articles about Medjugorje began to proliferate in the mainstream Catholic media.

Coming somewhat in advance of this flood of publicity about Medjugorje was an increase in the number of organized pilgrimages. Father René Laurentin, who in the past decade has spent a great deal of time in the United States and has become one of the leading advocates of the Medjugorje apparition, has commented in his writings both on the lull in Marian devotion after the Second Vatican Council and on the upsurge of recent interest in Mary and in Marian pilgrimages in the wake of Medjugorje. Laurentin has said that, when he first came to teach in the United States, he was told by Father Cole of the Marian Library, "Do not talk about apparitions. This European theme is of no interest to the American people. It is your particularism."[11] In 1984 and 1985, when Laurentin began to

speak about Medjugorje in the United States, he found that his
talks were received with restraint and reservation. He reported
something of a turning point in interest, however, in 1985, when
a "New York Catholic company" interviewed him at length on
the subject. It was two years later then, he says, when the rush
really began, Americans having rather suddenly become much
more interested in apparitions and pilgrimages to apparition
sites than the French, who had by then cooled in their enthusiasm.[12]

Important, especially in the past four or five years, for
spreading the word about Medjugorje in the United States have
been a number of Marian centers and prayer groups, formed
by people who had been on one or more of these pilgrimages.
There seem to have been three, somewhat distinct, motivations
for the founding of these institutions. First, and probably most
important, was the need felt by many of those who had returned
from Medjugorje to "repay" the Virgin for a grace they believed
they had received there. Like most other Marian apparition
sites, Medjugorje has been perceived as a place of healing
where the Virgin may grant one's most personal petitions. And,
many centers and prayer groups were started by people who felt
they had been healed or helped in some other way by Mary at
Medjugorje and who, in return, wanted to do their part in
spreading the messages they believe she has been delivering
there. A second motivation stems specifically from one of the
Virgin's reported messages about the need for prayer groups.
She is said to have told the Medjugorje seers, "Yes, there is a
need for a prayer group, not only in this parish, but in all parishes. A spiritual renewal is necessary for the entire church."[13]
And, it is clear that the organization of such prayer groups in
their home parishes by some returning priests and pilgrims has
been directly inspired by this directive.

The third motivation presupposes, and is derived from, the
apocalyptic end-time scenario in terms of which many devotees
of the Medjugorje apparition have understood the Medjugorje
messages. Crucial here are the ten secrets reportedly given to
each of the visionaries, which are understood to pertain to im-
minent, historic events of global importance. The conviction
that these secrets would be publicly announced in advance of
these events and the belief that there would be only a short period of time to distribute the information contained in these secrets were important factors in the founding of at least some
Marian centers. For many devotees of Medjugorje, it was important and, indeed, crucial that a nationwide network of centers be in place to distribute this important information just as

soon as it should be announced. There are, at present, 175 Marian Centers in the United States and Canada listed in *Mary's People* (a supplement to the *National Catholic Register*), most of which have issued from a founder's religious experience at Medjugorje.

In most of the apparitions reported in the United States in the past five or six years, the visionaries have had some connection with Medjugorje, and the typical modern American seer is a person who has returned from a Medjugorje pilgrimage. According to the *Los Angeles Times,* June 23, 1991, visionary Carol Nole of Nipomo, California, had received some 27 messages from the Virgin in the preceding three years. The most important of these messages, she said, was the directive of the Virgin to erect a cross on a hillside near her home. Although no date is given, the article notes that Nole had been to Medjugorje and that she believed in the visions there as well as in her own experiences. Nole's visions were drawing crowds to St. Joseph Catholic Church of Nipomo, and a group of supporters was hoping to find the money to buy the needed land and to fulfill the Virgin's request.[14]

Joe Reinholz, an eighty-one year old resident of Hillside, Illinois, reported that, after he had made a pilgrimage to Medjugorje, in 1986, he was directed to a spot in the Queen of Heaven Cemetery, where he was cured of blindness. He began reporting his experiences in 1991, and the place where he was cured, a crucifix in the military section of the cemetery, soon became the focus of a small, but steady, stream of pilgrims. Although, according to an article in the *Chicago Tribune* on July 24, 1991, only Reinholz had reported visions of Mary, others who had prayed at the site reported seeing the crucifix bleed or their rosaries turn to gold.[15]

Also in the summer of 1991, in Marlboro Township, New Jersey, the visions of fifty-four year old Joseph Januskiewicz were beginning to attract public attention. Januskiewicz had made a pilgrimage to Medjugorje in 1988, where he felt that he had been healed from a back injury and long-time hearing loss, and, six months after his return, Mary began appearing to him daily in his back yard. Januskiewicz said that these daily visits continued for eighteen months and that Mary then told him she would limit her appearances to the first Sunday of each month. Januskiewicz constructed in his back yard a well-landscaped shrine with both a large crucifix and a large statue of Mary, and, almost every month since the summer of 1991, on the designated apparition Sundays, this shrine and the seer's brief evening experiences there have drawn thousands of people to this quiet little town.[16]

While visionary Estela Ruiz of Phoenix, Arizona, had never been to Medjugorje, her experiences began in September, 1988, while her husband was on a Medjugorje pilgrimage. Ruiz, a middle-aged woman whose children had grown and who had begun to embark on her own career as a teacher, said that, at the time, she had begun to grow away from her husband, who was becoming more devout and more devoted to Mary, and that, on that September day, as she thought of her absent husband and seemed to feel his spirit with her, she was walking by a painting of Our Lady of Guadalupe and heard a voice calling out to her. Ruiz's first reported vision of Mary was on December 3, 1988, and she continues to this day to have apparitions and other unusual experiences.[17]

These are only a few of the many apparitions that have been reported and that have attracted some public attention in the United States in the past few years, but these stories show very well the way Medjugorje has affected the lives of some American Catholics in some rather extraordinary ways.

Medjugorje's impact on contemporary American devotion to Mary may be summarized along several lines. First, it has contributed to an atmosphere in which claims of extraordinary experiences are met with less skepticism and find a more sympathetic audience. Second, it has been the catalyst for literally thousands of personal religious experiences, from the more common experiences of seeing sun miracles or one's rosary beads changing color, to the less common and more dramatic experiences of conversions, healings, locutions, and visions. Some of the persons who have had, and who continue to have, some of the more dramatic of these experiences, specifically, locutions and visions, have themselves attracted some attention and have become the focal points for significant Marian movements (which I will examine in the next section of this essay). And finally, the messages reported at Medjugorje have focused attention on, and contributed to, a popular resurgence of interest in Mary's "universal motherhood."

Important for the emergence of this image in the devotion associated with Medjugorje are several reported messages at Medjugorje which suggest that Mary's current apparitions are for all people. According to the Medjugorje visionaries, Mary said that "In God there are no religions, there are no divisions, but you men have made divisions."[18] She further exhorted people to respect all members of all religions, noting that "God wants that you love all and that you esteem all."[19] To be sure, she is also said to have rejected the notion that all religions are the same or have the same amount of grace: "It does not amount to the same thing to pray in any community. The power of the Holy Spirit is not equally strong in all churches and the power of the Holy Spirit active in the priests varies. All believers do not pray in the same way."[20] But, in the Medjugorje messages, such differences seem to be more a result of human weakness than of any partiality of divine grace. And so, in the framework of Medjugorje, Mary has frequently been seen as issuing a call to everyone, regardless of creed, and as declaring herself to be a "Mother of All." This idea of the universal motherhood of Mary is especially strong in two of the currently popular American apparitions, Conyers (Georgia) and Cold Spring (Kentucky).

Mary as "Our Loving Mother" at Conyers, Georgia

The American apparition that has probably received the most attention in the national media in the past few years is that reported by a Conyers, Georgia, housewife, Nancy Fowler. According to the account written by Judith Child and published in two volumes of messages Fowler says she has received from Mary and Jesus, Fowler began having peculiar experiences in 1983. At that time, she was married, with a three year old son, and was working as a registered nurse. Shortly afterwards, she accepted another nursing job with more prestige and pay, but it required her to work on weekends. It was at this time that she began to be assailed by demons and sometimes saw thousands of eyes peering at her from the darkness. This began a period of her life, marked by severe insomnia and "fear-filled days," during which she would see "spirit forms like dark shadows in half-animal and half-human shapes floating past her."[21]

Fearing for her sanity, Fowler sought out help, for example, from a priest who told her that her experiences were not reality. But, even as this priest was speaking to her, according to Child, she could see the shapes of demons in silhouette on the wall. She also sought help outside the Church, but precisely what kind of help or from whom is not specified. It was not until she gave up her new job, went to Confession, and began to attend Mass that she found some measure of relief. Fowler confided in another priest at this time, who advised her to send the demons away "in the Name of Jesus," and this, she said, was successful.

The published accounts of Fowler's experiences refer to these peculiar torments as "mystical experiences," and they describe her as struggling for some years with these experiences and also wrestling with the thought that she was being called to be a

prophet. While they do not make it clear just how these struggles developed into a state of severe depression, that is apparently what happened, and, in February of 1987, they report that
Fowler was "full of despair and not wanting to live, feeling like
there was no hope."[22] Then, the Lord appeared to Fowler in a
silent apparition which, apparently, ended her depression.

In October of that year, she felt called to make a pilgrimage to
Medjugorje, and at Medjugorje, she said, she heard a voice
which reiterated her call to become a prophet. "You are a
prophet," the voice said, "I have chosen you before you were
born. My prophets speak the words that I give them. It is necessary that you be completely obedient to Me. I have called you to
holiness. Be a good wife and mother and pray devoutly. I will
show My people that holiness is for everyone in all walks of life.
Now say the Our Father and Hail Mary in honor of My
Mother."[23]

Fowler's first apparition of Mary came in the next year, and
two years later, in 1990, according to the accounts, Mary told
Fowler to make her experiences public and promised her that
she would appear to her and give her messages for her children
of America on the 13th of every month. Early in 1991, on the
appointed days, crowds of about 60 persons began gathering at
the Fowler home, and, by August, the crowds had grown so
large that County officials, citing zoning restrictions, were talk-
ing about prohibiting the gatherings. By that time, however, a
couple who believed in the divine origin of Fowler's experiences
had purchased some nearby property, which was apparently ex-
empt from the restrictions; a corps of volunteers moved in
quickly to prepare it for the influx of pilgrims, and, on September 13, 1991, then, a large crowd gathered for the first of Fowler's apparitions on what has come to be called "The Farm." The
apparitions of Mary have continued there ever since, on the
thirteenth of every month, drawing crowds of up to eighty thousand people, and, while it is these pre-announced apparitions in
which Mary gives public messages to "her children of America"
which have brought Conyers to the attention of both the local
and national media, Fowler has been reporting apparitions and
auditions of Mary and Jesus at other times as well. All of these
experiences have played a part in the formation of a distinct
image of Mary at Conyers which is worthy of attention.

According to Fowler, Mary wishes to be known through her
Conyers appearances as "Our Loving Mother." The messages
which give rise to this designation and which put it into a concrete form date from May, 1991, when, Fowler said, Mary told
her that "too few mothers are honored anymore, too few."[24] Par-

ticularly important, however, was an apparition of Mary on May 9, in which Fowler said she was directed to photograph the statue of Mary which she kept in her prayer room and to have this made into a holy card. On the back of this card should be printed the "Fatima prayer," and underneath this, Mary said, should be written, "Let this prayer be echoed all over the world." The title of the card would be "Our Loving Mother," which, along with the location, Conyers, Georgia, should also appear on the back of the card. Fowler said that Mary promised: "Those who look upon this card and venerate my image will receive special graces. Many healings will be attributed to those who honor this picture. The picture is to be distributed widely, everywhere as 'Our Loving Mother' and many healings will occur."[25] On the following day, May 10, Fowler said that Mary reiterated that the image would bring many graces.

Also on that day, according to Fowler, Mary specifically compared Fowler's role in bringing this image to the world to the role of Catherine Labouré, whose visions of the Virgin on the Rue du Bac in Paris in 1830 gave rise to the so-called Miraculous Medal. Mary told her, "Sister Catherine was the instrument who was chosen by God to bring the Medal of the Immaculate Conception and you, Nancy, are the instrument chosen by God to give the world my image with the title, 'Our Loving Mother.' I implore you, do not delay in bringing this about. Many, many graces await mankind through this image."[26]

Although the image of the Mary who is appearing at Conyers is allegedly that of a loving mother, the messages attributed to Jesus and Mary have a style and agenda which seem to be at odds with this and which are reminiscent of some of the best known Marian apparitions of the past, especially Fatima and La Salette. While the connection with Fatima is perhaps clearest in the scenario of Mary's appearances on the thirteenth day of the month, the connection with La Salette is most evident in the nature and in the apocalyptic tone of the messages. In a message that seems especially to be modeled on the central messages of La Salette, Fowler said that, on September 10, 1990, Jesus told her, "The sins of mankind are offending the Holy Trinity of God. They are numerous and great and ever increasing. My mother is growing weak from holding My hand back from striking. It pleases me greatly when little souls come to Me to console Me but, there are too few."[27] Fowler says that Jesus and Mary have warned that the United States faces a coming chastisement unless people return to God and cease the behaviors that offend God. On March 19, 1991, for example, she said

Jesus exhorted people to "Put God back in your schools, in your government, in your leaders, in every man, woman, and child. Then, and only then, will you be one great nation under God."[28]

It is important to note that the messages from Conyers are quite specifically anti-abortion. For example, Fowler said that the Blessed Virgin appeared to her on March 13, 1992, with the infant Jesus in her arms, and said, "My children are not carrying their crosses. My children are murdered all over the world. Tell the people of the United States, tell the people of the world, abortion is murder. The cup of salvation will turn into the cup of wrath unless you stop. Please listen."[29] As this statement suggests, here, as in the rhetoric of many of the groups protesting abortion now, abortion is understood as an especially heinous form of murder. A particularly interesting message is that of December 31, 1990. Here, according to Fowler, Jesus appeared to her and told her that at Conyers he was giving the greatest graces outside of Mass. "Nowhere," he said, "are My graces being poured forth like they are here." But, he lamented that people were not responding. According to Fowler, Jesus said, "Where are My children? Where are My children at the Mass? Where are My children? I tell you, they are seeking their own selfish selves." He then went on to list the violations of commandments that he had tolerated and the suffering he had endured, all under the metaphor of murder: People had, he said, murdered the unborn, the born, the old, the young, the well, the disabled. He then invoked the images associated with his reviling at the crucifixion. Fowler said he told her that people "slander My name, mock me. Spit on Me. Throw My words away." He then addressed Fowler and her role as his prophet. Fowler said he told her, "My precious daughter, you see My suffering face. Look at Me. You see My love. My children, where have they gone? You are ready to speak My words and there is no one here to listen."[30] For these and other offences, Fowler said, Mary has come to warn America that the time is running out and that, if repentance does not come soon, "Devastation will be great."[31]

Both the messages reported at Conyers and what would seem to be the existential situation of the seer who reported them reflect anxiety about deviating from the traditional role and duties of a mother. If the published accounts are accurate, Fowler's experiences began in the context of a conflict between a promising career in nursing and a rather traditional set of maternal and religious obligations, and the demonic attacks which signalled this conflict ceased only when she clearly and unequivocally decided to devote herself to the latter. At least one of the

messages which Fowler says she received counseled women to
be submissive to their husbands,[32] and, even as she was receiving what she understood to be her call to a prophetic vocation,
she was admonished to be "a good wife and mother and pray
devoutly."[33] The theme of "Mary as Our Loving Mother" at
Conyers, therefore, needs to be seen as a part of an apocalyptic
scenario at least as threatening as those associated with the apparitions at La Salette and Fatima, and, in the Conyers messages, it is only a return to traditional gender roles and the
moral and religious obligations consonant with them which can
forestall the impending chastisement.

The Call to All Mothers at Cold Spring, Kentucky

Mother imagery also pervades the messages connected with
the apparition at Cold Spring, Kentucky. This apparition came
to public attention in the aftermath of a large gathering at Cold
Spring on the night of August 31, 1992, and this discussion will
focus on some of the events and messages which led up to this
gathering, as reported in a privately published volume edited
by Gerald Ross.[34] The principal subjects here are Father Leroy
Smith, pastor of St. Joseph Church in Cold Spring, where this
gathering took place, and a visionary from a nearby Ohio sub-
urb of Cincinnati.

Father Smith made a pilgrimage to Medjugorje in October,
1988, the first of several which he undertook while he was pastor
of St. Theresa Catholic Church in nearby Southgate, Kentucky, and, upon his return, he formed a prayer group in this
parish. In July, 1991, Smith was transferred to St. Joseph parish
in Cold Spring, and, by this time, he had organized and was
leading three other groups with devotional agenda related to
Medjugorje. First, there was a weekly Friday night prayer
group consisting of people who had accompanied him on one of
his Medjugorje pilgrimages, and this group reportedly moved
with him to St. Joseph Church. Second, there was a Medjugorje prayer group which met monthly, on Monday evenings,
with several priests in attendance — for Confessions, a recitation of the Rosary, the Chaplet of Divine Mercy, and a homily
and Mass — with a period of fellowship and a discussion of
some spiritual topic following. These meetings reportedly drew
several hundred people from Kentucky, Ohio, and Indiana.
Also, Smith had organized a Mother of God Marian Movement
Priests Laity Cenacle which met once a month on Sunday. It is
perhaps not surprising, in the light of Smith's involvement and
leadership in these apparently very popular Marian devotions,

that an anonymous visionary from the Cincinnati area should have been told in a vision to contact him, and, indeed, that he should be understood by this visionary as one of three priests in the United States commissioned by the Virgin Mary as special facilitators of her devotion.

While the identity of this visionary is not revealed in the Cold Spring literature, some basic biographical data can be gleaned from the first-person accounts of her experiences contained in Ross's volume, which bears the title, *Personal Revelations of Our Lady of Light.* The visionary is female, and she understands that she has been called by Mary because, like Mary, she is a mother who is concerned with the welfare of her children. Indeed, we are told that she has several children, at least one of whom is a daughter, and several grandchildren. Her experiences are said to have begun on January 31, 1990, with a "strange but comforting dream" in which she found herself in a church looking at a statue of the Pieta. Suddenly, she said, the face of Mary came to life and was marked by "intense suffering and longing," and she herself then could feel Mary's pain and agony as she looked down on her crucified Son. Then, as her dream continued, where the Pieta had been, she saw Jesus alone, glowing brilliantly and apparently filling the whole room. While other people were present at the scene, she said, they did not seem to notice anything, even when she called out to them, and she said that Jesus reached out his hands to her and that, when she put her hands in his, she felt great happiness. And, she said Jesus told her, "I am always with you. You will remember this. This is no dream."[35]

Her first vision of Mary came about a year and a half later, on September 1, 1991, while she was visiting a friend's farm in Indiana. She and four companions were sitting around a campfire that evening, she said, when they noticed, above a clump of trees, a light which seemed to have "the shape of a lady turned sideways." The lady turned toward them, and the woman reporting these visions recalled being afraid and saying aloud, "If you're not from the Lord, You're not welcome here." But then, she said, she heard in her mind the words, "I am from the Lord. Because you honored my Son, I have come to you." She and one of her companions then knelt and began to recite the Rosary, and the lady then told her, "I am the Lady of Light. Take my light and spread it into the darkness of ignorance overshadowing the earth."[36]

About two months later, on October 26-27, 1991, this anonymous visionary, accompanied by her daughter, attended a Marian Conference in Chicago, and there, she said, she had several visions of Mary. In these visions, Mary told her that she had not forgotten the United States, that she was coming to the mothers of America because she needed them to help her do her work here, and that it would be her task to help Mary reach those mothers.

The messages which this seer has said she received from Mary at that time are characterized by an apocalyptic urgency reminiscent of the messages at Conyers. Mary told her, she said, that the children of America were spoiled, selfish, and lacking in faith. The time was growing short, and mothers needed to change their lives into holy ones. They needed to be examples to their families and lead them back to God. If mothers would lead their children to her, Mary allegedly said, she would protect them "under her mantle of motherly love." Americans had strayed far from God, so far, indeed, that Mary had devised and was carrying out a special strategy to reach them. Mary had told her, she said, that it had been necessary for her to appear elsewhere first — that is, in the now well known contemporary European apparitions — so that, by calling faithful Americans to those holy spots, they could take the peace they found there home with them. This, she said, was the only way to awaken the spirits of Americans.

It is interesting that the messages reported by this visionary are addressed specifically, not just to mothers, but to all mothers, including those who are non-Catholic. Mary, she has said, considers it important that non-Catholics "who are misinformed" about her be told that she is real, because they are her "missing children and she has much love to give them." They need to know that Catholics do not worship her; that they do not pray to her in the sense of adoration, but rather "to and with her as an intercessor"; that she is not the equal of Jesus, and that she performs no miracles, but only requests them.[37] Mary told her, "I am everybody's Mother, and my messages here are for all, not just for you."[38]

It was in May, 1992, that Mary issued her most urgent call to mothers. It was then that, the visionary said, Mary gave her a letter dedicated to the Mothers of the world. In that letter, Mary called for the mothers of the world to unite. She characterized the world as being in "utter chaos" and noted that the homeless and helpless had lost their way and needed help. She cast her appeal for these people in terms of the mothers who cry for them and the mothers among them who have no way to care for their children. According to the letter, Mary asked, "Can we, as mothers, turn our eyes away and turn deaf ears to their pleas for help?" Should the mothers to whom she was addressing herself be tempted to turn away with the thought that as individuals they could do nothing, Mary issued words of encouragement and an exhortation to join together. She said, "If we join hands, mothers, we can sweep this country and the world with a tidal wave of aid and comfort to all who are in need."[39] She urged mothers, who, she said, were in a sense in charge of all children and not just their own, to throw away apathy and start again.

Mary's specific directives to mothers, as reported by the Cold Spring visionary, are cast in terms of the issues that have loomed large in the recent debate in the United States over the role of religion in personal and public life. According to the seer, Mary has called for mothers to remember the salvation of children "who have been abandoned,"[40] to restore families "to a throne of dignity,"[41] and to organize children into prayer groups, even in schools.[42] There are also messages condemning abortion. At the October Marian Conference in Chicago, the visionary said, Mary told her she was sending a powerful message to all mothers of aborted children. The message was for their salvation, and those mothers should know that there is no error that is not forgiven by Jesus, if they only ask. She allegedly said, "He will send them peace if they will surrender their wills to him."[43] It is significant, perhaps, that right to life groups have much support and are of an especially conservative cast in the Covington, Kentucky, area, where Cold Spring is located.

It was also in May, 1992, that this seer received a message that set the stage for the gathering at St. Joseph Church at Cold Spring on September 1 of that year, which attracted the attention of the national media and which became, for the public, the focal point of this seer's experiences. In October, 1991, Mary had told her, she said, that America lies in spiritual darkness: "You are in darkness now, but if you will follow me, the Light, I shall lead you into a brighter future."[44] Thus, Mary said, she wanted to be known in America as "The Lady of Light." On May 9, 1992, while attending a Marian Conference at Notre Dame, the seer said that Mary told her that she wanted September 1 designated as the day of "Our Lady of Light" and as a day of prayer, and at that time, she promised her she would send a special sign.[45] It was apparently the publicizing of this promise which led to the gathering of a large crowd at St. Joseph Church on August 31 — and the expectation of a sign at midnight. People apparently saw various things that night — certainly all of them did not see the Virgin Mary, as some press reports have suggested — but there was apparently a consensus among those who had gathered there that Mary was present in some special way.

Some Conclusions from Conyers and Cold Spring:
The Mother as Protector of the Unborn and of the Family

It is time to focus specifically on two of the high-profile social issues which assume some importance in the messages of these recent apparitions, that is, abortion and the family, and the way these are understood to relate to the images of motherhood in general and to the image of Mary's universal motherhood in particular which characterize these messages.

The importance of the issue of abortion and its close association with motherhood for many contemporary Roman Catholic Marian devotees are perhaps best summed up in the "Special Edition II" (Winter 1993) issue of the Pittsburgh Center for Peace's newspaper, "Our Lady, Queen of Peace." This publication, which is decidedly apocalyptic in tone, assembles a number of prophecies associated with the recognized apparition of Fatima and uses these as a framework for understanding the prophecies of a number of recently reported apparitions both in the United States and abroad. To summarize the apocalyptic message of this publication: "As human beings reach new levels of discord throughout the world and as countless countries, societies, nations and homes break apart, something strange is developing. In every part of the world, apparitions, miracles, and messages from heaven are being reported." These messages are said to announce a "new era of peace and joy and love,"[46] but this new era will be realized only after passing through the present period of tribulation.

The issue devotes two of its twenty pages to a discussion of abortion. The messages of an anonymous American male visionary set the context for this discussion, which focuses on an allegedly miraculous replica of Our Lady of Guadalupe, which has been on several missionary tours of the Americas. According to the anonymous visionary, Mary has promised to end abortion and bring about a new era of protection of human life,[47] and the missionary image of Guadalupe is seen as facilitating this effort. It is reported that, as this image has been put on display before abortion clinics and at Right-to-Life rallies, it has facilitated the kinds of miracles that have typically been associated with Marian apparitions — rosary beads changing color, the smell of roses, photographs showing various miraculous images, and conversions. In a statement, then, which echoes the message reported by the anonymous Cold Spring visionary, it is said that "God wants those guilty of abortion to be reconciled with *Him* and those killed by abortion to be saved." According to the article, this will be accomplished "through the blood shed by the innocents and our reparatory prayer, sacrifice, sacramental receptions and desire for their salvation."[48]

A full page is also set aside in this publication, just after this material on abortion, for the announcement of a special "Apostolate of Holy Motherhood." The call for this special apostolate is said to have come through another American visionary who calls herself "Mariamente," and who in 1987, when she had visions and received messages from Mary and Jesus, was a mother in her mid-thirties with three young children. Mariamente said that Mary told her that this apostolate was necessary for the welfare of "families of the earth floundering in sin and error which has become so rampant, and is choking off their very life."[49] As she admonished people generally to throw off the snares of the world, such as luxuries and material wealth, Mary expressed special concern that "so many mothers neglect their duty for other things. This is often unnecessary and solely for the purpose of accumulating more wealth, when their true wealth, their children, go unattended."[50] The apostolate of motherhood would thus be an apostolate of "prayer and duty in the home," with Mary herself as the model for mothers who would imitate her virtues as they focused on these domestic tasks.

In the apocalyptic messages which frame the Cold Spring apparition, the chief symptoms of America's ignorance and spiritual darkness are the neglect of children and the demise of the American family. The remedy here is for women to respond to their motherly instincts, to resume their role as caretakers of children and the family, and to bring people back under Mary's protective mantle. This role will ultimately encompass such social action as protesting abortions and reintroducing prayer into schools.

In both the Conyers and the Cold Spring messages, the universal dimension of Mary's motherhood functions chiefly, it seems, to underline and support a radical diagnosis of America's spiritual darkness focused on the family (all families and all children are in danger) and an aggressive program of outreach to address it (outreach must be to all people). In both cases, however, the intended audience appears to be primarily Roman Catholics who are to serve as the leaders and models for returning children and families to their rightful place at the center of American life.

The place and role of non-Catholics here is, in fact, somewhat ambiguous. While there seems to be a sense that there will be support for this mission among many conservative non-

Roman Catholic Christians — which may be the reason there are directives to take these messages to non-Catholics — it is Catholics, very clearly, who are seen as leading the way in this great mission to restore the integrity and spiritual health of the family. There is no sense here of different religions teaching the same thing, with only superficial differences in symbol and practice, which we will find among the non-Catholic spiritual seekers to whom we will now direct our attention.

Apparitions and Locutions in New Age Marian Devotion

Recent interest in apparitions of Mary has not been confined to Catholics, and, particularly in the past several years, many non-Catholics have taken an interest in Medjugorje. An especially significant figure among non-Catholics who have been caught up in Medjugorje is Lutheran journalist Wayne Weible. In October, 1985, someone suggested to Weible that Medjugorje would make a good topic for study, and, since he wrote a weekly news column, Weible began to study the books and videotapes on Medjugorje. He published four columns on Medjugorje in December of that year and then made pilgrimages to the site. Convinced now of Medjugorje's authenticity and importance, Weible has become a leading spokesperson for this apparition, has published a newsletter and a book, and speaks regularly at Marian Conferences. Medjugorje has also captured the attention in recent years of some women who might be characterized as "new age spiritual seekers," and, while it would be interesting to see how and why a Protestant male such as Weible has been attracted to Mary, it will be more interesting, I think, to examine the published accounts of the experiences of these three "new age" women. Indeed, these accounts may provide some insight into the reason so many people today of various religious backgrounds are being drawn to images of the Virgin Mary and what images of Mary are resonating with and shaping these people's experiences.

Peggy Tabor Millen is a self-described "seeker on the spiritual path."[51] Nominally a Methodist, Millen holds degrees in neuropsychology and communication disorders, and she has pursued metaphysics, attitudinal healing, *A Course in Miracles,* and Siddha Yoga. In March, 1989, Millen joined twenty-eight other people on a pilgrimage to Medjugorje sponsored by the Institute for Attitudinal Healing, and her book, *Mary's Way,* published in 1991, chronicles her experiences on that pilgrimage and the lessons she says she learned from them.

To explain the universal appeal of Mary at Medjugorje, Millen explicitly draws on the alleged message from Mary at Medjugorje that humans have created the divisions among religions and that in God there is no separation. She argues that Medjugorje is "catholic" only in the sense of "universal" and not with reference to a particular denomination.[52] Millen says that Mary appears there as "the Universal Mother who nurtures, protects, and guides."[53] Mary's choice of six ordinary young people precisely for their ordinariness suggests to Millen the universality of her call to all people.[54] Millen's first experience of praying the Rosary underlined for her this experience of universality and oneness. Millen said she was previously contemptuous of Catholic statues, rosaries, and crucifixes and regarded such things as "unenlightened." But, when she herself prayed with Rosary beads in her hands, she found that these were really no different from the physical aids to faith of other religions, such as crystals and mandalas. These are, she said, symbols of the "One Source," reminders for people to stay on the path, and tools for them to use "in our practice of oneness."[55]

Millen's most significant religious experience came in front of what she calls the "Mary altar" in St. James Church at Medjugorje. While praying before a statue which she called "the Blue Madonna," she said, she was suddenly aware of "the Oneness of all being and the incredible healing and all-encompassing Power of the Universe."[56] This feeling of "all-encompassing love" was what she had been searching for her whole life. She said she then heard a voice which directed her to "take this and go out into the world."[57]

For Millen, pilgrimage involves a shifting of priorities. Physical pilgrimage means a shift in environment and a change of focus for a defined period of time. But, the inner pilgrimage means a shift of priorities "so that we become one with who we already are."[58] There are four lessons that Millen says she learned at Medjugorje which sound much like a primer in both modern feminist theology and new age spirituality. First, Millen says, she learned that Mary is the "feminine energy that can change the world."[59] She finds that the world has had enough of the masculine side, which she characterizes as aggressive and manipulative; rather, she says, it is time for the feminine side of nurturance and intuition. She found that it is time to embrace the earth and one another, and, if there seems to be an apocalyptic tone about Mary's messages, she concludes that the reason is that people themselves have created the apocalypse. Second, the pilgrimage gave her room to confront "the major issues that occur daily" and to do this from a place of deep peace. Third, she learned to release expectations of all kinds, including her expectations of what a spiritual experience is. Fourth, Millen says she learned that "truth transcends" and that everyone is guilty of making judgments based on sectarian beliefs.

Millen characterizes Mary as the "real woman who lived life from her heart" and finds her to be the true symbol and archetype of the heart itself.[60] She calls her the "Mother of Divine Love"[61] and says that, as Mother, Mary represents the "inclusive love of her progeny."[62] Here, Millen again echoes the universal call that she hears in some of the messages of Medjugorje to respect every person's religious faith. She says that, while her book is entitled "Mary's Way," it could just as easily have been called "Jesus' Way" or Buddha's Way," since the "curriculum" is the same for all. Once the trappings of dogma, doctrine, and form are stripped away, Millen concludes, "there is only one way to God."[63]

In her book, *Longing for Darkness: Tara and the Black Madonna,* published in 1990, China Galland recounts her spiritual journey from a strict Roman Catholic upbringing to a rather eclectic Buddhist spirituality. Galland's journey started with her divorce at age twenty-one. After being married for two years to a man who was, apparently, abusive, Galland says that she was advised by a priest that, for her safety and that of her children (she had one child and was several months pregnant), she should leave the marriage and file at once for both a civil divorce and an ecclesiastical annulment. She followed his advice, remained a Roman Catholic, and avoided dating while awaiting an annulment of her marriage from Rome. After a year without any word, she said, it was suggested that she send a canon lawyer to Rome, but she noted that it could take seven years for a decision to be made through normal channels. She had no money of her own and no enforceable order for child support, and this, she said, made the idea of retaining a lawyer and flying him to Rome "a cruel joke." She says that she then made "the first adult decision" of her life, left the Roman Catholic Church, and "buried" her spiritual life.

In January of 1977, however, after the failure of her second marriage, she tried to return to Catholicism. She went on a retreat to a California monastery, and there, in front of a statue of the Blessed Mother, she began to pour out her frustration and sorrow. She felt that, after so many years, she had come home again only to find that she was a stranger. Although she longed for the comfort of the Blessed Mother, Galland says, she found her too remote because of her perfection. Galland described the

Blessed Mother as "impossibly good, inhumanly pure," and this, she says, put "a glass curtain" between them. By contrast, Galland found herself filled with faults, and she discovered that she had built her life outside the Church.[64]

At that time, Galland was living very close to the San Francisco Zen Center's Green Gulch Farm, and she began to go there on Sunday mornings. She was attracted by the child care, by the "poetic lectures" with no talk about God, and by the fact that there were women priests there.[65] She began to take seriously the Buddha's popular aphorism, "Look within, thou art the Buddha," which she saw as superior to the teachings of Catholicism which, she said, "came from above and had to be taken on faith."[66] Galland also learned about the Buddha Tara, who had defied the traditional Buddhist belief that enlightenment could be attained only in a male body and who had taken a vow to be enlightened only in a woman's body. Electrified by this defiant woman of Buddhist tradition, who appears in one form as a "black Buddha," Galland set off to learn as much about her as possible, beginning a search that would take her around the world. But, as Galland began to study this female and black form of the Buddha, she was led as well to a study of images of the Black Madonna.

While she was investigating the images of the Black Madonna in the American Southwest, Galland discovered a poster of Robert Lentz's icon of the Madonna of El Salvador, the Mother of the Disappeared. This Madonna was painted in a Byzantine style and placed against the backdrop of a Central American jungle, but what especially captured Galland's attention was the white handprint smudged in the lower left corner of the icon. When this white handprint was left on a door, Galland had been told, it marked people out as targets for the El Salvador death squads, and, if people who found this mark on their door did not leave, they too would disappear. And, in this icon, Galland realized, the Madonna herself was "marked" and stood in solidarity with those who had disappeared.

The power of the "Madonna of the Disappeared" suddenly took shape and indeed "exploded" for Galland out of the intersection in this icon between the spiritual and the political. Galland says she was thus brought to reject the image of Mary as a passive sufferer which, she felt, was the predominant way Mary had been portrayed in Catholic tradition. Rather, Galland says, she now received "great comfort in the fact that Mary was an earthly mother, that she went through a pregnancy as a teenage mother, that she had known homelessness, that she had borne at least one child."[67] Having witnessed her child's death, Mary also

knew "the depth of a mother's sorrow." Galland surmised that to
have imagined Mary as other than a passive sufferer "would
have challenged social authority," but now in her prayers she
began to imagine Mary differently, as a "fierce mother." And
indeed, she concluded that Mary is needed now by many other
people as well, "a fierce Mary, a terrific Mary, a fearsome Mary,
a protectress who does not allow her children to be hunted, tor-
tured, and devoured."[68]

Although Galland said that she was initially reluctant to take
the apparition at Medjugorje very seriously, she was finally led
to make a trip there in October 1988 after she had completed
most of her study. While there, she was invited to photograph
the visionaries during their experiences, and, while engaged in
this task, Galland says, she felt that the two visionaries who
were present, Marija and Ivan, were indeed seeing Mary. She
put her camera down on the floor and bowed low, touching her
forehead to the floor as a sign of respect. Later, she described
herself on that occasion as being flooded with joy and happiness, which she took as a clear indication that "something true
and good" had happened to her at Medjugorje.[69]

But, Galland also found things at Medjugorje which troubled
her. She was curious about the universality of Mary's messages,
but she found in her interviews that there was a difference of
opinion about whether one had to be Catholic or not to respond
to Mary's messages. She was also bothered by the fact that there
was an apocalyptic tone to the messages and decided that the
idea of living in the end times was not something that she could
"sanely entertain."[70]

Like Millen, Galland found that the practices called for by
Mary at Medjugorje — prayer, fasting, reconciliation — were
the traditional spiritual practices found throughout the world,
and she was also led to reflect on the relationship between the
Buddha Tara and the Virgin Mary. She recalled that all the
Buddhas are said to appear in billions of forms, appearing according to the needs of devotees, and this led her to wonder
whether Tara might not be appearing as Mary, that is, in a form
which the West would recognize. From the Buddhist perspective, she decided, this was indeed possible. Although she would
not go so far as to say that Mary is Tara or that Christ is Buddha, Galland found that Buddhism gave her a different context
and a different way to think about her experiences.[71]

The new-age seeker whose claims of encounters with Mary
are perhaps the most direct and explicit and whose writing,
moreover, has probably attracted the most public attention is
Annie Kirkwood, a nurse and mother of several children and

author of the 1991 book, *Mary's Message to the World*. According to the introduction to her book, based on information provided by her husband, Byron, and the editors of Blue Dolphin Press, Kirkwood receives her communications from "Mother Mary" in the form of locutions. Kirkwood hears internally, in her mind, what Mary says, in much the same way, apparently, as quite a few Roman Catholics in recent years believe they have heard Mary. Indeed, when she first had such an experience, Kirkwood protested that she was not Catholic and could therefore not be receiving messages from Mary. She thought that her Catholic friend, Marty, was the one who should logically be receiving such communications. In subsequent experiences, however, Mary reassured Kirkwood that she was not Catholic either, but Jewish. She reportedly told Kirkwood that she had chosen her because, "You are also a mother, and so interested in your children's welfare as I have always been — but mostly because of your pure heart and your pure motives in seeking the truth of God."[72] Kirkwood was told that she was also chosen because she was not associated with any religion and was a "simple and seeking soul." Mary told her that it would be among common folk that her word would be spread, and she exhorted Kirkwood to tell the story of the way she was chosen and the way, because she was not a Catholic, she had at first rejected the experience as not real.[73]

In Kirkwood's locutions, Mary insists that she has come for all people, not just for Catholics, and that she will not be limited by cultural differences. She told Kirkwood that she would be using many different people to reach the world, that not all of them would belong to the Catholic Church, and that she loves people no matter what culture they live in or what religion they believe in.[74] In a message that clearly echoes some of the messages of Medjugorje, Kirkwood reported that Mary told her, "I cannot be limited because I am commissioned by God the Creator. God is not limited. He is limitless and above all religions and dogmas of man."[75]

The messages from Mary reported by Kirkwood are in some ways much like those of other modern Marian apparitions. First, like many of those messages, they are apocalyptic in tone and warn of a coming catastrophe. According to Kirkwood, Mary told her that her appearances throughout the world have been for the sole purpose of warning people about the times ahead.[76] As in other apparitions, Mary exhorted people to pray and said that, through their prayers, people could lessen the severity of what was to come.[77]

The content of these messages, however, addresses, not the traditional religious concerns of Roman Catholics, but the new age concerns of ecology and personal growth. According to Kirkwood, Mary has addressed herself to the "residents of planet earth."[78] She has warned that certain natural disasters, for example, violent weather and earthquakes, are impending. These disasters are the result of human acts, past and present, reflecting a complete disregard of the earth as a planet. Some of these messages suggest that these disasters are primarily a means for the earth to renew itself ("the time is drawing near when you will be shaken and frightened, not because of any punishment, but to renew the land and minds of mankind").[79] Others, however, carry the suggestion that some punishment is involved in a kind of natural retribution ("It is not God who will be punishing you but the planet herself").[80]

In a particularly interesting prediction that combines moral transgression and this natural retribution, Kirkwood said that Mary warned that New York "will not stand again as the giant trade center." She said that it had polluted the world the most "with its greed and worship of power and money." Mary predicted that the year 1995 "will be the year that the trading centers of the world will be destroyed by the planet herself."[81] Mary also issued a number of other predictions for this decade, including nearly daily UFO sightings, the appearance in increasing numbers of civilizations from other planets, a decline in the power of the Catholic Church, and a call by religious leaders for the unity of all religions.[82]

Kirkwood said that Mary expressed to her a frustration in not being able to interest people in preparing for these changes, even though they were already beginning to happen. She was giving Kirkwood the same message, she said, that she had already given at Fatima, Lourdes, Mexico, and in many other places: There had to be a destruction of the land for this planet to continue to exist.[83] Kirkwood said Mary told her, "I will be blessing all who seek to find the Truth with God's blessing. He is the One whom I represent. His Love is what I give to all men. It is His Healing Power which I leave behind each apparition."[84]

Some Conclusions from the New Age Writings:
The Mother as Protector of the Self,
the Oppressed, and the Earth

For all of these three women, the universality of Mary seems to imply, as it does not in the messages of Conyers and Cold Spring, a fundamental oneness or unity of all of the world's peoples. And, for all three, the suggestion is that there is an essential unity in the world's religions that may be obscured by their various doctrines, symbols, and practices. Mary's appeal to all the people of the world is a nondenominational call to cast aside their differences in favor of concerns directed, in differing degrees, to the well-being of oneself, one's society, and one's planet.

Millen's recollections of her pilgrimage to Medjugorje and her devotion to Mary are related chiefly to issues of personal well-being and are cast primarily in terms of personal growth. Mary as the archetype of the heart is the model here that all can imitate in order to realize in themselves the qualities of intuition and nurturance, which are feminine qualities that have the potential to renew both the self and society.

Galland's discussion has more of a social dimension in the sense that her story began with the experience of being disenfranchised or alienated from the Catholic Church, and she found that she could reclaim her connection with this community and its symbols only through another non-Western religious tradition. For Galland, Buddhism provides the spiritual basis and freedom from which she is able to reexamine her relationship with the Blessed Mother. Working from the Buddhist premise of "take what you need and leave the rest," Galland rejects the apocalypticism and sectarianism that have often been associated with the image of Mary, and she reimagines her as a fierce, determined, and independent mother, who, like the Madonna of the Disappeared ones, is ready to risk her life in the defense of her children. The universality of Mary's motherhood here means that she is in solidarity with those who are suffering and that this solidarity transcends religious context.

Mary's locutions to Kirkwood, while they speak of an impending catastrophe if changes in life and lifestyle are not immediately forthcoming, represent the most universal and global of these three new age Marian interpretations. Here, Mary's universal motherhood implies and encompasses a concern for the planet, Mother Earth herself, who is in need of cleansing and renewal. Mary's audience here is explicitly said to include everyone, and Mary specifically says here that she will not be bound by cultural differences either in her choice of visionaries or the audience of her messages.

General Conclusions

The image of Mary that clearly dominates contemporary Marian apparitions in the United States and the popular discourse that surrounds them is that of a universal mother, concerned for all her children. Indeed, although one often sees Mary referred to in the literature of these apparitions as "Lady," "Queen," and "Virgin," it is as the Blessed Mother that she gives voice to her concern for the spiritual future of America, however that is defined, and it is by reference to her "motherhood" that she expresses her concerns and issues her directives. However, there are differing and, indeed, mutually conflicting interpretations of what Mary's universal motherhood means.

In the interpretations that surround the experiences of both the visionaries and devotees of Marian apparitions and the interpretation of the messages that Mary has reportedly given, there is a selectivity of context and focus that affects and largely determines the meaning of the apparition itself. For the followers of Conyers and Cold Spring apparitions, or at least those who closely adhere to the seers' own interpretations and the interpretation of other recent apparitions set forth in the *Our Lady, Queen of Peace* newspaper, the central image of Mary's motherhood comes to focus in, and serves the preservation of, the family in its "traditional" sense and the protection of the unborn. Mothers here are the key to restoring the dignity of the family, placing their children under Mary's protective mantle and bringing them back to God, and thus there is a strong call for all women to embrace their traditional roles as mothers and their traditional duties in the home.

For the "new age" women, on the other hand, who have directed their attention for the most part to some of the messages of the more ecumenical apparitions, such as Medjugorje, the image of Mary's motherhood has come to focus in a concern, not with motherhood as such, but with certain qualities associated with motherhood. These include the "feminine" qualities of intuition and nurturance which are seen as necessary to counterbalance the masculine tendencies of aggression and destruction. They also include, however, the qualities of fierceness, independence, and determination that may allow one to triumph over hostile forces that may be threatening one's children and one's world. There is here a call to restore one's spirituality as a means of achieving inner peace and then to take action on behalf of oppressed peoples and the oppressed earth.

If forced to confront each other, these two groups would undoubtedly have some rather spirited debates about the meaning of Mary's universal motherhood. But, the fact that both groups focus on, and seek to allay, their anxieties through images of Mary as a universal mother testifies to the power of these images in our time and to the diversity of the voices which are calling Mary blessed in this, the last decade of the twentieth century.

NOTES

[1] Elizabeth A. Johnson, "Marian Devotion in the Western Church," in *Christian Spirituality II: High Middle Ages and Reformation,* ed. Jill Raitt (New York: Crossroad, 1987), 392-414.

[2] William Christian, Jr., "Religious Apparitions and the Cold War in Southern Europe," in *Religion, Power and Protest in Local Communities,* ed. E. Wolf (Berlin: Mouton Publishers, 1984), 249.

[3] John O'Connor, "The Liberation of the Virgin Mary," *Ladies Home Journal,* December 1972, 75, 126-127.

[4] Ibid., 75.

[5] Ibid., 126.

[6] Ibid., 127.

[7] Richard N. Ostling, "Handmaid or Feminist," *Time Magazine,* 30 December 1991, 62-66.

[8] Ibid., 65.

[9] Ibid.

[10] Ibid., 66.

[11] René Laurentin, *Our Lord and Our Lady in Scottsdale: Faithful Charisms in a Traditional American Parish* (Milford, OH: Faith Publishing Company, 1992), x.

[12] Ibid., x, xiii.

[13] Peter Batty, "Collected Words of Our Lady, Queen of Peace, at Medjugorje," in *Our Lady, Queen of Peace* (Dublin Medjugorje Centre: November 1985), 16.

[14] Miles Corwin, "Vision Quest," *Los Angeles Times,* 23 June 1991, A3, A29.

[15] Maria Donato, "In search for miracles, believers head to Hillside," *Chicago Tribune,* 24 July 1991, Section 1, 1, 10.

[16] Deborah Kovach, "Awaiting a Miracle," *The Times* (Trenton, NJ), 6 August 1992, A1, 16; Carmen Juri, "6,000 flock to shrine, hoping to see Mary," *The Star-Ledger* (Newark, NJ), 7 September 1992, 1, 9.

[17] "Our Lady of the Americas: An Interview with Visionary Estela Ruiz," in *Our Lady, Queen of Peace,* ed. Thomas Petrisko (Pittsburgh Center for Peace: Winter 1992), 8.

[18] Tomislav Vlasic, "The Message of Medjugorje," in *Our Lady, Queen of Peace* (Dublin Medjugorje Centre: November 1985), 5.

[19] Ibid.

[20] Batty, *op. cit.,* 18.

[21] Judith Child, "The Conyers Story Part II," in *To Bear Witness that I am the Living Son of God, Volume II* (Newington, VA: Our Loving Mother's Children, 1992), v.

[22]Ibid., vii-viii.

[23]Ibid., viii.

[24]Our Loving Mother's Children, *To Bear Witness that I am the Living Son of God, Volume II* (Newington, VA: Our Loving Mother's Children, 1992), 43.

[25]Ibid.

[26]Ibid., 44.

[27]Ibid., 40.

[28]Ibid., 25.

[29]Ibid., 51-52.

[30]Ibid., 86-87.

[31]Ibid., 77.

[32]Ibid., 35.

[33]Ibid., viii.

[34]Gerald G. Ross, ed., *Personal Revelations of Our Lady of Light* (Fort Mitchell, KY: Our Lady of Light Publications, 1992).

[35]Ibid., 8-9.

[36]Ibid., 10.

[37]Ibid., 14-15.

[38]Ibid., 17.

[39]Ibid., 45.

[40]Ibid., 44.

[41]Ibid., 45.

[42]Ibid., 24, 25, 44.

[43]Ibid., 15.

[44]Ibid., 37.

[45]Ibid., 23.

[46]*Our Lady, Queen of Peace: Special Edition II,* ed. Thomas Petrisko (Pittsburgh Center for Peace: Winter 1993), 2.

[47]Ibid., 17.

[48]Ibid.

[49]Ibid., 18.

[50]Ibid.

[51]Peggy Tabor Millen, *Mary's Way* (Berkeley, CA: Celestial Arts, 1991), 17.

[52]Ibid., 10.

[53]Ibid., 13.

[54]Ibid.

[55]Ibid., 26.

[56]Ibid., 27.

[57]Ibid.

[58]Ibid., 29.

[59]Ibid., 25.

[60]Ibid., 40.

[61]Ibid.

[62]Ibid., 48.

[63]Ibid., 34.

[64]China Galland, *Longing for Darkness: Tara and the Black Madonna* (New York: Penguin Books, 1990), 15.

[65]Ibid., 16.
[66]Ibid., 20.
[67]Ibid., 273.
[68]Ibid., 275.
[69]Ibid., 314.
[70]Ibid., 321.
[71]Ibid., 310-311.
[72]Annie Kirkwood, *Mary's Message to the World* (Nevada City, CA: Blue Dolphin Press, 1991), ix.
[73]Ibid., x.
[74]Ibid., xii.
[75]Ibid., xiii.
[76]Ibid., 3.
[77]Ibid., 6-7.
[78]Ibid., 3.
[79]Ibid., 2.
[80]Ibid., 15.
[81]Ibid., 16.
[82]Ibid., 15.
[83]Ibid., 27.
[84]Ibid., 30.

Mary and the Church of the Future

Carol Frances Jegen, B.V.M.

To speak of Mary and the Church of the future is to speak of Mary in this time of New Pentecost inaugurated by the Second Vatican Council. In this context, it is helpful to recall the spirited, and somewhat divisive, debate that occurred during the Second Vatican Council regarding its Marian teaching. Two different orientations toward Marian devotion struggled to highlight Mary, either in her exalted privileges or in her life of faith as a human person, mother of Jesus of Nazareth. The closest vote in the entire Council, a narrow margin of forty, situated the teachings about Mary in the Dogmatic Constitution on the Church, *Lumen Gentium*.[1] In so doing, the Council pointed to a significant shift of emphasis regarding Marian devotion in our times. The title of that final chapter is highly significant, "The Role of the Blessed Virgin Mary, Mother of God, *in* the Mystery of Christ and the Church." This Council proclaimed emphatically that the needed emphasis on Mary in the life of the Church now and in the future is the emphasis on Mary *with us* in every part of our lives as Christians.

Lumen Gentium, Light to All Nations, was the central ecclesiological document of this Council called to reform and enliven the entire Church in our times. *Lumen Gentium* was keynoted by a phrase from the prophet-servant theology of Second Isaiah with its clarion call to a prophetic way of life initiated by God's own Spirit. In unmistaken terms, the First Servant song makes clear that the power to bring justice and light to all nations comes from the Spirit of God. How straight-forwardly the prophet proclaims Yahweh's action: "Upon (my servant) I have put my spirit; he shall bring forth justice to the nations" (Is 42:1).

175

Keynotes are highly significant in the artistic works of music and of literature. Keynotes set a tone for all that follows in the composition. In regard to *Lumen Gentium*, many other Scripture texts could have been chosen to keynote this central Council document on the Church. But, under the inspiration of the Holy Spirit, this Isaian text was selected, thereby keynoting the needed ecclesiological emphasis in our times as one of prophetic witness to all nations.

Lumen Gentium refers to the Church as the People of God. *Lumen Gentium* calls everyone in the Church to holiness. And, may we not say that, in climaxing this Conciliar teaching with the chapter on Mary, Vatican II presented Mary as the way to genuine holiness for all called to live in this union with Christ, for those called to share in his prophetic vocation?

Fortunately, the Second Vatican Council gave us a second document on the Church, the Pastoral Constitution on *The Church in the Modern World, Gaudium et Spes*. Very significantly, this historic document emerged during the Council, largely through the initiative of our Third World bishops in whose countries live two thirds of our human family. *Gaudium et Spes* is addressed "to the whole of humanity" (*GS* 2).

The needs of the world keynote this Pastoral Constitution in its opening sentences: "The joys and the hopes, the griefs and the anxieties of the (people) of this age, especially those who are poor or in any way afflicted, these too are the joys and hopes, the griefs and anxieties of the followers of Christ. Indeed, nothing genuinely human fails to raise an echo in their hearts" (*GS* 1). Those joys and hopes, those griefs and anxieties are presented in the context of the vast changes going on in the social order. The psychological, moral and religious changes in attitudes and values, particularly on the part of young people, form a backdrop, as it were, for a consideration of the complex problems facing the Church of the future as it responds to the needs of the whole human family.

Problems of special urgency are highlighted in the second part of this Pastoral Constitution. The Preface to Part II states:

> Of the many subjects arousing universal concern today, it may be helpful to concentrate on these: marriage and the family, human culture, life in its economic, social and political dimensions, the bonds between the family of nations and peace (*GS* 46).

To work with these human problems, a new Vatican structure was proposed, and unprecedented encouragement of dialog was given with no one excluded. The new Pontifical Commission

Justice and Peace, with its worldwide network, was initiated in the following mandate:

> In view of the immense hardships which still afflict the majority of (people) today, the Council regards it as most opportune that some agency of the universal Church be set up for the world-wide promotion of justice for the poor and of Christ's kind of love for them. The role of such an organization will be to foster progress in needy regions, and social justice on the international scene (GS 90).

Now, as we recall these prophetic teachings of *Gaudium et Spes*, we are reminded that demanding agenda were set for the Church of the future. As we ponder the agenda a quarter of a century later, well might we ask how much progress has been made. And, for our particular purpose in this volume, we need to ask: Where is Mary in all these plans, in these joys and hopes, in these griefs and anxieties?

Several times in this Vatican II era I have suggested that the final chapter of *Lumen Gentium*, "The Role of the Blessed Virgin Mary, Mother of God, in the Mystery of Christ and the Church," can be a bridge uniting the two major documents on the Church, *Lumen Gentium* and *Gaudium et Spes*.[2] That is to say, *Lumen Gentium* climaxes its basic ecclesiology by presenting us with the person, Mary, who for centuries has been called a "type of the Church." In Mary, we begin to see what the Church is called to become. In Mary, we can begin to see the Church of the future. In Mary, we can see the way a Church needs to respond to human needs in every generation. Most of the major issues of our future are indicated in *Gaudium et Spes*. In Mary, we can find ways to approach those issues. With Mary, we can become a prophetic Church, influencing the future of a world entering a new century, a new millennium.[3]

Mary in Luke-Acts

The story of the Christian communities' earliest attempts to influence the future of their world is found in the Acts of the Apostles, that New Testament book which gives us an account of the Pentecost event. And, lest we think that we are no longer in a time of New Pentecost because such a special outpouring of the Holy Spirit was confined only to the years when Vatican II was in session, we need to recall that all of Acts depicts the first Pentecost era, not merely the second chapter that gives us the familiar Pentecost scene.

Recent studies in Acts highlight the narrative character of the book. New Testament scholar, William Thompson, S.J., writes:

> Luke's story reveals a world of characters and events, images and symbols, metaphors and stories, which focused their attention and focuses our attention on the Christian mission. The narrative invites us to enter that world, let it interact with our own world of meaning, and gradually shape in us a stance toward our mission today. If we choose to read the story, pray with it and study it with care, we will gradually attune ourselves to its vision and values, its affections and attitudes, its passions and convictions.[4]

A similar orientation to Luke-Acts is given by Lucan scholar, Robert Tannehill, in his second volume of *The Narrative Unity of Luke-Acts*, wherein he claims, "If some in the modern church find Acts strange and irrelevant, this reaction may in part reflect the church's loss of a clear and compelling mission."[5] In highlighting the significance of the narrative pattern in Acts, Tannehill comments: "Luke-Acts does more than share a grand vision. It tells a story from which we are able to learn."[6]

Just how does Mary fit into that story? What can we learn from her? Some scholars would reply, "precious little," in the light of Mary's single mention in the entire Book of Acts. Only in the first chapter does Mary seem to play a role. There, the Mother of Jesus is with the early community in its prayerful preparation for the coming of the Holy Spirit (Ac 1:14).

How significant is this one text on Mary, the only one in the entire Book of Acts? I suggest it is a text of paramount importance in the life of the Church in every period of its history, including our own. Here, we see Mary, Mother of God, in the mystery of Christ and the Church sustaining those earliest Christians in a prayerful receptivity to the Spirit of the risen Jesus. The singularity of this Marian text is one of emphasis. It is Luke's way of highlighting the centrality of prayerfulness in the life of the Church. Everything that follows in the entire Book of Acts — the Church's growth, organization, persecution, martyrdoms — all depend on a genuine life of prayer. Here, in the very beginning of its life as a Christian community, Mary, the Mother of Jesus, is presented as the woman of prayer *par excellence* who guides the followers of Jesus in a prayerful, discerning life of faith.

In relating this text from Acts to the prayers of Jesus as indicated in the Lucan Gospel, Tannehill emphasizes that this prayer of the community prepares them for a new development of great importance. It is a text that helps us see the way the

Church's mission is always dependent on prayerful discerning of divine direction and even of divine prodding.[7]

Tannehill's remarks are pertinent here because they clarify the relation of the Christian community's prayerfulness to genuine discernment of God's action in their lives. Today we are quite aware that discernment is more than decision-making. Discernment is the prayerful recognition of the movement of the Holy Spirit in the lives of individual persons and communities. Discernment is basic to the vitality of the Church, especially in regard to its mission and ministries in any period of its history.[8]

In Luke-Acts, Mary is clearly a woman of prayerful discernment, one who knows from experience the singleness of heart that prayerful discernment demands. Mary also helps us appreciate the necessity of sound theological understanding as a necessary ingredient in the discernment process. Mary knew her Jewish Scriptures; Mary knew the covenant history of her people.

Just as *Lumen Gentium's* final chapter on Mary can be considered a bridge between Vatican II's Dogmatic and Pastoral Constitutions on the Church, so, too, the first chapter of Acts can be considered a bridge between the Gospel of Luke and the Acts of the Apostles. Furthermore, a characteristic Lucan use of parallelism suggests a certain comparison between the Infancy Narrative of the Lucan Gospel and Acts' description of the infant Church. In both situations, Mary's prayerfulness is singled out for special comment.

Twice in the Infancy Narrative Luke highlights Mary's prayerfulness. After the shepherds' visit to her new-born son, "Mary treasured all these things and reflected on them in her heart" (Lk 2:19). Surely, this surprising visit called for reflection. Rugged shepherds from the neighboring hillside were not the most likely visitors to expect for one who had been called "Son of the Most High" and to whom the Lord God had promised the throne of David (Lk 1:32).

Luke concludes the second chapter of his Gospel describing two temple episodes with a strong, simple reminder, "His mother meanwhile kept all these things in memory" (Lk 2:51). Mary needed to remember Simeon's prophetic words, that her child would be opposed by many; that she would be pierced with a sword — "so that the thoughts of many hearts may be laid bare" (Lk 2:35). Mary, with Joseph, had gone through the agonizing process of searching for Jesus in sorrow before they found him in the Temple (Lk 2:45-50). Such suffering situations called for a prayerfulness strong enough to enable one to ponder without understanding and to discern gradually the mysterious ways of a loving God.

From one point of view the Lucan Infancy Narrative can be considered a small book of prayer. All of the key characters: Zachary, Elizabeth, Mary, Joseph, Simeon, Anna and Jesus, are presented as prayerful persons. Even John the Baptist in the womb of Elizabeth rejoiced at the presence of God. In these early chapters, three canticles are inserted, quite possibly from the early Jewish-Christian liturgy: the prayer songs of Mary, Zachary and Simeon. The angels' song of praise on Christmas night is probably a special Lucan composition.[9]

Mary's great song of prayer, her Magnificat, sings of God's great, ongoing actions in human history. Mary's song, like Zachary's, proclaims the active presence of God in the future: "His mercy is from age to age on those who fear him" (Lk 1:50). Furthermore, Mary proclaims the surprising actions of this great and glorious God: the lowly are raised to high places; the hungry are given every good thing (Lk 1:52,53).

In these early chapters of Luke, perhaps the scene of Mary's prayerfulness which parallels the early chapters of Acts most directly is that of the Annunciation (Lk 1:26-39). There, Mary's prayerful, honest, questioning dialog is answered with the promised gift of God's Holy Spirit. From beautiful experience, Mary knew the way to prepare for and receive the Holy Spirit, the power of the Most High. Not only at the first Pentecost, but all through the Church's life, would Mary be able to help the followers of her son prepare for and receive the gift of God's Spirit.

Luke's Infancy Narrative concludes with the summary statement: "Jesus, for his part, progressed steadily in wisdom, and age and grace before God and (everyone)" (Lk 2:52). To progress steadily in wisdom and grace requires a prayerful spirit. Surely, Jesus' growth in prayerfulness was guided by Mary with Joseph's help. *Lumen Gentium* reminds us that Mary's maternal love also extends to the faithful in their development as disciples of Jesus (*LG* 63). Mary, Mother of God, in the mystery of Christ and the Church, continues to help the members of the Church grow in wisdom and grace, in genuine prayerful discernment. Mary knows from experience that everything else in the life of the Church depends on this maturing in prayer.

Mary in History

A study of Mary in Luke-Acts may be considered a study of the Mary of faith. That is to say, some of the same questions and concerns related to the study of the Jesus of history and the Christ of faith also pertain to Mary. Luke-Acts gives us the Mary of faith as known and loved by the earliest Christian communities. However, very little specific information is recorded about the Mary of history, the human Mary who lived with Jesus and Joseph.[10]

In the recent major ecumenical study, *Mary in the New Testament*, eminent scholars point to Lk 8:19-21 as one of three key synoptic texts on Mary.[11] There, Jesus praised her as one among those who heard the word of God and acted on it. Mary is presented as a first disciple, a role that continues in the community of disciples gathered in the Upper Room, prayerfully awaiting the coming of God's Spirit (Ac 1:14). However, if we are searching for historical detail on Mary, those two scenes are not very helpful. And, when we turn to the Infancy Narratives of both Matthew and Luke, we are studying a *genre* different from the rest of the Gospels.[12] As theological histories, those introductory chapters do not give us the detailed pictures of life that we are accustomed to see in today's TV documentaries. Consequently, in the light of the New Testament, discovering the historical Mary may be considered an even more challenging task than is discovering the historical Jesus.

Historical, geographical, and cultural studies can help us appreciate Mary's life situation in the Middle East of her day. An intriguing "geographical" consideration of the early Jerusalem community's devotion to Mary is found in Carroll Stuhlmueller's article, "Old Testament Settings for Mary in the Liturgy."[13] Interestingly enough, the movement of the community from one place of worship to another is related to their appreciation of Mary's role in their lives of faith. However, in such studies we learn more about early devotion to the Mother of Jesus than we learn about Mary herself.

The lives and works of today's liberation theologians have helped us realize anew that faith experience is the necessary basis for all genuine theological insight. The ordinary and extraordinary events of everyday life, as seen through the mind and heart of faith, are the starting points for theological endeavor.

In the events of daily life, such as the birth of a child or the loss of a loved one, we are able to express a certain quality of compassionate love and understanding when we have undergone similar experiences. When our life experiences begin to correspond more and more with the life experiences of the faith community as presented in our Scriptures, then the possibilities for new faith insights increase, and the process of discernment moves ahead with new wisdom.

Here, it may be helpful to recall the way the Exodus has been paradigmatic for persons oppressed in slavery situations, such as our African-Americans, and how significant the Exodus story has been in the development of Black Theology.[14] Another contemporary example would be the Latin American mothers of the disappeared. These valiant women have found new meaning in the mystery of Mary's loss of Jesus at the age of twelve.

Mary's maturing prayerfulness depended on her experiences as seen in the light of faith. Significantly, in the Infancy Narrative Luke highlights her prayerfulness in relation to the experiences of the shepherds' visit and the loss and finding of Jesus in the Temple (Lk 2:19, 51). Both experiences were unexpected and surprising. As such, they called for prayerful discernment on Mary's part.

Mary's faith perspective was formed by the heritage of her Jewish people. Her growing union with God strengthened her conviction that Israel's God would be ever faithful to the promises made to all generations of Abraham's descendants. Mary knew well the way Yahweh was involved in their history. Undoubtedly, she learned more about those remarkable ways of God from listening to her son as his teaching ministry developed. Mary was singularly blessed in those groups of listeners who heard Jesus' word and acted on it (Lk 8:19-21).

To hear the word of God and to act on it call for prayerful discernment. Mary was well acquainted with key situations of discernment in the lives of her people: of Abraham responding to Yahweh's invitation to "Go forth from the land of your kinsfolk" (Gn 12:1); of Moses facing the implications of God's command to "lead the Israelites out of Egypt" (Ex 3:11). Although we do not know precisely the way Mary became aware of Jesus' decision to move on to Jerusalem, aware as he was of impending suffering and death, we do know Mary was with Jesus on Calvary (Jn 19:25-27).

Mary of Nazareth knew the challenge of discernment as she was asked to "conceive and bear a son and give him the name Jesus" (Lk 1:31). Mary of Pentecost knew from experience that the followers of Jesus would need to grow in prayerful discernment. They would face futures of unprecedented challenges, not unlike the centuries of demanding experiences her people had shared with their God.

Before we reflect on some of the challenges calling for prayerful discernment in today's Church and try to learn from the stories of the Church as recorded in Acts, let us ponder briefly the human Mary of the Pentecost event. In so doing, we may be able to gain fresh insight into some of the ways Mary is actively present with us in this time of New Pentecost.

In the Upper Room, Mary, the Mother of Jesus crucified, was in the midst of those who had failed and even denied her son when he needed them most. How well she must have been aware of the human frailty of those who would carry on her son's mission. What heroic forgiveness this whole experience called for on the part of Mary.[15] Mary's forgiving heart may well have been the most powerful word she spoke during that entire time of prayerful preparation for the coming of the Holy Spirit of her risen son. As Mary continued to guide those first Christians in the ways of prayerful discernment, her spirit of forgiveness must have provided an atmosphere of compassion in which those early communities faced the future.

It is this human, prayerful, discerning Mary in the mystery of Christ and the Church that Vatican II presents to us as we face our future which that same Council called "an hour of supreme crisis" (*GS* 77). Here, I want to emphasize Mary's human experience, the experience of the Mary of human history whose maternal love continues to be with us in the Church today. For centuries, the Church has emphasized Mary's intercessory role. But, often this prayerful Mary has been presented in such exalted ways that her human understanding, gained from life experience, has been somewhat overshadowed.

Vatican II's emphasis on Mary with us in the day to day life of the Church brings Mary into our lives, into our "joys and hopes, our griefs and anxieties" (*GS* 1). In our many situations calling for prayerful discernment, what strength and wisdom we can gain through our awareness of Mary's special presence in the life of the Church today!

Granted, we know few historical details of her life. Granted, Mary lived in a very different cultural milieu. But, the more we reflect on the ways Mary is depicted in the New Testament, the more we come to understand her as a strong, courageous woman who can relate to our human situations with a strong, compassionate, understanding heart, because she has lived a life of faith in the midst of extraordinary difficulties.

Our pressing concern is not so much the Mary *of* history as it is the Mary *in* history, in our history as a pilgrim Church, struggling to be faithful to the Spirit of her risen Son. In the words of *Lumen Gentium*, "By her maternal charity, Mary cares for the (followers) of her Son who still journey on earth surrounded by dangers and difficulties . . ." (*LG* 62). An awareness of her presence can give us unbelievable strength as we continue to renew and reform the Church of the future.[16]

A Future for the Church

In a recent article in *America*, Richard McBrien, Professor of Christian Ethics at the University of Notre Dame, addressed the question of today's conflicts within the Church.[17] McBrien made a strong case for the important role of those who are "the products and supporters of the Second Vatican Council — of the council as shaped and fashioned by its working majority, not by its defeated minority."[18] McBrien named persons loyal to Vatican II, as liturgists and religious educators, justice and peace officers, campus ministers, social science personnel, administrators of our Catholic colleges and universities, theologians, spiritual writers and directors, many sisters, priests and bishops.[19]

In his great concern about fidelity to Vatican II, was not McBrien pointing to the contemporary Church, tenaciously committed to the "apostles' instruction" (Ac 2:42) as we know it in our times? This question of fidelity to the teaching of the apostles was the first major integral element of an authentic Christian community as described in Luke-Acts. In this classic Lucan summary statement, the earliest description of a Christian community is given:[20] "They devoted themselves to the apostles' instruction and the communal life, to the breaking of bread and the prayers" (Ac 2:42). If we consider Acts as a New Testament book that holds vision and values capable of informing and influencing us in our shaping of the future of the Church and society,[21] then this Lucan editorial summary is of crucial importance.

Not without struggle did the earliest Christian communities come to realize that fidelity to the teaching of the apostles meant fidelity to Jesus, their risen Lord. Docetist and Gnostic interpretations of the Incarnation began to plague the infant Church. Jesus' very identity as Word Incarnate was in question. Today's problems and questions regarding Jesus and his good news are not the same as those of earlier centuries. Perhaps they are more critical. But, the struggle to remain faithful to the Gospel in its Vatican II orientation confronts us with the same challenge the earliest Christians knew — to continue steadfastly to the apostles' instruction, to the Jesus of the Gospel.[22]

In *Christology at the Crossroads*, Salvadoran Jesuit Jon Sobrino claims that problems within the Church are basically problems with the Church's understanding of Jesus at a given point in history.[23] The implications of such a profound statement are manifold and deserve utmost attention for all those Christians concerned with the future of the Church.

In this regard, I wish to highlight the fact that no one grew to understand Jesus more authentically than his mother, Mary. In her prayerful influence on the early Church, surely Mary must have helped those Christians realize the centrality of Jesus' witness and teaching *in* and *for* their own lives. Fidelity to her Son, Jesus, was the underlying issue in the communities' adherence to the "apostles' instruction and the communal life, to the breaking of bread and the prayers" (Ac 2:42).

In this Lucan editorial summary, the "communal life" is the integral element related immediately to the communities' adherence to the apostles' instruction. A more detailed description of this communal life is given in the verses following immediately in the second chapter of Acts:

> Those who believed shared all things in common; they would sell their property and goods, dividing everything on the basis of each one's need. They went to the temple area together every day, while in their homes they broke bread. With exultant and sincere hearts they took their meals in common, praising God and winning the approval of all the people (Ac 2:44-47).

Recent studies of the Qumran texts have helped us appreciate the profound implications of this description of communal life. In such a faith community, only if there were a prayerful sharing of mind and heart with one another, did the sharing of material goods have any authentic meaning.[24]

In Acts, this picture of the Christian community presents us with a prayerful, discerning way of life. In the Greek text, this communal life is named *koinonia*, an almost untranslatable word. *Koinonia* implies a mutual sharing of life. In the context of Christian community, the sharing of faith life depended first and foremost on the way the members of the community were prayerfully attuned to the Spirit of the risen Jesus and thereby actually empowered to continue the mission of Jesus as members of his Body, the Church. In the spirit of *koinonia*, each person's maturing life of prayer also called for a sharing of faith insights with other members of the community. Through such prayerful sharing and dialog, the community grew in their ability to discern where and when and how the Spirit of the risen Jesus was prompting them to carry out the mission of Jesus.

Once again, it is helpful to recall the scene in the first chapter of Acts in which Mary is singled out by name in that prayerful community awaiting the coming of the Holy Spirit. Once again, it is helpful and necessary to relate this pre-Pentecost scene to those texts in the Lucan Gospel highlighting Mary's prayerfulness. Mary listened, pondered, and dialogued with her God whose word she heard and acted on (Lk 1:26-39; 2:19, 51; 8:19-21).

Like the text in Acts, the key synoptic texts on Mary's prayerful listening presents her in a communal context. Mary was one among others who heard the word and acted on it, thereby enjoying a new familial relation with Jesus as his mother, his sisters, and his brothers (Lk 8:19-21; Mk 3:31-35; Mt 12:46-50).

Perhaps the standard exegesis of this synoptic text does not place sufficient emphasis on the communal implications that are implied. Often, the intimacy of familial relations is emphasized, but not the community dynamics implied therein. Again, if we try to be more realistic about Mary's human reactions to Jesus, especially during his ministry, we will find ourselves more aware of Mary's role in nurturing dialog and discernment among those first followers of her Son. Mark's Gospel presents us with perplexed reactions to Jesus. Apparently, some of his extended family did not agree with his message and wanted to stop his preaching and teaching (Mk 3:21). In such situations, did Mary recall Simeon's prophecy that her Son would be a sign of contradiction (Lk 2:34)? Just how much prayer and dialog were necessary to help Mary and those sincere Jewish disciples grow in their understanding and acceptance of her Son's messianic identity as one that was described by Second Isaiah as "a man of suffering, accustomed to infirmity" (Is 53:3)?

Our awareness of Luke's historical sense helps us relate these synoptic texts, including Luke's, to the prayer text on Mary in Acts. Now, in this Vatican II era, we must relate these texts also to our own historical vantage point in the history of the Church. Like Jesus, the Church is called to grow in wisdom and grace as it advances in age. Vatican II's call to holiness is a call to prayer, including communal prayer in all that can mean for discernment. Surely, Mary in the Mystery of Christ and the Church continues to nurture the Church's ways of dialog that can make for genuine discernment.

In today's Church, one of the movements that hold great promise for prayerful dialog and discernment is that of the small faith communities. In a recent International Conference held in December, 1991, at the University of Notre Dame, members of small Christian communities from Africa, Asia, South and North America, and Europe gathered to share their experiences. One way to describe the gathering would be to name it another Pentecost event. The influence of the Holy Spirit in forming vital Christian communities in a variety of cultures throughout the world was obvious and inspiring. In every situation, from Tanzania to Taiwan, from Brazil to the

United States, the descriptions of community experiences included prayerful discernment on the social conditions of each country. The Notre Dame meeting itself could be described as an experience of prayerful discernment about the Church of the future.[25]

If the Church today and tomorrow is going to respond to "the joys and the hopes, the griefs and the anxieties of the (people) of this age" (*GS* 1), then the Church must be more open to internal structural change, in order to witness more authentically to the need for structural change in society. The dynamics of small Christian communities can be exceedingly helpful in this process. These faith communities can be considered new structures that point the way for a new future in the Church. Prayerful dialog is at the very heart of these small faith communities as the members discern together the way to respond to the critical needs of our times.[26]

In the Church of the United States, since Vatican II we have witnessed another phenomenon that can be considered the beginnings of needed structural change within the Church. I am referring to the consultations which preceded and accompanied our bishops' pastoral letters on peace, on the economy, and on women's concerns. Such widespread consultation dialogs are a positive contribution of the Church of the United States to the universal Church.[27] Could not these consultations be described as new expressions of *koinonia*, well attuned to the early Church's community life as influenced by the prayerful presence of Mary?

One of the most encouraging structural developments that can be considered another expression of *koinonia* since Vatican II is that of Pastoral Councils: parish, diocesan, and national. Although we have not yet succeeded in establishing a National Pastoral Council in the United States, we have benefitted from the Catholic Bishops' Advisory Council inaugurated in 1969.

I had the unique privilege of being a member of that Advisory Council during the first five years of its existence. What new life for the Church was experienced at every meeting when bishops, priests, religious, lay women and men could dialog freely about every agenda item for the USCC and NCCB meetings and make recommendations accordingly![28]

The guiding principle in all of these new Church structures is that of *shared responsibility*. Here again, we can turn to Mary, the handmaid of the Lord, who continues to share responsibility with Jesus for the salvation of the world. *Lumen Gentium* reminds us of the way Mary embraced "God's saving will with a full heart and impeded by no sin, she devoted herself totally as a

handmaid of the Lord to the person and work of her Son"
(*LG* 56). Now, with us in the mystery of the Church, Mary can
help us see the need for, and the implications of, shared responsibility with her risen Son, Jesus. Therein lies new hope for the
Church of the future.

As we continue to face the need for structural change in the
Church of the future, let us recall one of the first structural
changes as recorded in the Book of Acts. In chapter six, we are
presented with the question of food distribution for some of the
Church's poorest members, the widows who spoke Greek instead of Hebrew. Luke tells us, "The twelve assembled the community of the disciples" (Ac 6:2) and suggested ordaining
deacons to help take care of their new situation. Luke adds,
"The proposal was unanimously accepted by the community"
(Ac 6:5).

Nowhere in all of Acts is the communities' prayerful involvement more significant than it is in the story of the Council of
Jerusalem as related in Acts 15. The early difficulties regarding
the circumcision of Gentiles was settled after considerable discussion and dialog. Again Luke informs us of the way "the
whole Jerusalem Church" was involved (Ac 15:22). How telling
is the key statement of the letter sent from that Jerusalem
Church to the Church of Antioch: "It is the decision of the Holy
Spirit, and ours too, not to lay on you any burden beyond that
which is strictly necessary . . ." (Ac 15:28)!

These two examples from Acts, regarding food distribution
and circumcision, illustrate the wisdom of the early Church in
adapting religious practices to cultural needs. In response to the
needs of Greek-speaking widows, a major adaptation took place
in the organizational structure of the early Church. The diaco-
nate came into existence. In the circumcision controversy, respect for the cultural conditioning of Gentile converts brought
about a needed change in the initiation rituals for new members
of the Church. Circumcision, sign of Jewish identity, was not to
be part of the Christian initiation rite. Both of these needed
adaptations resulted from prayerful dialog and discernment on
the part of the community.

If we accept Luke-Acts as a "story from which we are able to
learn,"[29] then I suggest that, from these two stories, we learn the
critical importance of distinguishing cultural differences from
tenets of faith. Two of the documents of Vatican II faced this key
issue. The Constitution on the Liturgy, *Sacrosanctum Concilium*,
encouraged liturgical adaptation to correspond to cultural
needs.[30] The Decree on the Church's Missionary Activity, *Ad
Gentes*, can be considered a major breakthrough regarding mis-

sionary activity and cultural adaptation. Let us ponder briefly some pertinent texts from *Ad Gentes*. In Chapter III, "On Particular Churches," we read:

> From the customs and traditions of their people, from their wisdom and learning, from their arts and sciences, these Churches borrow all those things which can contribute to the glory of their Creator, the revelation of the Savior's grace, or the proper arrangement of Christian life . . . If this goal is to be achieved, theological investigation must necessarily be stirred up in each major socio-cultural area. . . . Thus it will be more clearly seen in what ways faith can seek for understanding in the philosophy and wisdom of these peoples. . . . Christian life can be accommodated to the genius and the dispositions of each culture (*AG* 22).

Now, in our great concern for the Church of the future, can we learn more from Luke-Acts regarding cultural needs and corresponding changes in Church practices? In this regard, surely the whole question of women's leadership roles in the Church is a major issue calling for discernment and change. The vast differences between the role of women in Jesus' cultural milieu and in our own must be faced honestly. Fortunately, some of these issues have been raised in the many discussions regarding the proposed pastoral letter on women's concerns.[31]

In the ongoing dialog and discussion on the role of women in the Church, let us be mindful of Mary's prayerful influence in the Church today. In her own transition from Jewish to Christian life, Mary knew how necessary structural changes were in the life of the faith community. Mary knew also that wise structural change would not be possible without the community's prayerful attuning to the Holy Spirit. Her concern for the developing life of the infant Church continues in her concern for the developing life of the Vatican II Church. With her active presence in the Mystery of Christ and the Church, may we nurture prayerful, discerning, adapting communities in every part of the Church's life. And, as we look ahead to the Church of the future, let us consider seriously the use of such modern communications as teleconferences which could help unite sections of the universal Church in new dialogical ways. Without vital community life in the Church of the future, is there much hope for the Church's influence on the future of the world?

A Church for the Future of the World

Following the lead of Vatican II that gave us two Constitutions on the Church, *Lumen Gentium* and *Gaudium et Spes*, our present consideration of Mary and the Church of the future must include the Church's potential influence in the modern world. This consideration is necessary, and in many ways challenging, because it touches the heart of Christian spirituality, including some orientations of Marian devotion.

For some Christians, a life of faith has little to do with the major concerns of the modern world. Such concerns are dubbed political issues that have nothing to do with the mission of the Church. Persons of this mentality understand salvation primarily as a matter of eternal life. Such an "otherworldly" spirituality emphasis is often suspicious of efforts that focus on the major problems of this world: global hunger; war and peace; ecology. Yet, it is precisely such issues of this world that *Gaudium et Spes* addresses. Chapter Four, entitled "The Role of the Church in the Modern World," proclaims that, as members of the earthly city, the members of the Church "have a call to form the family of God's children during the present history of the human race, and to keep increasing it until the Lord returns" (*GS* 40).

In discussions of the Church's involvement in the concerns of this world, often the fact of original sin is introduced as a reminder that the evil in the world is universal, persistent, and quite capable of thwarting all efforts for good. A logical consequence of this mentality is to give in to discouragement about effecting any substantial change in society and to focus almost exclusively on the other world, the world of heaven in which all of us will share the joys of eternal life.

When original sin is mentioned, a well-known aspiration to Mary readily comes to mind: "O Mary, conceived without sin, pray for us who have recourse to thee." This prayer can bring us to a needed consideration of the meaning of Mary's Immaculate Conception. This Marian dogma is crucial in our consideration of Christian spirituality today as we are called to embrace the "joys and hopes, the griefs and anxieties of the (people) of this age, especially those who are poor or in any way afflicted . . ." (*GS* 1). Some implications of the dogma of the Immaculate Conception can be exceedingly helpful in our present study of the Church's impact on the future of the world.[32]

One of the most insightful recent works on the meaning of original sin is that of the Jesuit theologians, Zoltan Alszeghy and Maurizio Flick.[33] These scholars focus on *dialogical alienation* as the core of the sin situation afflicting the world. Their insights relate directly to the first eleven chapters of Genesis. There, we find a progressive deterioration of the communing dynamic that God bestowed on creation in the beginning. The primary breakdown in communing love is that between God and human persons. Then, the dynamics of dialogical alienation make their way into the relation between man and woman, typified in the Adam and Eve story; between family members, typified in the Cain and Abel story; between the human community and the earth, typified in the flood story; and, finally, between the family of nations, as typified in the impossibility of dialog in the Tower of Babel story.[34] In the midst of this profound theological presentation, the Genesis writer inserts the text:

> I will put enmity between you and the woman,
>   and between your offspring and hers;
> He will strike at your head,
>   while you strike at his heel (Gn 3:15).

In this theological framework of dialogical alienation, perhaps we can see more clearly the relation of Mary's prayerfulness to her Immaculate Conception. From the very beginning of her life, Mary was oriented to a loving dialog with God. Mary's prayerfulness witnesses to the undoing of dialogical alienation with God and makes room for the communing love in every other aspect of human life. In this or any other consideration of Mary's Immaculate Conception, as Karl Rahner reminds us, it is of key importance to realize that God's redeeming action in Mary is also at work in our lives.[35]

Once again, if we turn to Luke-Acts, we can see anew the prominence of the Marian text in chapter one. Mary, leading the community in prayer, is key to the Pentecost event in chapter two. There, the amazing way in which the peoples from many nations begin to understand one another is presented as a reversal of the Babel experience. The dialogical alienation of original sin begins to be undone and transformed as the Holy Spirit begins again to renew the face of the earth.

Here, I wish to recall the emphasis placed on prayerful communities in the first part of this present study. The formation of such communities is a visible expression of God's redeeming action at its very roots. The action of the Holy Spirit in the formation of such communal structures includes the power for transforming societal structures as well. In all areas of life: personal, familial, communal, societal, and international, transforming situations of dialogical alienation into situations of loving dialog and discernment is a clear sign of God's action in our world.

Gaudium et Spes pointed to such needed changes in our times, particularly in the societal and international areas of life. I wish to focus now on one major problem facing the future of the world, the one which continues to cause untold "grief and anxi-

ety, . . . especially on the part of the poor . . ." (*GS* 1). I speak
of militarism, of the scourge of violence and war that has
plagued the human family throughout its history.

Gaudium et Spes devotes the entire Chapter Five to "The Fos-
tering of Peace and the Promotion of a Community of Nations."
The chapter begins with the statement, "In our generation
when men (and women) continue to be afflicted by acute hard-
ships and anxieties arising from ongoing wars or the threat of
them, the whole human family has reached an hour of supreme
crisis in its advance toward maturity" (*GS* 77). The phrase,
"hour of supreme crisis," sometimes translated "moment of supreme crisis," signals an unprecedented urgency to the whole
consideration of modern warfare and the quest for peace.

No other document of the entire Council contains such
strong condemnatory language. No other Council document
presents such a global challenge, not only to the members of the
Church, but to all members of the human family. In this final
chapter, *Gaudium et Spes* asks the Church to face, not just one
critical problem of the future, but to face the possibility of not
having a future — the possibility of really terminating life on
this planet, an action which would be blasphemous in an ultimate sense against the Creator of the universe. In the words of
Chapter Five:

> For enmities and hatred must be put away and firm, honest
> agreements concerning world peace reached in the future. Oth-
> erwise, for all its marvelous knowledge, humanity, which is al-
> ready in the middle of a grave crisis, will perhaps be brought to
> that mournful hour in which it will experience no peace other
> than the dreadful peace of death (*GS* 82).

The section on total war highlights the present "horror and
perversity of war" because of the "multiplication of scientific
weapons" (*GS* 80). In this context, the Council proclaims, "All
these considerations compel us to undertake an evaluation of
war with an entirely new attitude" (*GS* 80).

A major aspect of this "entirely new attitude" is the perspective on the arms race, referred to as a "crushing anxiety" for the
entire world. Again, the language is uncompromisingly strong:

> Therefore, it must be said again: the arms race is an utterly
> treacherous trap for humanity, and one which injures the poor to
> an intolerable degree. It is much to be feared that if this race
> persists, it will eventually spawn all the lethal ruin whose path it
> is now making ready (*GS* 81).

Then, as a clarion call, the Council sounds the challenge, "It is
our clear duty, then, to strain every muscle as we work for the

time when all war can be completely outlawed by international consent" (*GS* 82).

Throughout this entire chapter, peacemaking efforts are presented in relation to the kind of sincere dialog that makes for mutual trust. In the section entitled, "The Nature of Peace," we are reminded, "This peace cannot be obtained on earth unless personal values are safeguarded and (people) freely and trustingly share with one another the riches of their inner spirits and talents" (*GS* 78). Building peace with vigor is designated as a "work of supreme love for (humankind)" (*GS* 82). In this context of working for peace, *Gaudium et Spes* emphasizes the need for peace education as it states:

> Hence arises a surpassing need for renewed education of attitudes and for new inspiration in the area of public opinion. Those who are dedicated to the work of education, particularly of the young, or who mould public opinion, should regard as their most weighty task the effort to instruct all in fresh sentiments of peace. Indeed, every one of us should have a change of heart as we regard the entire world and those tasks which we can perform in unison for the betterment of our race (*GS* 82).

The chapter continues with suggestions and directives for peacemaking efforts in "Building Up the International Community," as the second major section is entitled. The Church is presented as allowing and invigorating honest dialog, not only among "all those who compose the one People of God, both pastors and the general faithful," but also among persons of other faiths, even those "who oppress the Church and harass her in manifold ways." Because, "if we have been summoned to the same destiny, which is both human and divine, we can and we should work together without violence and deceit in order to build up the world in genuine peace" (*GS* 92).

These statements on the need for honest dialog resonate with the section on "Reverence and Love for Enemies," found in the second chapter of *Gaudium et Spes* which is entitled, "The Community of Mankind." There we read:

> Respect and love ought to be extended also to those who think or act differently than we do in social, political, and religious matters, too. In fact, the more deeply we come to understand their ways of thinking through such courtesy and love, the more easily will we be able to enter into dialog with them (*GS* 28).

This whole question of dialog in the context of love of enemies brings us once again to the Mary of Pentecost, the human Mary whose forgiving heart made possible the formation of a forgiving, reconciling community. Mary understood the implications of reconciliation as voiced in the Letter to Ephesians, as no one else could. Her Son, Jesus, had reconciled us to God through his cross which put enmity to death (Eph 2:16). Mary knew the way "It pleased God to make absolute fullness reside in him, and by means of him, to reconcile everything in his person, both on earth and in the heavens, making peace through the blood of his cross" (Col 1:19).

How Mary must have understood the Eucharistic action of her Son! How she must have pondered those words, ". . . this is my blood, the blood of the covenant, to be poured out in behalf of many for the forgiveness of sins" (Mt 26:28)! Often, I wonder whether this forgiving aspect of the Eucharistic mystery is the one needing special emphasis today. Just as the Mary of Pentecost helped form communities who relied on the breaking of bread and prayer (Ac 2:42), so her influence in the Church today brings us to a new awareness of the reconciling power of the blood of the new covenant. In every Eucharist, we are nourished with her Son's forgiving, reconciling love. In every Eucharist, we are strengthened in our efforts at reconciling dialog. In special ways now, we are reminded that our recent American martyrs were Sisters of the Precious Blood.

This very year, 1993, began on the feast of Mary's Solemnity, a celebration which has coincided deliberately for several years with the World Day of Prayer for Peace. At first sight, the relation between these two themes may not seem too obvious. In the light of Vatican II's liturgical renewal, the feast of Mary's Maternity, her Solemnity, was moved in the liturgical calendar. Originally placed on October 11 in commemoration of the declaration of Mary as *Theotokos* by the Council of Ephesus in 431,[36] this feast, newly titled the Solemnity of Mary, Mother of God, was placed on January 1, the octave day of Christmas. Around the same time, the World Day of Prayer for Peace was established, also on January 1, the beginning of a new year. The more we realize Mary's role as peacemaker, the more we can see the wisdom in placing these two feasts on the same day. Especially in the mystery of Pentecost does Mary show us the way to peace. Her prayerful witness in the community of disciples opened the way for the reconciling power of her Son and his Spirit to be operative. How significant that *Gaudium et Spes* refers to the Holy Spirit as the befriending Spirit (*GS* 3)! Now, in the Mystery of Christ and the Church, Mary's peacemaking influence continues as she helps us respond to the empowerment of God's Spirit enabling us to make friends with everyone, especially our perceived enemies.

The 1993 World Day of Peace message of John Paul II is entitled, "If you want peace reach out to the poor."[37] In many ways,
this message reiterates the teachings of *Gaudium et Spes* and re-
lates them to the destitution, injustice, and violence of today,
including the tragic situations in Bosnia-Herzegovina and in
Somalia. One of the most significant statements for us, living in
the United States, is the following:

> To reject all temptations to secure economic dominance over
> other nations means to renounce a policy inspired by the pre-
> vailing criterion of profit and to replace it with a policy guided
> by the criterion of solidarity toward all and especially toward the
> poorest (#2).

In the context of the impossible conditions imposed by the
international debt, once again, in this Peace Day message, the
arms race is called into question. The tragic consequences of
drug cultivation and traffic are decried also. One of the strongest statements on the futility of war is given in the face of today's
ethnic, tribal, and racial violence. In new ways, we hear the
teachings of *Gaudium et Spes*:

> Recourse to violence, in fact, aggravates existing tensions and
> creates new ones. Nothing is resolved by war; on the contrary,
> everything is placed in jeopardy by war. The results of this
> scourge are the suffering and death of innumerable individuals,
> the disintegration of human relations and the irreparable loss of
> an immense artistic and environmental patrimony. War worsens
> the sufferings of the poor; indeed, it creates new poor by de-
> stroying means of subsistence, homes and property, and by eat-
> ing away at the very fabric of the social environment. Young
> people see their hopes for the future shattered and too often, as
> victims, they become irresponsible agents of conflict. Women,
> children, the elderly, the sick and the wounded are forced to flee
> and become refugees who have no possessions beyond what they
> can carry with them. Helpless and defenseless, they seek refuge
> in other countries or regions often as poor and turbulent as their
> own (#4).

John Paul II concludes his message with a section on the role
of evangelical poverty and the making of peace. Clearly distinguishing evangelical poverty from socio-economic poverty, he
clarifies the key role in peacemaking played by those who are
poor in the sense of the Beatitudes.[38] He writes: "Those who are
poor in the Gospel sense are ready to sacrifice their resources
and their own selves so that others may live. Their one desire is
to live in peace with everyone, offering to others the gift of Jesus'
peace (cf. Jn 14:27)" (#5).

One Gospel scene in Mary's life is recalled in this Peace Day Message: the flight into Egypt. Again, we are reminded of the human Mary and Joseph suffering the terrifying anguish of refugees in flight from death-dealing violence. In the lives of the millions of refugees today, surely this Gospel story takes on ever greater significance. Once again, we are faced with Mary's compassionate love at work now in the Mystery of Christ and the Church, inspiring worldwide concern and action for the plight of refugees and for the works of peace.

This year, 1993, we celebrate the tenth anniversary of our United States Catholic Bishops' Pastoral Letter, *The Challenge of Peace: God's Promise and Our Response*. This historic document begins by quoting directly from *Gaudium et Spes*: "The whole human race faces a moment of supreme crisis in its advance toward maturity" (*CP* 1).[39] We can be grateful that the whole human race has new hope for peace because of the treaty START II. During the next ten years, we should see a seventy-five percent reduction of the nuclear weapons possessed by the United States and the former Soviet Union. However, it is of crucial importance to understand these statistics in the light of the megatonnage of explosives available as we entered the decade of the nineties. Recalling that one megaton is one thousand tons of explosives, we need to be aware that eleven megatons were used in the three major wars: World War II, the Korean War, and the Vietnam War. By 1990, 18,000 megatons of explosives were available in the world's nuclear arsenals.[40] A recent Newsletter of the International Physicians for the Prevention of Nuclear War reports that, even after the implementation of START and START II, the arsenals of the nuclear powers will still contain 12,000 nuclear weapons.[41] When it comes to the question of disarmament, we still have a long, long way to go.

One of the most significant and encouraging aspects of *The Challenge of Peace* is its treatment of nonviolence. This section begins with a clear reference to the example of Jesus' life and his teaching (*CP* 111). Although this Pastoral Letter also reiterates "just-war" theory, its presentation of nonviolence is a helpful sign of the Church's growth in the wisdom of the Gospel with respect to peacemaking.

The Challenge of Peace includes a section on Prayer. The first article encourages us to "enter into a closer communion with our Lord." We are reminded that personal and communal prayer nourish that communion, "for it is in prayer that we encounter Jesus who is our peace and learn from him the way to peace" (*CP* 290). The second article speaks of the way prayer renews our faith and confirms our hope in God's promise

(*CP* 291). The third article makes explicit reference to Mary in the following words: "We call upon Mary, the first disciple and the Queen of Peace, to intercede for us and for the people of our time that we may walk in the way of peace. In this context, we encourage devotion to Our Lady of Peace" (*CP* 292).

Perhaps more prayerful reflection on the title of this Pastoral Letter would help us understand Mary's present role as Our Lady of Peace. The full title is *The Challenge of Peace: God's Promise and Our Response*. Is there anyone in all of Christian history who was more trusting of God's promise and more faithful in response? Here, the words of Elizabeth to Mary in the Lucan portrayal of the Visitation readily come to mind: "Blest is she who trusted that the Lord's words to her would be fulfilled" (Lk 1:45).

If there is anything needed in the Church's role in the peace-making efforts of the world today, first and foremost it is faith in God's promise of the gift of peace. Unless we really believe God will bless our efforts toward peace on earth, we will never be able to make the whole-hearted responses called for by today's situations of unprecedented violence. Above all else, the Mary of history is a woman of faith.[42] *Lumen Gentium* acclaims her as the Church's model and excellent exemplar in faith and charity (*LG* 53). Because she is a woman of faith, Mary can be called Queen of Peace and Lady of Peace.

The May, 1992, issue of *U.S. Catholic* was devoted to the question, "Can Catholics make peace with war?" Included was an interview with Bishop Walter Sullivan of the Richmond, Virginia, diocese and current bishop president of Pax Christi USA.[43] In the interview, Bishop Sullivan faced the difficulties of the Church of the future in becoming a Church of peace and peacemakers in the face of such complex questions as patriotism and national security. Basically, Bishop Sullivan is hopeful about the growing commitment to peacemaking on the part of Catholics, but he is very realistic about the conversion process needed for such a commitment. He highlights peace as a way of being and living in union with the person of Jesus from whom all peace comes. Bishop Sullivan states emphatically, "You cannot associate violence with Jesus Christ — that's an absolute contradiction. Jesus is one who forgives."[44]

For Bishop Sullivan, along with thousands of Catholics in the United States, *Pax Christi*, the International Catholic Peace Movement, has been a vital influence in nurturing and strengthening one's commitment to the cause of peace in our world of violence. *Pax Christi* began soon after World War II, as Catholics from wartorn France and Germany came together in a spirit of forgiveness and reconciliation. *Pax Christi* has a strong spirituality base underlying its many programs for peace and justice. Its statutes include a brief statement of purpose: to work for peace for all people, always witnessing to the peace of Christ.[45] Often, *Pax Christi* members meet in small groups to prayerfully study and discern wise actions for peace. *Pax Christi USA* frequently focuses on Mary's witness, inspiration, and power in the lives of today's Christians dedicated to the peace-making of the Gospel.[46]

In their strong encouragement to the Catholics of the United States to become active peacemakers, our bishops included two powerful statements in their Pastoral Letter that call for continual remembrance on the part of men and women determined to follow the peacemaking ways of Jesus and of Mary. In section 333, the bishops proclaimed, "We are called to be peacemakers, not by some movement of the moment, but by our Lord Jesus. The content and context of our peacemaking is set, not by some political agenda or ideological program, but by the teaching of his Church" (*CP* 333). In section 276, they reminded us of the price of peacemaking:

> To set out on the road to discipleship is to dispose oneself for a share in the cross (cf. Jn 19:20). To be a Christian, according to the New Testament, is not simply to believe with one's mind, but also to become a doer of the word, a wayfarer with and a witness to Jesus. This means, of course, that we never expect complete success within history and that we must regard as normal even the path of persecution and the possibility of martyrdom (*CP* 276).

On this note of martyrdom, let us return once more to Luke-Acts. In the seventh chapter, we find the story of Stephen, the Church's first martyr. One of the most significant aspects of that story is Stephen's prayer for forgiveness: "Lord, do not hold this sin against them" (Ac 7:60). How similar this prayer is to that of Jesus on Calvary: "Father, forgive them; they do not know what they are doing" (Lk 23:24)! In relation to this martyrdom story of Stephen, we can raise the question of Mary's influence in nurturing the heroic spirit of forgiveness in the lives of those who are called to follow her Son.

I want to conclude our consideration of Mary and the Church of the future by suggesting that Mary, who is acclaimed as first disciple of Jesus, is, above all, the first disciple of forgiveness and reconciliation. No other aspect of Jesus' life and mission is more needed in our times. No other disciple lived this forgiveness and reconciliation more fully than the Mary of Pentecost. Now, in our New Pentecost era begun by the Second

Vatican Council, may Mary's forgiving, reconciling spirit be with us who, with her, live in the Mystery of Christ and the Church. If we allow her to lead us on in Jesus' own ways of peacemaking, then, as never before, the coming generations will call her blessed.

NOTES

[1]For an excellent commentary on the implications of the Council's teaching on Mary, see Anne Carr, BVM, "Mary in the Mystery of the Church: Vatican Council II," in Carol Frances Jegen, BVM, ed., *Mary According to Women* (Kansas City: Sheed & Ward, 1985), 5-32.

[2]Cf. Carol Frances Jegen, BVM, "Mary: Woman for Our World," *Chicago Studies* 27/1 (1988): 50.

[3]In a recent lecture at the University of Tulsa, a strong case was made for the Church to be prophetic in our times. Cf. Joan D. Chittister, OSB, "New World, New Church: Political, Pastoral or Prophetic," *Warren Lecture Series in Catholic Studies*, No. 22, Oct. 25, 1992.

[4]William G. Thompson, SJ, unpublished manuscript, "Acts of the Apostles: Witnessing the Risen Lord," 1992, 4.

[5]Robert C. Tannehill, *The Narrative Unity of Luke-Acts: A Literary Interpretation*, Vol. 2: *The Acts of the Apostles* (Minneapolis: Fortress, 1990), 1.

[6]Ibid., 2.

[7]Ibid., 19. However, here Tannehill pays no attention to Mary's significance in this scene.

[8]For a brief historical study on discernment, see *Discernment of Spirits*, the authorized English edition of the article, "Discernement des Esprits," in the *Dictionnaire de Spiritualité*, trans. Sister Innocentia Richards (Collegeville: The Liturgical Press, 1970). The section on St. Ignatius of Loyola, by Joseph Pegon, SJ, is particularly helpful. In the Introduction, Jesuit Edward Malestesta writes: "The discernment of spirits, while always necessary for an authentic Christian life, becomes imperative with a new urgency and intensity in a time of crisis such as our own" (9).

[9]Raymond Brown, *The Birth of the Messiah* (Garden City, N.Y.: Doubleday, 1977), 250-53; Joseph A. Fitzmyer, "The Gospel According to Luke I-IX," in *The Anchor Bible* (Garden City, N.Y.: Doubleday, 1981), 309, 358.

[10]Cf. Donald Senior, CP, "New Testament Images of Mary," *The Bible Today* 24/3 (1986): 143-51.

[11]Raymond Brown, Karl P. Donfried, Joseph A. Fitzmyer, John Reumann, eds., *Mary in the New Testament* (Philadelphia: Fortress, 1978), 167f.

[12]Cf. Brown, *The Birth*. The introductory section on "Scholarship and the Infancy Narratives" is particularly helpful, as is Appendix VIII, "Midrash as a Literary Genre."

[13]Carroll Stuhlmueller, CP, "Old Testament Settings for Mary in the Liturgy," *The Bible Today* 24/3 (1986): 159-66.

[14]James A. Cone, *Black Theology of Liberation* (Philadelphia: Lippincott, 1970), 64f.

[15]At the Mary Symposium at Saint Mary's College, Notre Dame, during the recent Marian Year, when I introduced the topic of Mary's forgiving spirit at Pentecost, I was surprised at the somewhat extraordinary resonance of the participants. Since that time, my conviction has deepened about the importance of this Marian theme for our times. Cf. Carol Frances Jegen, BVM, "The Justice Dimension: Mary as Advocate of Peace," in *Mary Woman of Nazareth*, ed. Doris Donnelly (New York: Paulist Press, 1989), 133-45.

[16]For further reflections on Mary's maternal presence in the life of the Church, see Carol Frances Jegen, BVM, "Mary, Mother of a Renewing Church," *The Bible Today* 24/3 (1986): 153-57.

[17]Richard P. McBrien, "Conflict in the Church: Redefining the Center," *America* 167/4 (1992), 78-81.

[18]Ibid., 81.

[19]Ibid.

[20]For helpful comments on the significance of Lucan summary statements, see Tannehill, "The Communal Life of the Jerusalem Believers," 43f.

[21]Thompson, 58.

[22]Unfortunately, many Christians do not have an adequate understanding of the privileged place of Conciliar teaching in the life of the Church. Such ignorance presents particular difficulties in the area of Marian doctrine and devotion.

[23]Jon Sobrino, SJ, *Christology at the Crossroads*, trans. John Drury (Maryknoll: Orbis, 1978). Cf. Chapter One, "The Starting Point for Christology." Sobrino quotes Assman, "What is surprising is the lack of any sense of crisis about the meaning of Christ in the very midst of an acute crisis about the meaning of the Church" (2).

[24]Cf. Bertil Gartner, *The Temple and the Community in Qumran and the New Testament* (Cambridge: University Press, 1965).

[25]A summary of this historical meeting is found in *International Papers in Pastoral Ministry* 3/3 (1992), University of Notre Dame.

[26]The development of small Christian communities in the United States includes a *Buena Vista Federation* which publishes a Newsletter, *Buena Vista Ink*, available from Buena Vista, Inc., P.O. Box 5474, Arvada, CO 80005.

[27]In the early stages of the discussions regarding the proposed Pastoral on Women's Concerns, Bishop Joseph Imesh remarked informally that, if the Pastoral did nothing else, it was one more witness of the Church in the United States to the importance of dialog. Bishops in other countries were amazed that we would undertake such a process in the writing of pastoral letters.

[28]A brief history of the early years of the Advisory Council is given in *Shared Responsibility at Work*, ed. Michael J. Sheehan and Russell Shaw (Washington, D.C.: United States Catholic Conference, 1975). Another helpful document in regard to pastoral councils is *A National Pastoral Council: Pro and Con*, Proceedings of an Interdisciplinary Con-

sultation August 28-30 in Chicago, Ill. (Washington, D.C.: United States Catholic Conference, 1971).

[29]Tannehill, 2. Also see his comments on p. 81 regarding the resolution of the difficulties caused by language and cultural differences.

[30]*Sacrosanctum Concilium* states: "the Church . . . respects and fosters the spiritual adornments and gifts of the various races and peoples. . . . Sometimes in fact she admits such things into the liturgy itself, as long as they harmonize with its true and authentic spirit" (*SC* 37). For a recent article on inculturation and the liturgy in the United States, see Mark R. Francis, "Holding Hands at the Our Father: U.S. Liturgical Inculturation?," *Liturgy 90*, January, 1993.

[31]The December 3, 1992, issue of *Origins* 22/25 contains statements made by bishops at their November, 1992, meeting. Bishop Lucker's concerns are pertinent in relation to the whole question of honest dialog. He asks what happened to the statements deleted from the third draft. Archbishop Weakland reminded the Conference that the "traditional reasons given for the non-ordination of women, the ones that were consistently taught in our history, centered on the inferiority of women."

[32]For a more extensive study of the meaning of the Immaculate Conception, see Carol Frances Jegen, BVM, "Mary Immaculate: Woman of Freedom, Patroness of the United States," in *Mary According to Women*, 143-63.

[33]Zoltan Alszeghy and Maurizio Flick, "A Personalistic View of Original Sin," *Theology Digest* 15/3 (1967): 190-96.

[34]Cf. Carol Frances Jegen, BVM, *Restoring Our Friendship with God* (Collegeville: Michael Glazier/Liturgical Press, 1989), especially 52f.

[35]Karl Rahner, *Mary, Mother of the Lord* (New York: Herder and Herder, 1963), 44, 49.

[36]Here, it is helpful to recall that Vatican II began on October 11. Pope John XXIII wanted to put the entire Council under Mary's special protection and chose the anniversary day of the *Theotokos* proclamation.

[37]The entire text was published in *Origins* 22/28 (December 24, 1992), 476-79. This statement comes at the conclusion, 479.

[38]For a more extensive development of the Beatitude spirituality implied here, see Carol Frances Jegen, BVM, *Jesus the Peacemaker* (Kansas City: Sheed & Ward, 1986), Chapter Five, "Programming for Peace."

[39]National Conference of Catholic Bishops, *The Challenge of Peace: God's Promise and Our Response* (Washington, D.C.: United States Catholic Conference, 1983). This Pastoral Letter was approved on May 3, 1983, at the Bishops' Meeting held in Chicago. Several groups of Catholics kept a continual prayer vigil in the hotel during the deliberations. Students and faculty from Mundelein College were scheduled for that evening at 10:00, soon after the document had been passed by an overwhelming majority. Bishop Lucker and others came to our room in the hotel and prayed with us in gratitude. It was truly an "upper room" experience of Pentecostal joy.

[40]Ruth Leger Sivard, *World Military and Social Expenditures*, 1989, p. 14. Annual reports can be obtained from World Priorities, Inc., Box 25140, Washington, D.C. 20007.

[41]*Vital Signs* 5/4 (December, 1992), 1.

[42]Significantly, the U.S. Catholic Bishops' Pastoral Letter on Mary is entitled, *Behold Your Mother, Woman of Faith* (Washington, D.C.: United States Catholic Conference, 1973).

[43]"Should Catholics belong to a peace church?," *U.S. Catholic*, May, 1992, 38-43.

[44]Ibid., 40.

[45]Two recent booklets on Pax Christi spirituality are *Ambassadors of Reconciliation* (Brussels: Pax Christi International, 1992); Jozef Hanssens, *The Gospel of Peace for Our Time* (Brussels: Pax Christi International, 1992).

[46]Cf. Joan Chittister, OSB, *Mary, Wellspring of Peace* (Erie, PA: Pax Christi USA, 1987). For a recent and most timely Pax Christi USA publication, see Doris Donnelly, *Seventy Times Seven: Forgiveness and Peacemaking* (Erie, PA: Pax Christi USA, 1993).

Index of Persons

204